The Carter Presidency

The Carter Presidency

A re-evaluation

John Dumbrell

Manchester University Press
Manchester and New York
Distributed exclusively in the USA and Canada by St. Martin's Press

Published by Manchester University Press
Oxford Road, Manchester M13 9PL, UK
and Room 400, 175 Fifth Avenue, New York, NY 10010, USA

Distributed exclusively in the USA and Canada
by St. Martin's Press, Inc., 175 Fifth Avenue, New York,
NY 10010, USA

British Library Cataloguing-in-Publication Data
A catalogue record for this book is available from the British Library

Library of Congress Cataloging-in-Publication Data
Dumbrell, John, 1950–
     The Carter presidency: a re-evaluation/John Dumbrell.
        p.   cm.
     ISBN 0–7190–3617–8
     1. United States—Politics and government—1977–1981.   2. United
States—Foreign relations—1977–1981.   3. Carter, Jimmy, 1924–   .
4. Human rights—Government policy—United States.   I. Title.
E872.D86   1993   92–40686

ISBN 0 7190 3617 8 *hardback*

Phototypeset in Linotron Sabon
by Northern Phototypesetting Co. Ltd, Bolton

Printed in Great Britain
by Biddles Ltd, Guildford and King's Lynn

Contents

Preface

In several important respects Jimmy Carter's Presidency (1977–81) was characterised by failure. Carter was a one term President who had considerable difficulty even in securing re-nomination by his own party in 1980. His popularity ratings fell at times to alarming depths. To many Americans in the Reagan and Bush eras, Carter's Presidency continued to evoke images of national malaise and weakness: of humiliation at the hands of Middle Eastern oil producers and revolutionaries in Iran.

Despite all this, the record of Jimmy Carter is subject to that same cycle of academic evaluation and re-evaluation which has altered our perceptions of other Presidencies in recent American history. Presidential reputations wax and wane according to the preoccupations of succeeding generations. In Carter's case, as is shown in Chapter 1 below, his Presidency began to achieve a measure of (journalistic rather than academic) rehabilitation by the later 1980s. To some extent, this rehabilitation was associated with negative perceptions of Carter's successor, Ronald Reagan, as well as with positive views of Carter's own post-White House career. Yet it was also linked to the apparent relevance of Carter's 'world order' and 'global community' concerns for the post-Cold War world. From an early 1990s viewpoint, Carter's leadership seemed in many ways far-sighted, as well as comparatively untouched by cynicism and corruption. It appeared that Jimmy Carter's custody of the Presidential office could stand comparison with that of other modern Chief Executives. (Whatever one's view of Reagan, it is worth recalling that, of Carter's three immediate predecessors, Lyndon Johnson withdrew ignominiously from the nomination race in 1968; Richard Nixon resigned in disgrace in 1974; while the other, Gerald Ford, was never elected to the executive office at all.)

This book shares the perspective of those commentators who have come to contest the negative (and especially the Reaganite) condemnation of Carter. Particular attention is drawn to the political and institutional context within which President Carter operated. Vietnam and Watergate created opportunities for a virtually unknown Democrat to assume office. They also created problems. As is indicated in Chapter 1, Carter's period in office was not sustained by the strong liberal consensus – on foreign policy, on the role of the President and on economic issues – that had guided previous Democratic incumbents. Sailing very often in uncharted waters, Carter sought a new, post-liberal and post-imperial, species of leadership.

In attempting to evaluate Carter's Presidency, this book focuses on his principal 1976 campaign theme: 'competence and compassion'. Carter saw managerial efficiency as an important part of the solution to America's post-liberal problems. His competence in office is assessed explicitly in Chapters 2 and 7, but implicitly throughout. Even more central to Carter's vision than competence, however, was 'compassion': the restoration of moral purpose to American political life. The main focus of this book is this 'compassion' in its major operational form: the human rights policy.[1] Intersecting with a general re-awakening of interest in human rights in the late 1970s, Carter's human rights commitments lay at the heart of his promise to restore consensus by reinvigorating the nation's moral purpose. At home, human rights policies were developed as a way of refashioning liberalism to meet the demand of an economically hostile environment. Internationally, human rights initiatives were designed to unite left and right behind a new, morally coherent and purposive foreign policy.

Chapter 3 (on women's rights) and Chapter 4 (on black civil rights) consider Carter's domestic human rights policies. Chapter 5 discusses the Administration's 'world order' and 'global community' orientations. It examines the implications of human rights policy for two dramatically contrasting areas of US interest: the Soviet Union and Northern Ireland. Chapter 6 continues this discussion in the context of the revolutionary upsurges in Nicaragua and Iran. Chapter 7 offers some judgements on the human rights initiative in foreign policy, and considers the circumstances surrounding the Administration's return in 1979–80 to a more orthodox Cold War approach. The final chapter attempts a general evaluation of the Carter Presidency's competence and compassion.

Notes

1   My human rights focus and the exigencies of space inevitably mean that not all areas of policy are examined in detail. Further coverage of important policy areas is contained in E. C. Hargrove, *Jimmy Carter as President: Leadership and the Politics of the Public Good* (Baton Rouge: Louisiana State University Press, 1988) and Richard C. Thornton, *The Carter Years: Toward a New Global Order* (Washington DC: Washington Institute Press, 1991). See also, in particular, William B. Quandt, *Camp David: Peacemaking and Policies* (Washington DC: Brookings Institution, 1986).

Acknowledgements

Research for this book was undertaken at the Jimmy Carter Presidential Library in Atlanta. I would like to thank the Library staff, especially Martin Elzy, and also the US Embassy, who provided a grant. I am grateful to those authors of papers given at the 1990 Hofstra Presidential Conference who allowed me to consult their work. (Detailed reference to particular papers is given in the footnotes.) The latter section of Chapter 5 was originally presented in a paper given to the 1991 annual meeting of the Political Studies Association of Ireland, in Belfast. Thanks also to Donna Hunter, who read and commented on Chapter 3, and to Jenny Williams, who word processed the manuscript.

The book is dedicated to the memory of my father, William Henry Dumbrell.

John Dumbrell

Note on sources

This book is based primarily on sources available at the Jimmy Carter Presidential Library, Atlanta, Georgia. The following abbreviations are used in the notes:

CQ	Congressional Quarterly
CQWR	Congressional Quarterly Weekly Report
DPS	Domestic Policy Staff
MC transcript	Miller Center (University of Virginia) interview transcript, available at the Carter Library
PHF	Presidential Handwriting File
SF	Subject File
SO	Staff Offices
WHCF	White House Central File

1

The Carter Presidency

Competence and compassion 同情

During his 1976 Presidential campaign, Jimmy Carter repeatedly invoked, before a variety of audiences, the theme of 'competence and compassion'. Soon after the nomination, for example, he addressed a Democratic fund-raising party in Hollywood hosted by Warren Beatty. Reacting to criticism levelled at him for attending such a modish, privileged gathering, Carter declared:

public servants like me . . . have a special responsibility to bypass the big shots, including you and people like you and make a concerted effort to understand people who are poor . . . who are stymied, who have some monumental problem and at that same time to run the government in a competent way, well organized, efficient, manageable, so that those services that are so badly needed can be delivered.[1]

By 10 October, when Carter gave two speeches on the subject in Indiana, 'competence and compassion' had become the campaign's leading leitmotif. Addressing a fund-raiser in South Bend, the candidate applied the theme to domestic concerns:

There are only two basic things we need in government. One is competence. Can the government be managed properly? Can it be efficient, economical, purposeful? Can it be open so that people can understand and control it, so it can represent what we are? Can this be possible in our own country? I think so.

And the other component part I think would be compassion. The need for government to understand those who don't make decisions for themselves.

According to Carter, competence and compassion 'are not incompatible':

As you will know, someone who is strong and sure and powerful is in a much better frame of mind to reach a helping hand to someone who is weaker. But if you are insecure and not quite so powerful as you would like to be, your inclination is to struggle and to step on others.[2]

The second Indiana speech of 10 October, delivered at Notre Dame, extended the theme to foreign affairs. (At the same university the following May,

President Carter was to make his famous declaration that his foreign policy was sufficiently 'confident' to be 'free of that inordinate fear of communism' which had once led the US to embrace dictators.)[3] In the 1976 speech, Carter criticised the *realpolitik* of the Nixon–Kissinger–Ford era:

> I think all of us realize that the question of supporting human rights throughout the world is a very difficult one. It requires a balancing of tough realism on the one hand, and idealism on the other. Of our understanding of the world as it is, and the world as it ought to be. The question, I think, is whether in recent years we have ignored those moral values that have always distinguished the United States of America from other countries.[4]

In his Inaugural Address the following January, the new President promised a 'competent and compassionate' government.[5] The theme was directly associated with national healing. The divisions of the 1960s, of Vietnam and of the Watergate period, could be transcended by an Administration which sought to restore moral rectitude alongside technocratic competence. Carter was, in political commentator Eric Sevareid's phrase, a 'wheeler-healer',[6] riding to power on the promise of national reconciliation. Competence and compassion also intermeshed with Carter's populism. At one level, this reflected Jimmy Carter's personal synthesis of Southern Populist–Progressive and Baptist traditions.[7] At another, it was a matter of style and symbol – partly conscious, partly instinctive. Numerous speeches and gestures spoke to Carter's belief that being a good, competent President involved proximity – spatial, cultural and emotional – to 'the people'. The Inaugural Address embodied a promise 'to stay close to you, to be worthy of you, and to exemplify what you are'.[8] Presidential competence would involve listening to Franklin Roosevelt's 'forgotten man'; it would involve 'depomping' the Presidency. At a 'town meeting' in Massachusetts in March 1977, Carter appealed for public input into his Administration: 'I'll tell my staff to bring these letters directly to me. You need not say that you were glad to have me with you and what a good job I did and so forth. Just say, "This is what I think you ought to do to be a good president".'[9] Arrogance, mystification, secrecy: these were the enemies not only of compassion but also of competence.

Populism, the appeal to national reconciliation and the professed unity of competence and compassion underlay Carter's understanding of political service. The same concerns were made explicit in the crucial 'crisis-of-confidence' address in July 1979. The President reminded his television audience of his populistic promises, and acknowledged his own failure yet to achieve that blending of competence and compassion, of managerial and moral values, which alone could heal the national wounds. At the head of a list of criticisms of his Administration, Carter placed the following remark by 'a Southern governor': 'Mr. President, you are not leading the Nation – you are just managing the government.'[10] So did Jimmy Carter, the 'engineer-preacher',[11] appeal once more to the need to synthesise morality and technocracy. In a sense, he was presenting himself as a kind of Presidential Robert Pirsig, whose mid-1970s bestseller (*Zen and the Art of Motorcycle Maintenance*) offered a similar agenda of harmonising apparent opposites. The 'competence and compassion' theme went deeper than the promise to mend recent national wounds. It went to the heart of American democratic traditions, to the dialectic of Jeffersonian and Hamiltonian values. In the unlikely shape of a Baptist from rural Georgia with a background in engineering, the Democrats in 1976 were offering nothing less than a revitalisation of the American political tradition: the restoration of that democratic balance between republican virtue and efficiency which had been distorted by the rise of giant corporations, a global foreign policy and an overweening attachment to Presidential power. If it could only connect morality and reason, the passion and the prose, the US might effectuate 'an undiminished, ever-expanding American dream',[12] 'a rebirth of the American spirit'.[13]

Any such rebirth, Carter argued, would have to be grounded in an unequivocal acceptance of limits. Hubris abroad had led to the defeat in Vietnam. At home all economic indicators appeared to point to the need for retrenchment, consolidation and diminished expectations. The days of unrestrained use of American power abroad, and of big spending liberalism at home, were over. The government had to be the government of 'the people', not of any special interests. Carter saw it as his duty to educate 'the people' in the realities of the new 'age of limits'. In his Inaugural Address, he declared: 'We have learned that "more" is not necessarily "better", that even our great nation has its recognized limits, and that we can neither answer all questions nor solve all problems.'[14] A year later, in the 1978 State of the Union Message, the President warned against expecting too much of government, which of itself could not 'eliminate poverty', 'provide energy' or 'mandate goodness'. Only 'a true partnership between government and the people' could aspire to such things.[15] The 1979 Message returned to the 'competence and compassion' theme, clearly situating it amid the need to recognise limits: 'In our government it is a myth that we must choose between compassion and competence. Together, we build the foundation for a government that works – and that works for people.' The US people needed to change its attitude: 'We cannot afford to live beyond our means . . .'[16]

So, if Carter's doctrine of 'competence and compassion' had a messianic streak, it was a messianism appropriate to lowered expectations, post-imperial moderation and modest democratic and populistic virtues. Americans had, in Carter's view, to turn back to the true American tradition. In the 1979 'crisis-of-confidence' address, the President asserted that America, while losing confidence in the future, was 'also beginning to close the door on the past'. The true American tradition was one where citizens could 'serve as the ultimate rulers and shapers of our democracy' and where 'self-indulgence and consumption' no longer held sway.[17] It is on the basis of

this commitment to competence and compassion, predicated upon as acceptance of limits, that Carter's Presidency should be judged.

The Carter Presidency: a brief narrative

Carter's 1976 victory over Gerald Ford was narrow and regionally based.
The Georgian took only 50.1 per cent of the popular vote. Almost 80 per cent
of his electoral vote came from the South and North-east. Yet the new
President was able to enjoy a honeymoon, maintaining 70 per cent Gallup
approval ratings in the early months. He did run into trouble over the
nomination of Theodore Sorensen to head the Central Intelligence Agency.
However all other major appointments were confirmed by the Senate. (Even
Sorensen was not actually rejected, but rather withdrew.) After a fierce battle,
Paul Warnke was confirmed as chief arms control negotiator. For the first half
of the Presidency, the Democrats controlled the Senate, 61–38, and the
House of Representatives, 292–143. The new White House team 'hit the
ground running'. The President issued a (qualified) Vietnam draft evasion
amnesty on the day following his inauguration. An extensive list of legislative
proposals was presented to Congress. These included plans for executive
branch reorganisation, new ethics-in-government laws, welfare reform,
hospital cost containment and a new energy resource-maximisation package.
Early problems with Congress revolved around the President's vetoing of
water projects he felt to be wasteful, as well as the dropping of a $50 tax
rebate proposal.

The style of the new Administration was decidedly populist, homely and
(lower case) republican. Cabinet members were to drive their own cars.
Carter's first important television address, on 15 April 1977, described the
energy crisis as 'the moral equivalent of war'; it would be the Administration's first priority. The House of Representatives passed an energy package
in August 1977, and a new Department of Energy was established under
James Schlesinger. On 7 September, a major Administration foreign policy
initiative was signalled, with the signing of the treaty designed to hand over
control of the Panama Canal to Panama after 1999. After intense Administration lobbying, two separate Panama Canal treaties were ratified by the
Senate in March–April, 1978.

The year 1977 saw a spelling-out, especially in the May Notre Dame
speech, of a new attitude towards the policy of containing communism.
Human rights, rather than anti-communism, would guide the new Administration. Efforts to speed up talks for a new Strategic Arms Limitation Treaty
(SALT II) stalled in Moscow. Soviet leaders rejected Secretary of State Cyrus
Vance's arms cuts proposals. At the end of June, the President announced his
intention not to proceed with the B-1 bomber. American ground troops
would be withdrawn from Korea. In terms of Carter's popular standing, the
most damaging event of 1977 was the September resignation of Bert Lance,

director of the Office of Management and Budget. Carter's defence of Lance, who was accused of financial improprieties – he was later acquitted of the charges – while a private banker in Georgia, appears to have severely impaired the President's early popularity. Between July and October 1977, Carter's Gallup approval rating dropped from 59 to 48 per cent. In December, Democratic national chairman Kenneth Curtis resigned, complaining about White House attitudes to the party.

Many of the Administration's 1977 legislative proposals remained bogged down in Congress in 1978. The President called for a 'new spirit'. An energy bill was passed late in the session, though it fell short of the President's recommendations. Carter was defeated in his proposal for a consumer protection agency. In October, however, he won passage of a major reform of the civil service. March saw White House invocation of the Taft–Hartley Act – traditionally a last resort, especially for Democratic Presidents – to end a widespread coal strike. In the defence area, Carter announced, against senior advice and to the consternation of NATO allies, his intention to defer production of the neutron bomb. Worries about declining popularity prompted a high-level Administration conference at Camp David in April. Staff changes followed. In June, the passage of 'Proposition 13' in California signalled the arrival of the 'taxpayer's revolt'. The President's own tax reform measures remained on a committee table in Congress.

The year 1978 was one of foreign policy triumphs, though also of rumblings against the Shah in Iran which foreshadowed trouble for the Administration. The Panama Canal treaties were ratified. By the year's end, the US and the People's Republic of China had agreed to establish diplomatic relations. The US would abrogate its 1954 treaty with nationalist Taiwan. By the close of 1978, also, the SALT II negotiations were back on track. The final treaty was signed at the Vienna summit in June 1979. Above all, in September 1978, there were the Camp David Middle East peace accords, mediated by personal Presidential diplomacy. These led to the signing of a Middle East peace treaty, involving Israel's retreat from Egyptian territory, the following March. Historic as it was, the treaty did not settle the question of the status of the Palestinians. The accords did help Carter at home. His approval rating shot up seventeen points. The Democrat's showing in the mid-term Congressional races also showed relatively modest losses – a reasonable performance for a first-term President. In December, however, Democratic activists at a mid-term conference in Memphis demonstrated their support for the figure now regarded as Carter's main rival within the party: Senator Edward Kennedy.

The 96th Congress, which convened in January 1979, had Democratic majorities of 276–157 in the House, and 58–41 in the Senate. The main business before Congress was again a major energy package. Carter tried a new slogan, the 'new foundation'. His legislative programme was now clearly consolidative. The Presidential budget for fiscal year 1980 was described by the White House as 'lean and austere'; (the fiscal 1979 budget had been 'lean and tight'). Yet defence spending was to increase. With the crisis in Iran – the Shah fell in January 1979 and Ayatollah Khomeini returned in February – energy issues at last captured national attention. As Iranian supplies dried up, the US experienced a 10 to 15 per cent shortfall in gasoline supplies. In May, however, Congress rebuffed Carter's request for standby authority to impose rationing. On 28 March 1979, the accident at Three Mile Island nuclear plant alerted the American public to yet another dimension of US energy difficulties.

In June, oil producing countries announced a 50 per cent price rise. Inflation was now running at 13.3 per cent, compared with six per cent in 1977. The 'misery index' – the aggregation of inflation and unemployment which Carter had used to attack Ford in 1976 – now stood at 19.3. (In 1976 it had been 15.3.) Stuart Eizenstat, his chief domestic policy adviser, warned the President that the Administration was in deep crisis. Carter retreated to Camp David to consult various governmental and private figures. On 15 July, he delivered his 'crisis-of-confidence' address, culminating in a call to Congress to enact his energy legislation. After eliciting mass Cabinet resignations, Carter, in effect, fired four Cabinet members: Joseph Califano of Health, Education and Welfare (HEW); Michael Blumenthal of the Treasury; James Schlesinger of Energy; and Brock Adams at Transportation. Hamilton Jordan was designated White House chief of staff. A public opinion poll published in the *Washington Post* on 14 September 1979 gave Carter the lowest job approval rating of any President for three decades.

Most of the energy package (a windfall profits tax, a synthetic fuels programme, a standby gasoline rationing and conservation programme and a solar energy initiative) was passed by Congress in 1979 and 1980. By this time decontrol of oil prices had been greatly accelerated, and Carter had also won important victories in the field of commercial, especially transport, deregulation. On 17 October 1979, he signed a bill establishing a new Department of Education, to be headed by Shirley Hufstedler. On 4 November, attention shifted dramatically to Tehran, where revolutionary Iranian students were holding about sixty-five US Embassy personnel hostage.

Prior to November 1979, the centre of the foreign policy stage was held by SALT II and the upcoming fight for Senate ratification. Congressional and public opinion were now generally regarded as having swung rightwards on defence issues. Just before the Vienna summit, Carter announced his support for the MX missile. The relatively hawkish National Security Adviser, Zbigniew Brzezinski, achieved new public prominence. On 15 August, Andrew Young, US Ambassador to the United Nations and ideological adversary to Brzezinski, resigned after meeting, without official permission, a Palestinian Liberation Organisation representative. The US agreed with NATO to deploy new (cruise and Pershing II) missiles in Europe unless the

Soviets made theatre nuclear withdrawals. The fall of Anastasio Somoza's regime in Nicaragua, itself largely the result of US human rights policies, prompted fears in Washington about the extension of Soviet influence in Central America. A temporary crisis arose over the supposed presence of a Soviet 'combat brigade' in Cuba. By this time, Soviet–Cuban influence in Africa was increasingly dominating US perceptions of that continent. When, on 28 December 1979, Soviet forces invaded Afghanistan, all American suspicions of the rival superpower seemed confirmed. Carter moved to apply economic and political sanctions – most famously the suspension of grain sales and official US withdrawal from the 1980 Moscow Olympics. Prospects for SALT II ratification were now zero.

The debilitating agony of the Iranian hostage crisis continued. Carter refused the students' request that the Shah, who was in the US for medical treatment, be returned to Iran. The Shah left for Panama in mid-December. On 7 November 1979, three days after the hostages were taken, Edward Kennedy announced his candidacy for the Democratic nomination. Yet the initial effect of the Iranian crisis on Carter's popularity was positive. By early December his approval rating stood at 61 per cent, falling back to the mid-50s in early 1980.

Carter's defence budget for fiscal year 1981 amounted to $154.5 billion. In December 1980, Congress approved a figure of $159.7 billion, the first time in thirteen years that the legislature had approved a defence appropriations bill above the President's budget request.

Carter announced his anti-inflation programme on 14 March. It included a proposed balanced budget for fiscal year 1981. The economy was now clearly in recession once more. Labour leaders blamed the Administration's restrictionist policies for the loss of 1.8 million American jobs. It seemed as if the White House had failed, by neglect or by design, to manage the synchronicity of the economic and the electoral cycles. Unemployment stood at 7.8 per cent in May 1980. Inflation stood at over 13 per cent. In foreign affairs, Brzezinski was now in ascendance. All attempts to have SALT II ratified were abandoned. The 'Carter Doctrine', under which the US undertook to use force in the Middle East/Persian Gulf area if its interests were threatened, was promulgated. Presidential Directive 59 was issued. This envisaged the controlled use of nuclear weapons on military and industrial targets in the Soviet Union. Carter was now looking to increases in military spending by 4.5 per cent per annum until 1985. This did not prevent Ronald Reagan, the future Republican Presidential contender, from berating Carter for supposed softness in foreign and defence affairs, as well as for economic mismanagement.

The President did well in the early primaries, though Kennedy managed four important spring victories in Northern industrial states. A disastrous hostage rescue mission was launched in April. Cyrus Vance, who opposed the mission and was in more or less open disagreement with Brzezinski, resigned and was replaced as Secretary of State by Edmund Muskie. The President at last left the White House 'rose garden' and took to the campaign trail. He won eleven straight primary victories. Kennedy still managed some important victories, notably in California on 3 June. Around the same date, Congress overrode a Presidential veto, thus killing a proposal for an oil import fee. The President was further embarrassed by the involvement of his alcoholic brother, Billy, as a lobbyist for the Libyan government. The Democratic convention, which Kennedy supporters attempted unsuccessfully to declare 'open', nominated Carter but revealed major breaches within the party. In November, Reagan won by an electoral college landslide (489–49). Carter took only six states (Minnesota, Georgia, West Virginia, Hawaii, Rhode Island and Maryland) as well as the District of Columbia. In terms of the popular vote, 50.7 per cent went for Reagan, 41 per cent for Carter, and 6.6 for the liberal Republican Congressman (running as an independent) John Anderson. The Carter White House turned its attention to securing a hostage release – fifty-two Americans were now held – during the 'lame duck' period. The final near-crisis came over Poland, where, in December 1980, a Soviet invasion was anticipated. The President sent a stern warning letter to the Soviet leadership. Carter's Farewell Address returned to the theme of human rights. Immediately after Reagan's Inauguration, the hostages were released. Carter commented: 'We've had some notable accomplishments, some failures, and more than our share of bad luck. But we were bucking the tide on a lot of issues.'[18] Early in the year, Robert Strauss, Democratic Presidential campaign chairman, had put the point more bluntly: 'Poor bastard – he used up all his luck getting here. We've had our victories and defeats, but we've not had a single piece of good luck.'[19]

Carter's changing reputation

By the early 1980s, it had become the fashion to ridicule both Carter's 'compassion' and his 'competence'. The former was regularly dismissed either as merely gestural tokenism – even cynicism – or as naively subversive (especially in foreign affairs) of true American interests. During the later part of the Carter Presidency, Gary Trudeau's *Doonesbury* cartoon mocked the Administration's putative 'Department of Symbolism', offering token responses to 'some of the most important rhetorical issues of our time'[20] On the Reaganite right, Jeane Kirkpatrick denounced Carter's human rights policies as having 'alienated non-democratic but friendly nations', paved the way for 'anti-Western opposition groups to come to power in Iran and Nicaragua', and generally having contributed to reduced American influence in the world.[21] Leftist critics of his 'compassionate' foreign policy dismissed it either as inherently, and increasingly, militaristic; or, alternatively, as an expression of post-Vietnam capitalist restructuring, dictated by US business interests.[22]

On the 'competence' question, the most familiar complaint about Carter and his team concerned their supposed bumbling amateurism and political naivety. Sanford Ungar, writing in April 1977, had portrayed the new President's staff as 'a group of rank amateurs'.[23] In its dealings with political Washington, especially with the Congress, Carter's White House appeared both naive and foolishly haughty. Ward Just described the supposed estrangement from Washington in 1978:

he and his people remain remote, removed from the Washington experience. With very few exceptions, he transplanted his campaign staff intact to the White House, and that may be the major difficulty, because successful campaigns do not necessarily make successful bureaucrats; in any case, they govern as if the process is somehow beneath them.[24]

To many commentators, the problem was not one of simple incompetence. Carter's problems derived rather from his 'outsider' status: the way in which he had gained election by attacking not only the Nixon–Ford legacy, not only big government and the bloated bureaucracy, but also Washington itself. Dilys Hill and Phil Williams wrote in 1984: 'It is one of the ironies of the Carter Presidency that the very disillusionment which had led many Americans to vote for an outsider for president also made it enormously difficult for that president to function effectively.'[25] The 'outsider' thesis seemed to offer an explanation for this phenomenon of a one-term President, whose most impressive political performance appeared to have been the initial securing of the Democratic nomination.[26]

Another recurring theme was Carter's celebrated 'fuzziness' on the issues. A commonly told joke had the young Jimmy confronting his parent to explain the chopping down of a peanut plant. When asked if he were the guilty party, Jimmy replied: 'Daddy, I cannot tell a lie. Maybe it was, and maybe it wasn't.' Some commentators felt that fuzziness had served him well in the 1976 nomination race. He was, in James Wooten's phrase, 'the Lon Chaney of 1976, the man of a thousand faces'.[27] Later, however, his 'fuzziness', his lack of what Betty Glad called any 'basic philosophy',[28] was seen as having collapsed into simple ineffectuality. Even in some serious political studies of the 1980s, and not only from the pens of Reagan supporters, Carter's Presidency was treated as little more than an object of ridicule. Recalling Carter's 1976 *Playboy* interview and a well publicised incident of 1979, George Reedy wrote:

Virtually nothing of any moment was done during his administration and to the extent that he will be remembered in popular legend it is as the born again president who 'lusted in his heart after women' and who beat off an attack from a killer rabbit charging his canoe.[29]

(A Herblock cartoon in the *Washington Post* on 4 September 1979 showed Carter's campaign strategists examining the results of a poll in which 31 per cent supported the rabbit.)

Extremely influential in reinforcing negative views were the contributions from James Fallows and ex-HEW Secretary Joseph Califano. The former, who had worked in Carter's White House as a speech-writer, published two pieces in the journal *Atlantic Monthly* in 1979 under the title, 'The Passionless Presidency'. Drawing together received journalistic wisdom, Fallows added anecdotes and supplied a general aura of insider-authenticity. 'Carter and those closest to him', wrote Fallows, 'took office in profound ignorance of their jobs'. The arrogant Georgians in the White House had 'little sense of what power is and how it might be exercised'. Their only real interest was in winning elections; they undertook work which was not directly related to political campaigning 'with the spirit of enlisted men on manoeuvres'. They resented all criticism, seeing it simply as anti-Southern snobbery. As for the President: 'Like the southern defensiveness, Carter's notion of populism and privilege gave him a reason to resist learning things in the usual way.' His populism 'was reflected in his pride, even arrogance, about having seen all sides of life close-up in his small town and in his disdain for the elite "socially prominent" (a favorite phrase) professionals whose privilege shielded them from such knowledge.' It was partly a matter of sheer incompetence: Carter's organisational naivety – he 'seemed to think that organizations would run in practice as they did on paper', – his failure to prioritise (the tendency to 'think in lists, not arguments'), his reluctance to settle the open warfare between Vance and Brzezinski, and so on. Carter's 'cast of mind' was also at fault. As an engineer, the President viewed problems 'as technical, not historical'. This led him to: 'forgo the lessons of experience and insist on rediscovering fire, the lever, the wheel'. (In June 1978, Richard Davy had written in the London *Times* that Carter had difficulty seeing things whole. He 'has shown the linear vision of an engineer, pursuing each problem separately toward its most logical solution.' Tom Wicker frequently made the same points in the *New York Times*.)[30] It was not a case of compassion having ousted competence. Rather, for Fallows, the Carter Administration, though itself incompetent, was 'passionless'; its leadership amounted to no more than an empty commitment to arid, directionless managerialism.[31]

This 'passionless Presidency' thesis was extended in Califano's memoir, *Governing America*. At times reading like a panegyric to Califano's old boss, Lyndon Johnson, this book depicted a Carter Presidency which was rudderless, with no ideological fire in its belly. Engaged in an unheroic retreat from the true faith (Great Society liberalism), Carter's Administration was also bedevilled by its inability 'to switch gears from campaigning to governing', by its political 'innocence' and needless 'animosity' towards the Washington press corps.[32]

A 1983 survey of historians ranked Carter twenty-fifth in a league-table of Presidential greatness. (Below him stood only Presidents B. Harrison, Taylor, Tyler, Fillmore, Coolidge, Pierce, A. Johnson, Buchanan, Nixon, Grant and Harding.) Opinion surveys during the 1980s consistently placed Carter low in public esteem.[33] By this time the Presidency had been well and truly 'repomped' by Ronald Reagan. (Many commentators pointed out in 1980 that Americans quite liked imperial Presidents.) As the 1950s appeared to the 1960s, so did the (especially late) 1970s appear to the 1980s: a decade where, in the (ironic) title of Peter N. Carroll's 1990 study, *It Seemed Like Nothing Happened.*[34] What did happen apeared largely negative: energy crisis, the perception of national decline, humiliation at the hands of terrorists in Tehran. The opening paragraph of John Updike's *Rabbit is Rich*, published in 1981 and set in 1979, described an America where:

the people out there are getting frantic, they know the great American ride is ending. Gas lines at ninety-nine point nine cents a gallon and ninety per cent of the stations to be closed for the weekend . People are going wild, their dollars are going rotten.[35]

The most obvious counter to negative memories of the late 1970s, to Reagan's attacks on the Carter record, and in particular to the Fallows–Califano 'insider' critique of the Administration, came in the form of sympathetic participant memoirs. These showed that criticism and ridicule had rankled. Press Secretary Jody Powell attacked Califano's *Governing America* as a 'Washington book' of 'the "if they had only listened to me" variety'.[36] Carter himself had scribbled in the margin of one of Fallows' *Atlantic Monthly* articles: 'Everybody has got to make a living.'[37]

Powell's memoir was frank in admitting the Carter team's inexperience, its 'pitiful lack of information about Washington':

Jimmy Carter lacked, to a greater extent than any modern President, a loyal coterie of friends and die-hard supporters among those people who remain permanently in Washington as administrations come and go. Once a man becomes President, making new friends is a difficult undertaking.

Yet, Carter and his staff were capable of learning and adjusting. Powell concentrated, in defending the Administration, on press hostility, including a disinformation campaign (possibly co-ordinated in 1980 by the shadowy 'Madison group' of conservative Senate staffers). As in Hamilton Jordan's Iran crisis memoir, especial venom was reserved by Powell for Kennedy's 1980 challenge.[38]

The foreign policy memoirs revealed a clear determination by both Brzezinski and Vance to avoid the direct expression of the relatively 'hard' or 'soft' attitudes with which the press associated them. Brzezinski wrote that he had frequently cautioned Carter: 'before you are a President Wilson you have to be for a few years a President Truman.' Emotionally, Carter 'thirsted for the Wilsonian mantle', and thereby opened himself to 'the unfair but damaging charge of vacillation'. Actually, Carter was 'tough, cool and determined', always '*his own* Secretary of State'. Brzezinski staunchly defended Carter's aspirations to moral leadership:

It was Carter's major accomplishment that, by the time he left office, there was more widespread appreciation worldwide that America stood again for principle and identified itself with the movement for more social and political justice.[39]

Vance's memoir presented a surprisingly lukewarm position on human rights. The former Secretary of State emphasised that he had always preferred 'quiet diplomacy' to 'public pressure'. The US should avoid attempting 'to impose our values on others', and understand 'the limits of our power and wisdom'. Vance emphasised that he had always been committed to a strong military posture, and to the view that competition, not co-operation, would be 'the principal feature' of US–Soviet relations.[40] Yet clear differences between the two advisers still emerged from the memoirs: notably over the question of whether or not Cold War paradigms should be applied to regional disputes. Most reviewers highlighted these differences: Norman Thomas wrote in 1986, for example:

The public perception of a tentative and halting foreign policy presided over by an indecisive president, marked by sharp changes in direction, and embarrassed by inexcusable gaffes . . . and frequent public squabbling . . . is not erased by these memoirs.[41]

Carter's own *Keeping Faith* memoirs were generally taken as confirming an emerging view of the thirty-ninth President as worthy, well meaning, but dull and ideologically confused. In a similar way, for an earlier generation, Eisenhower's memoirs appeared to confirm the (then) prevailing impression of Ike's blandness and intellectual mediocrity. Carter's straightforward description of his political position resurrected the old charges of 'fuzziness': 'a fiscal conservative but quite liberal on such issues as civil rights, environmental quality, and helping people overcome handicaps to lead fruitful lives'. Compared to the fireworks of the Nixon memoirs, Carter's book *was* dull. Ward Just noted that, where Nixon seemed to have written *RN* at three o'clock in the morning, *Keeping Faith* evoked the hour of 'three in the afternoon of a winter's day'.[42] Yet at least Carter, unlike Nixon – who, after all, had resigned in disgrace and was fortunate to escape criminal prosecution, – was prepared to admit mistakes. He acknowledged, for example. that his legislative requests should have been more clearly prioritised, and that the 1979 Cabinet resignations were poorly handled. Admittedly not without a touch of defensive pride, Carter allowed that the failure to overcome his 'outsider' status had been a problem. As with all other modern Presidential memoirs, *Keeping Faith* revealed its author's frustration – Brzezinski used the word 'disdain' – regarding domestic politics, and preference for foreign policy. Its description of the Middle East agreements exuded caution and modesty, as did Carter's references to it in his 1985 volume, *The Blood of Abraham*. Yet the detailed recapitulation of the Camp David negotiations in *Keeping Faith* actually constituted an understated yet revelatory exploration of an extraordinary achievement of personal diplomacy.[43]

Though they did not prompt any immediate revaluation of the Presidency, the Carter Administration memoirs did at least stimulate interest and call into question some of the cruder preconceptions about Jimmy Carter. Two sympathetic studies of his foreign policy appeared in 1986.[44] Gaddis Smith concluded that Carter had failed, but also that he had 'offered a morally responsible and farsighted vision'.[45] Yet the neo-conservative attack continued: for example in Joshua Muravchik's 1986 study of the human rights policy.[46]

Between 1980 and about 1988, the academic and journalistic tide was against Carter. Such sympathy as there was for *The President Who Failed* (the title of Clark Mollenhoff's 1980 study)[47] tended simply to echo Robert Strauss's point about poor Carter's bad luck. The British press followed the general American judgement. For its left flank, Carter was the betrayer of liberal social democracy and the post-1979 militarist. He stood to President Reagan as British Labour leaders of the 1970s stood to Mrs Thatcher. In 1987, Alexander Cockburn, the radical Irish journalist writing for the US magazine *The Nation*, declared: 'It was Wilson and Callaghan who paved the way for Thatcher, just as the Carter of 1978–80 oiled the hinge for Reagan.'[48] A *Spectator* editorial of 31 May 1980 allowed that the President was 'a man of more intelligence than his critics give him credit for', but went on to deliver the judgement of the British right:

The Ayatollah frustrates him . . . Soviet power demonstrates itself with brutal arrogance in Afghanistan, and the United States is powerless to respond effectively . . . The dollar slumps, inflation proceeds. There is no glimmer of a sensible and coherent energy policy or, alternatively, of a readiness to let the market do its work.

As for Reagan: 'If a peanut farmer from Georgia can make it to the White House and use his ancient mother as envoy extraordinary, there is no reason why an ageing ex-actor who calls his wife "Mummy" should not succeed him.'[49] Throughout the early 1980s, however, Carter did have at least one champion in the British press: Peter Jay, British ambassador to Washington between 1977 and 1979. Jay's defence of Carter in 1980 anticipated many of the arguments employed in the journalistic revaluation of Jimmy Carter which emerged in the late 1980s. Jay wrote in October 1980:

Mr. Carter is not senile, power-crazed, corrupt, stupid, indolent, reactionary, oppressive or megalomaniac. He is not even a male chauvinist pig. He is on the contrary exceptionally intelligent, inhumanely hard-working, profoundly liberal in his instincts, a democrat to his fingertips, genuinely compassionate towards the weak and the poor, honest, healthy and – though this is little recognised or deployed – capable of brilliant wit.

Carter had 'consistently confronted the toughest underlying issues in each region of the world'. His ruling paradigm for Soviet relations – competition and co-operation – was sensible. Had critics listened to his Annapolis speech in the early part of 1978, they would not have been surprised by the reaction to the Afghan invasion. Carter had resisted the blandishments of the military–industrial complex, while also reversing the post-Vietnam decline in military spending. His policies had increased NATO cost-effectiveness. He was the first President of the modern era not to be entrapped in Cold War orthodoxy, and his human rights initiatives should be applauded. His policy towards Zimbabwe/Rhodesia was a triumph, as were Camp David and the Panama Canal treaties. Admittedly, the US economy was in trouble and out of Carter's control. But there were domestic triumphs, especially regarding economic deregulation:

In retrospect, the years 1977–80 will be notable, in United States domestic affairs, for the bringing of a profound and quiet revolution: the de-regulation of huge tracts of American industry and commerce. Although the cooperation of Congress and the drive of Edward Kennedy played an essential part in this, it was a Carter Administration policy and carried through *against* special interests.

Jay listed other domestic and economic policy successes: urban renewal, creation of the Department of Education, civil service reform, extension of the deadline for the Equal Rights Amendment to the Constitution, minimum wage legislation, restoration of integrity to the social security system, child welfare measures, liberalisation of the farm reserve system, passage of the trade bill and consummation of the multilateral trade negotiations. Above all, Carter had finally got an energy bill passed. He:

succeeded (though not in the form he originally favoured) in accomplishing the single most necessary transformation for the US . . . namely a briefly staged and dramatic increase in energy prices charged to the consumer as well as comprehensive support for alternative energy developments.[50]

At the time, Jay's judgements appeared quixotic. By 1988, however, the journalistic tide had turned once again. In July 1988, the *Wall Street Journal* published an editorial entitled 'Jimmy, We Hardly Knew Ye'. It credited Carter with beginning the post-Vietnam revitalisation of the US military and, apparently straight facedly – in complete abandonment of previous *Journal* judgements on Carter – with economic prudence. It particularly applauded the appointment of Paul Volcker to head the Federal Reserve Board.[51] In a 1987 piece in *New Republic*, J. L. Pasley and A. P. Weisman offered a glowing account of the ex-President. Special praise was accorded to the Panama Canal treaties and to Carter's energy policy. Interestingly, the authors cited Carter's 1979 speech to Congress on oil price decontrol not as an example of the Georgian's political innocence but of his far-sightedness: 'I'd rather accept the political blame than spend another two years arguing with you about what ought to be done – when you *know* what ought to be done.' According to Pasley and Weisman, Jimmy Carter was right. Initially, the oil companies and OPEC enjoyed increased profits. But decontrol eventually led to the breaking of the cartel and to lower prices.[52]

To a degree, changing views of Carter derived from a kind of twenty–twenty hindsight. The accretions of history had put previously derided policies into new perspective. More directly, however, the change in Carter's fortunes derived from three factors, neatly brought together in an article written for the British *Independent on Sunday* by R. W. Johnson in April 1990: disillusionment with Reagan's performance, Carter's post-Presidential activities, and the ending of the Cold War. According to Johnson:

opinion polls in the US now show that Jimmy Carter is more popular than Ronald Reagan. This had a lot to do with Carter's achievement of an Egyptian–Israeli truce – remembered as the single greatest feat of US foreign policy in recent time. But it also has something to do with Carter continuing to crop up as a gentle, insistent peacemaker – in Nicaragua just, now in the Middle East – while Reagan receives terrible publicity for his 2m (dollar) fee for a speech in Japan . . .

One might add . . . that Carter kept the US trade and budget deficits under far better control than Reagan, that his Administration was immeasurably less corrupt, and that under Carter the American poor were decisively better off . . .

Largely forgotten is the . . . fact that Carter took office with a philosophy that has now been strikingly vindicated. The bi-polar, Cold War view of the world, Carter argued, was dangerously distorting US priorities.

In privileging human rights over geopolitics, Carter was playing 'America's strongest suit':

The Third World – spectators between the blocs – often had reservations about the merits of capitalism . . . But if you placed the emphasis instead on whether one had free speech, freedom of assembly and religion, free elections, a free press . . . – then America won every time.[53]

A year after the publication of Johnson's article, the British press was speculating about Carter's possible appointment as chair of a commission to mediate in Northern Ireland. In September 1991, *The Independent on Sunday* editorialised in favour of Carter succeeding Perez de Cuellar as Secretary-General of the United Nations![54]

By the late 1980s, the glitter was indeed beginning to rub off Reagan and the teflon Presidency. As E. J. Dionne argued in the *New York Times* in May 1989, after the Iran–contra scandal, Carter's 'hands-on' style of governing looked more like responsible management rather than a damaging obsession with detail.[55] In *Rabbit at Rest*, published in 1990, Updike's hero looked back on: 'eight years under Reagan of nobody minding the store, making money out of nothing, running up debt, trusting in God.'[56] Iran–contra also threw into relief Carter's own policies towards hostages. On the one hand, Carter could be accused of self-damaging over-dramatisation.[57] On the other, the hostages were eventually released. Whether Carter ever offered anything in the way of a 'deal' with the hostage-takers is a complex question. However, he certainly did not indulge in the kind of hypocritical and illegal trading associated with the Reagan Administration. Additionally, 1991 speculation about a Reagan–Tehran deal to delay hostage release – the thesis advanced by Carter's national security staffer Gary Sick[58] – served only to increase sympathy for Reagan's predecessor. In September 1989, *Time* magazine was hailing Carter was 'the best ex-president the US has had since Herbert Hoover'.[59] Carter's post-White House career has, by the standards set by other ex-Presidents, been glittering. His various activities – election monitoring from Nicaragua to Zambia, mediation in the Middle East and Africa, the Carter-Menil Human Rights Foundation, the various Carter Center projects, the brief involvement with the Jean-Bertrand Aristide regime in Haiti – all attracted positive coverage.[60] The new joke was that Carter had used the Presidency as a stepping-stone to something better. Neither his doveish statements on the 1990–1 Gulf crisis/war nor attempts to link him to the Bank of Commerce and Credit International scandal seriously damaged his reputation. *The Nation* in November 1990 saluted 'Citizen Carter: The Very Model of an Ex-President'. Andrew Young was quoted to the effect that Carter made him 'feel guilty for serving on corporate boards'; the ex-President 'shunned all that'. According to Kai Bird, *The Nation*'s columnist:

It is as if Carter decided to take the most liberal and successful policies of his failed Administration – human rights, peace-making and concern for the poor – and make them the centerpiece of a campaign for his own political resurrection.[61]

The human rights agenda gained additional attention with the ending of the Cold War and the search (once again) to find a new consensus to replace anti-communism.[62] The debate over American international decline [63] also brought back into focus Carter's early emphasis on the need for a post-imperial foreign policy which recognised the limits to US power.

In February 1990, the ex-President himself commented on the reassessment: 'it's gratifying to get good publicity for a change'. He placed himself in the tradition of 'Truman, Eisenhower, Hoover' – Presidents whose reputation became 'refurbished over time'.[64] In fact, academic judgement on the Carter Presidency has remained decidedly mixed.[65] Certainly, a number of papers presented to the major conference on the Carter Presidency, held at Hofstra University (New York) in 1990 were broadly sympathetic. A defence of Carter's leadership appeared in 1987 and a re-evaluative account of his foreign policy in 1991.[66] Yet the two major studies published in 1988,[67] both based on the White Burkett Miller Center (University of Virginia) oral history project, tended to refine rather than challenge received views. C. O. Jones's study of Carter's relations with Congress emphasised that the President's strategy was the result not of amateurish bumbling, but of a determination to put forward correct, coherent policy. In this view, Carter – especially early on – did not even attempt to succeed in traditional legislative bargaining.

According to Jones, Carter had a difficult task on his hands anyway. Congress was assertive and difficult to lead. But Carter's background and beliefs put him on a collision course with political Washington. E. C. Hargrove saw Carter as a highly conscientious political leader, grappling with disjointed and recalcitrant political structures. He concerned himself with comprehensive political solutions, rather than piecemeal accommodation to interest group demands. In Hargrove's conclusion, Carter is portrayed as a kind of heroic failure:

Most of the achievements were personal, and it is not clear that anyone else could have done as well. Carter's ineptness was most evident in those areas of leadership, especially with Congress, in which any brand of leadership would have had trouble succeeding.[68]

Carter and post-liberalism; the politics of human rights

The Carter Presidency was both response to, and expression of, the crisis of American liberalism. In its post-1945 form, US liberalism rested on three principal foundations: the strong Presidency, an internationalist foreign policy driven by anti-communist containment and social reform funded by economic growth. By the early 1970s, all three were teetering.

Vietnam, a Presidentially directed war, and the Nixon Administration left the 'imperial Presidency' exposed and vulnerable.[69] Jimmy Carter was certainly not in favour of a 'weak' Presidency. He explained in 1976:

I think our country is best served by a strong, independent and aggressive president, working with a strong and independent Congress in harmony, for a change, and with mutual respect, for a change, and in the open, for a change. The Congress of our country is inherently incapable of leadership.[70]

Yet Carter's view of the Presidency was a long way from the 'high liberal' view of the office encapsulated in John F. Kennedy's National Press Club speech of 1960.[71] His repeated stress on legality, openness and humility – 'the president is just a human being'[72] – was distinctly post-imperial. However, he also saw the office in highly populistic terms. As 'tribune of the people', the President should act as a champion against 'special interests' and 'inside deals'.[73] In this mode, Carter appeared, at least in his rhetoric, as a kind of latterday Theodore Roosevelt, rather than an upholder of the 'passive' or 'Whig' tradition of Presidential power.

Regarding foreign affairs, Carter's 1976 campaign autobiography declared that the 'time for American intervention in all the problems of the world is over'.[74] At Georgia Institute of Technology in early 1979, he declared that the US 'cannot control events within other nations'.[75] The President's task was, while avoiding any 'retreat into isolationism',[76] to build a post-liberal foreign policy, rooted in morality, recognition of limits and 'true' interests.

By the mid-1970s, American liberals were adjusting to the view that perhaps social reform could not be funded from economic growth. Carter's election actually took place as the US began to recover from its (then) worst recession since the 1930s. Stagflation, energy dependence (seen dramatically in the early 1970s OPEC price shock) and the erosion of the 'fiscal dividend' all threatened to undermine the assumptions of American liberalism. Lester Thurow held that the US had become a 'zero-sum society' in which social spending could not be extracted from the economic fat. It could be achieved only through painful redistribution. Social groupings (rather than traditionally defined economic classes) stood in direct competition for scarce resources.[77] In such a situation, traditional political parties and voting coalitions were bound to fragment. Pluralist thinkers, who had previously celebrated American 'polyarchy', began to address the problem of 'ungovernability'. They had seen 'the dark'.[78] The problem was partly economic, partly political, partly cultural. As early as 1969, Theodore Lowi argued that US liberalism had degenerated into a contest between special interests. 'Interest-group liberalism' involved the atrophy of public accountability, the creation of new structures of privilege and a new defensive conservatism. Even when Great Society programmes were directly aimed at 'uplifting the underprivileged', argued Lowi, their administration actually created 'new privilege'. Thus federal housing policy conformed to standards set by the building industry and 'became a major escape route for the middle class to leave the city', rather than 'a means of providing housing for all'.[79] In every area of governmental policy, from agriculture to urban affairs, powerful interest groups, mindful only of their narrow sectional advantage, had insinuated themselves. The 'common good' had disappeared into the interstices of interest group liberalism. Lyndon Johnson's Great Society had failed. In throwing dollars at the problems, the American state – so the newly pessimistic pluralists argued – had become over-extended, and was in danger of losing public respect. As Jimmy Carter himself pointed out in the 'crisis-of-confidence' address, the very optimism which supported American democratic liberalism showed signs of evaporating. A majority appeared to believe – for the first time in US history, as Carter pointed out in 1979 – 'that the next five years will be worse than the past five years'.[80] Daniel Bell argued in 1976 that capitalism's very success had undermined those cultural values – thrift, sturdy individualism – which had inspired that success.[81]

Some of these worries and criticisms developed into the neo-conservative, or New Right, critiques of liberalism itself. Carter's concern, however, was to adjust liberalism to what he saw as the reality of post-liberal conditions: to reinvigorate liberalism by resurrecting the 'common good', restoring consensus and accepting limits. 'Special interests' *could* be contained if there were 'disclosure' and 'expression by the President to the public of what is involved'.[82] Carter was anxious to place himself in the liberal 'great tradition' of Franklin Roosevelt and John Kennedy, while always emphasising the importance of limits. Speaking at the dedication of the JFK Library in Boston, Carter declared:

We have a keener appreciation of limits now . . . We are struggling with a profound transition from a time of abundance to a time of growing scarcity . . . but in this age of hard choices and scarce resources, the essence of President Kennedy's message – the appeal for unselfish dedication to the common good – is more urgent than it ever was.[83]

It is in this, post-liberal, context that Carter's cocktail of fiscal conservatism and 'human rights' liberalism should be seen. Stuart Eizenstat declared that his boss 'wanted to spend as little money as possible', but that he also 'wanted welfare reform, . . . national health insurance, . . . an urban policy'.[84] In 1976, Carter told an English interviewer:

The distinction between liberals and conservatives has been changed in the last few years . . . I would consider myself quite liberal on environmental quality, on human rights, civil rights, the race question. I would consider myself quite conservative on strengthening local government, on balancing the budget, on very careful planning and businesslike management of government.[85]

As noted above, his post-White House statements (beginning with his Farewell Address) tended to point up the liberal side. Yet in 1986 he made the following declaration of conservatism:

I've always looked upon myself as a conservative in some ways. I am a military-trained man. I always believed in a strong defence . . . I have always believed that the federal government should play a lesser role as compared to the state and local governments. I have also believed that our free enterprise system should be greatly deregulated and the highest level of competition prevail.[86]

Carter's post-liberalism was a conscious accommodation to what he saw as the needs of the times. It also reflected his personal temperament, his regional background and his religious inheritance. He believed in doing what was 'right'. In the Georgia Senate he had learned how difficult it was for 'the common good' to triumph over 'the intense concentration of those who have a special interest'.[87] In Georgian terms, Hugh Carter, the President's cousin, considered Jimmy to be 'moderate to liberal'.[88] *Keeping Faith* exhumed the legacy of Southern populism: 'to help the poor and aged, to improve education, and to provide jobs', but at the same time 'not to waste money'. Such beliefs, Carter acknowledged, involved 'inherent conflicts'.[89]

Jimmy Carter's religious position is perhaps best described as a kind of optimistic Niebuhrism. Attempts to portray him as a dogmatic fundamentalist were misconceived and mischievous. He frequently quoted Paul Tillich: 'Religion is a search.' Yes, man was fallen. But alleviation is possible, even if perfectibility is not:

there's an almost perfect concept expressed in the Christian ethic, that there's an ultimate pattern for government, but the struggle to reach it is always unsuccessful.

The perfect standard is one that human beings don't quite reach, but we try to.[90]

Alongside the 'common good', Carter exalted the good of the individual: not in the sense of wealth-maximising greed but in the sense of human rights. His predilection for quoting Kierkegaard was often mocked. (Norman Mailer famously failed to draw him on the subject.[91] One cannot help reflecting that no one ever tried to press Reagan on the subject of Kierkegaard.) But Carter's choice of quotation was telling: 'Every man is an exception.'[92] Governments must pursue the 'common good'. They should eschew divisive, special interests. Ultimately, however, salvation is about individual souls, albeit 'sick souls', and the reception of (undeserved) grace. Individuals bear rights, and these must be respected by political authorities.

Carter's commitment to human rights proceeded, at one level, from his religious views. However, the elaboration of the 'human rights' theme in the 1976 campaign[93] and after was primarily a way to restore unity to the fragmented Democratic party coalition. In 1978, Dennis Wrong wrote that, if Carter was an 'outsider', then it was 'increasingly hard to locate the mainstream to which he does not belong'.[94] Labour, blacks, women, Jewish people, environmentalists, Southerners, big-city politicos: they all appeared to be pulling apart. In the domestic sphere – it will be argued in Chapter 3 that 'human rights' had domestic as well as foreign policy implications – Carter hoped to restore unity. By focusing on individuals, 'human rights' might cut the knot of interest group liberalism. In foreign policy, it might restore consensus. It was, after all, a doctrine that could direct policy towards both the communist bloc and Latin American dictatorships.

The working out of Carter's human rights policies, both at home and broad, will be discussed in subsequent chapters. What is interesting in the immediate context, of a discussion of Carter's post-liberal ideas, is the way in which the policy intermeshed with the whole philosophical revival of liberal 'rights' theory. Essentially, modern liberal theory has turned, in Raymond Plant's words, 'away from the goals of human fulfilment just because these are contestable' and towards 'specifying that set of rules which would allow individuals to pursue their own good, subject to not interfering with the similar rights of others'.[95] Such concerns reside at the heart of the work of theorists like Ronald Dworkin and Bruce Ackerman.[96] American formulations of human rights go back much farther than this, of course: to the natural law tradition, to John Locke, to the 1776 Virginia Declaration of Rights and the Declaration of Independence. In this, Lockian, tradition, human rights are held to revolve around the rights to life, liberty and property. Most modern attempts to specify human rights, such as the 1948 United Nations Declaration of Human Rights, or the 1975 Helsinki Accords, emphasise the right to life and liberty, in the sense of freedom of thought, association, movement, religious observance and so on. The right to property tends to be maintained, but in limited form, consistent with high degrees of government intervention in the economy. The rule of law and citizenship rights are also widely accepted as coming within the compass of 'human rights', and would include freedom from torture or arbitrary arrest or detainment. Controversy attaches to the question of 'negative' ('freedom from') as against 'positive' ('freedom to') rights. Are rights essentially 'freedoms'? Or, are they also 'duties'? May 'human rights' be defined in social and economic terms – the right to work, to enjoy certain standards of living or diet, the right to leisure? Does the state, under 'human rights' doctrines, have to *provide* things as well as refrain from doing certain things? The whole epistemological basis of 'human rights' – usually assumed to be 'self evident' – may also be criticised, notably from the utilitarian and Marxist perspectives. Finally, 'human rights' raises problems of universality versus localism. How do we know that certain rights are universal and not merely the product of local circumstance and prejudice?[97]

Many of these issues raised problems for the Carter Administration. It engaged in the debate over economic rights. Critics of the policy pointed to some of the potential difficulties, accusing the US, for example, of cultural imperialism in applying its liberal democratic notions to countries with undeveloped economies. The Carter Administration also came up against the modern tendency for 'human rights' to be interpreted on a group rather than an individual basis: black rights, women's rights, the rights of children, and so on.[98]

The Carter Presidency in context

In January 1980, columnist Dom Bonafede attempted to analyse for the *National Journal* what he saw as the failure of Carter's populism. By 1980, Bonafede argued, much of the early populist enthusiasm had evaporated: 'Carter's cardigan sweater has been stored in mothballs, and he stopped carrying his own luggage a long time ago.' By way of explanation for Carter's political ineffectiveness, Bonafede pointed to:

a society polarized by single-interest politics, a Congress ridden by reform and fragmented in leadership, an overzealous press in pursuit of the sensational and the unsavory, and an emerging realization that our resources are finite and beyond salvation by governmental assistance.[99]

Judgements on the successes and failures of the Carter Presidency will be postponed until later chapters. For the moment, it is simply the intention to draw attention to the political context described by Bonafede.

Judgements on the Carter Presidency are bound to take account of the political and institutional fragmentation which accompanied it. At one level, the proliferation of single-issue (and 'narrow-band') lobbying was associated with the fragmentation of, especially, the Democratic party, and the rise of the 'consumer interest' as exemplified in the activities of Ralph Nader.

Organised labour had become weaker, while minority and white liberal groups had moved away from each other. Possibly as many as two thousand new lobbying groups – on issues ranging from gun control to grey power – were formed in the early to mid 1970s. Carter found himself in the position of having laboriously to piece together *ad hoc* coalitions for each and every domestic policy effort.[100] Interacting with the bureaucracy at all levels, fragmented lobbying raised newly complex problems of executive management and co-ordination. The 1978 debate in Congress over the price of natural gas involved some 117 lobby groups. Reacting to the rise of consumerism – with which, of course, Carter sought to identify himself – business interests also entered the fray in new guise. Co-ordinated business lobbying centred on Business Roundtable. The business lobby also fragmented, however. By 1978, some five hundred corporations had Washington offices, compared with about a hundred in 1968. These were the forces which defeated Carter's proposal for a consumer protection agency in 1978.[101]

In Congress, President Carter was confronted with a frustrating amalgam of assertiveness and fragmentation. During the Vietnam and Watergate years, the Congress had changed its attitude towards the White House. In foreign policy in particular, assertion had replaced deference, even in areas such as intelligence oversight, war-making and access to information. Reforms such as the 1974 Congressional Budget and Impoundment Control Act had strengthened the legislature's ability to challenge executive expertise. Alongside assertion had gone reform and internal democratisation. This had involved an (overdue) assault on the powers of committee chairmen, and on traditional leadership structures generally. The result was a Congress where power had become atomised – distributed among junior Members, proliferating subcommittees and staffers. Carter described in *Keeping Faith* the situation facing House Speaker 'Tip' O'Neill. He 'had a nearly impossible job trying to deal with a rambunctious Democratic majority that had been reformed out of almost any semblance of discipline or loyalty.'[102] It was also a Congress in which the very decentralisation of power had multiplied the points of access available to 'special interests'. Carter wrote in his diary on 9 June 1977 that the 'influence of the special lobbies', particularly in 'the automobile and oil industries', was 'almost unbelievable'.[103]

Vietnam and Watergate created opportunities for an outsider in 1976. Their legacy, however, was evidenced in public and press attitudes which produced yet more problems for the White House. The pre-Carter period witnessed a significant decrease in support for virtually all, but especially American national governmental, institutions. Harris polling in 1976 revealed that only 11 per cent of respondents felt 'a great confidence' in the executive branch; this compared with 41 per cent in 1966, 28 per cent in 1974 (before Nixon's resignation) and 13 per cent in 1975.[104] The irony of Carter's own position, of course, was that his own critique of 'Washington' to some extent reinforced such attitudes. The Harris poll findings did show some recovery in confidence in the early Carter years, yet Representative John Anderson's remark of 1977 was prescient:

(Carter) campaigned against Big Government and he has planted the seeds of doubt in the minds of the American public on the ability of government to solve problems. It may be almost something that comes back to haunt him.[105]

As will be noted in the following chapter, press attitudes towards Carter were complex. Media reactions to his Southernness, his 'outsider' image, his tendency to invoke national crisis, and his problematic relationship with political Washington, often pulled in different directions. The press was no more out to 'get' Carter than it had been to destroy Nixon. Yet there is no question that the Watergate era had produced a climate of journalistic combatativeness. This was especially the case in the area of personal and governmental ethics. As Bob Woodward later remarked:

We are pretty good at investigating and nailing someone who is guilty . . . If we can't verify an accusation, we just go on to the next one . . . You have to remember that our experience for the past ten or fifteen years has been that in the end the governmental official always ended up being guilty as charged.[106]

The political and attitudinal backcloth against which the Carter Administration operated did not make the President's job impossible, nor should it be used to excuse incompetence. It must be given due weight, however, when assessing how adequately the Administration fulfilled its commitments to competence and compassion.

Notes

1   Cited in Jules Witcover, *Marathon: The Pursuit of the Presidency 1972–1976* (New York: Viking Press, 1977), p. 525.

2   *The Presidential Campaign 1976: Vol. I: Part 2* (Washington DC: US Government Printing Office, 1978), pp. 999–1000. Carter's 1976 campaign speeches were largely self-written (see B. Carp and D. Rubinstein, MC transcript, p. 80).

3   See Gaddis Smith, *Morality, Reason and Power: American Diplomacy in the Carter Years* (New York: Hill and Wang, 1986), p. 66.

4   *The Presidential Campaign*, p. 994.

5   *Congressional Quarterly Weekly Report (CQWR)*, 22 Jan. 1977, p. 106.

6   See Michael Janeway, 'Campaigning', *Atlantic Monthly*, Oct. 1976, pp. 6–14, at 12.

7   See Erwin C. Hargrove, *Jimmy Carter as President* (Baton Rouge: Louisiana State University Press, 1988), pp. 6–8; William L. Miller, *Yankee From Georgia: The Emergence of Jimmy Carter* (New York: Times Books, 1978), pp. 202–16; N. C. Nielsen, *The Religion of President Carter* (London: Mowbrays, 1977).

8   *CQWR*, 22 Jan. 1977, p. 106.

9   Cited in Haynes Johnson, *In The Absence of Power: Governing America* (New York: Viking Press, 1980), p. 153.

10   *Congressional Quarterly (CQ) Almanac*, 1979, 45-E.

11   A. Etzioni, 'The Lack of Leadership', *National Journal*, 23 Feb. 1980, pp. 334–7, at 335.

12   *CQWR*, 22 Jan. 1977, p. 106 (Inaugural Address).

13   *CQ Almanac*, 1979, 47-E ('crisis-of-confidence' speech).

14   As note 12. See also Jimmy Carter, *Keeping Faith: Memoirs of a President* (London: Collins, 1982), p. 21.

15   *CQ Almanac*, 1978, 3-E.

16   *CQ Almanac*, 1979, 5-E.

17   *CQ Almanac*, 1979, 46-E ('crisis-of-confidence' speech).

18   Hamilton Jordan, *Crisis: The Last Year of the Carter Presidency* (New York: Putnam's Sons, 1982), p. 373.

19   *Ibid.*, p. 60.

20   See Donald S. Spencer, *The Carter Implosion: Jimmy Carter and the Amateur Style of Diplomacy* (New York: Praeger, 1988), p. 60. For a leftist critique of Carter 'tokenism', see Lawrence Shoup, *The Carter Presidency and Beyond* (Palo Alto: Ramparts Press, 1980).

21   J. J. Kirkpatrick, *Legitimacy and Force: Political and Moral Dimensions: Vol. I* (New Brunswick: Transaction Books, 1988), p. 144.

22   See, e.g., Fred Halliday, *The Making of the Second Cold War* (London: Verso, 1983), pp. 214–33; Jenny Pearce, *Under the Eagle* (London: Latin America Bureau, 1982); Holly Sklar, ed., *Trilateralism* (Boston: South End Press, 1980).

23   'Washington', *Atlantic Monthly*, Apr. 1977, pp. 6–14, at 12.

24   'Washington', *Atlantic Monthly*, Jan. 1978, pp. 6–11, at 8.

25   D.M. Hill and P. Williams, 'Introduction', in M. Glenn Abernathy, D. M. Hill and P. Williams, eds, *The Carter Years: The President and Policy Making* (London: Pinter, 1984), pp. 1–10, at 2.

26   See Austin Ranney, 'The Carter Administration', in A. Ranney, ed., *The American Elections of 1980* (Washington DC: American Enterprise Institute, 1981), pp. 1–36, 4.

27   James Wooten, *Dasher: The Roots and Rising of Jimmy Carter* (London: Weidenfeld and Nicolson, 1978), p. 33.

28   Betty Glad, *Jimmy Carter: In Search of the Great White House* (New York: Norton, 1980), p. 485.

29   G. E. Reedy, *The Twilight of the Presidency* (New York: NAL Books, 1987), p. 156.

30   R. Davy, 'President Carter's White House Record', *The Times*, 7 June 1978. See also T. Wicker, 'Another PR Solution', *New York Times*, 21 May 1978.

31   James Fallows, 'The Passionless Presidency', *Atlantic Monthly*, Part I, May 1979, pp. 33–48, 34, 41, 42, 45; Part II, June 1979, pp. 75–81, 77.

32   Joseph A. Califano, *Governing America: An Insider's Report from the White House and the Cabinet* (New York: Simon and Schuster, 1981), pp. 31, 402, 417. See also E. R. Kantowicz, 'Reminiscences of a Fated Presidency', *Presidential Studies Quarterly*, 16, 1986, pp. 651–65, at 662.

33   R. K. Murray and T. H. Blessing, 'The Presidential Performance Study', *Journal of American History*, 70, 1983, pp. 443–55. See also J. E. Holmes and R. E. Elder, 'Our Best and Worst Presidents', *Presidential Studies Quarterly*, 19, 1989, pp. 529–57; R. Dallek, 'The President We Love to Blame', *The Wilson Quarterly*, 15,

1991, pp. 100–7, 107; M. L. Whicker and R. A. Moore, *When Presidents are Great* (Englewood Cliffs: Prentice-Hall, 1988), p. 175.

34   P. N. Carroll, *It Seemed Like Nothing Happened: America in the 1970s* (New Brunswick: Rutgers University Press, 1990).

35   J. Updike, *A Rabbit Omnibus* (London: Penguin, 1991), p. 417.

36   Jody Powell, *The Other Side of the Story* (New York: Morrow, 1984), p. 31.

37   *National Journal*, 26 May 1979, p. 872.

38   Powell, *The Other Side of the Story*, pp. 52, 185, 208, 252; Jordan, *Crisis*, pp. 319–20.

39   Zbigniew Brzezinski, *Power and Principle: Memoirs of the National Security Adviser, 1977–1981* (London: Weidenfeld and Nicolson, 1983), pp. 432, 514–15, 520.

40   Cyrus Vance, *Hard Choices: Critical Years in America's Foreign Policy* (New York: Simon and Schuster, 1983), pp. 28–9, 46, 436.

41   N. C. Thomas, 'The Carter Administration Memoirs', *Western Political Quarterly*, 39, 1986, pp. 345–60, at 354.

42   See J. Dumbrell '3 a.m. in the White House', *Times Higher Education Supplement*, 21 Sept. 1990. See also *Washington Post*, 7 Nov. 1982 (R. G. Kaiser).

43   Jimmy Carter, *Keeping Faith*, pp. 74, 87, 121, 269–430; Brzezinski, *Power and Principle*, p. 521; Jimmy Carter, *The Blood of Abraham: Inquiries into the Middle East* (Boston: Houghton Mifflin, 1985), p. 145.

44   Gaddis Smith, *Morality, Reason and Power*; J. Michael Hogan, *The Panama Canal in American Politics: Domestic Advocacy and the Evolution of Policy* (Carbondale: Southern Illinois University Press, 1986).

45   *Morality, Reason and Power*, p. 247.

46   J. Muravchik, *The Uncertain Crusade: Jimmy Carter and the Dilemmas of Human Rights Policy* (Lanham: Hamilton Press, 1986).

47   C. R. Mollenhoff, *The President Who Failed: Carter Out of Control* (New York: Macmillan, 1980).

48   Alexander Cockburn, *Corruptions of Empire* (London: Verso, 1988), p. 471.

49   'What a Choice!', *Spectator*, 31 May 1980, p. 3. See also Anthony King, 'How Not to Select Presidential Candidates: A View from Europe', in Ranney, ed., *The American Elections of 1980*, pp. 303–28.

50   Peter Jay, 'Why President Carter has Clearly Proved his Right to a Second Term', *The Times*, 27 Oct. 1980, and 'The Profound and Quiet Revolution under Mr. Carter', *The Times*, 3 Nov. 1980.

51   *Wall Street Journal*, 18 July 1988 (p. 18).

52   J. L. Pasley and A. P. Weisman, 'He's Back! No, not Nixon – Jimmy Carter', *New Republic*, 19 Jan. 1987, pp. 14–15.

53   R. W. Johnson, 'Foreign View', *The Independent on Sunday*, 8 Apr. 1990.

54   'The World is Ready for an American at the UN', *The Independent on Sunday*, 1 Sept. 1991.

55   'Carter Begins to Shed Negative Public Image', *New York Times*, 18 May 1989.

56   J. Updike, *Rabbit at Rest* (London: Penguin, 1991), p. 9.

57   See, e.g., James McGregor Burns, *The Crosswinds of Freedom* (New York: Random House, 1990), p. 571.

58   *New York Times*, 15 Apr. 1991; also, Gary Sick, *October Surprise* (London: I.

B. Tauris, 1991).

  59   S. W. Cloud, 'Hail to the Ex-chief', *Time*, 11 Sept. 1989.

  60   Positive journalistic treatment of Carter may be found in: M. Ingwerson, 'Polls and History Begin to Deal Kindly with Jimmy Carter', *Christian Science Monitor*, 19 July 1988; M. McGrory, 'Exceptional "ex" ', *Washington Post*, 28 Sept. 1989; G. Sperling, 'Jimmy Carter Rediscovered', *Christian Science Monitor*, 14 Nov. 1989; W. King, 'Carter redux', *New York Times Magazine*, 10 Dec. 1989; 'A Dismembered Ron, a Refurbished Jimmy', *Newsweek*, 2 April 1990; 'Jimmy Carter's Second Coming', *Economist*, 15 Dec. 1990; B. Crick, 'Carter puts Atlanta in the fast track', *The Guardian*, 31 Aug. 1992. See also 'Jimmy Carter Works the World', *Human Rights*, 17, 1990, pp. 22–5; Mark J. Rozell, 'Carter Rehabilitated', paper presented at the Eighth Presidential Conference, Hofstra University, Nov. 1990; R. N. Smith and Timothy Walch, eds, *Farewell to the Chief* (Worland: High Plains, 1990); Jimmy and Rosalynn Carter, *Everything to Gain* (New York: Random House, 1987), p. 156.

  61   Kai Bird, 'Citizen Carter', *The Nation*, 12 Nov. 1990, pp. 559–64, at 560. See also Gary Reichard, 'Early Returns: Assessing Jimmy Carter', *Presidential Studies Quarterly*, 20, 1990, pp. 603–20; F. L. Schick, *Records of the Presidency* (Phoenix: Oryx Press, 1989), p. 237; Jimmy Carter, 'Keynote Address: The United States and the Advancement of Human Rights Around the World', *Emory Law Journal*, 40, 1991, pp. 723–31.

  62   See R. W. Johnson, 'Foreign View'; also, J. A. Rosati, 'Jimmy Carter: A Man before his time? The Emergence and Collapse of the first post-Cold War Presidency', paper presented at the Eighth Presidential Conference, Hofstra University, Nov. 1990.

  63   For two sides to the dispute, see Paul M. Kennedy, *The Rise and Fall of the Great Powers* (London: Unwin Hyman, 1988) and Henry R. Nau, *The Myth of American Decline* (Oxford: Oxford University Press, 1990).

  64   A. Harris, 'Citizen Carter', *Washington Post*, 22 Feb. 1990. See also R. M. Christenson, 'Carter and Truman: A Reappraisal of Both', *Presidential Studies Quarterly*, 13, 1983, pp. 313–23.

  65   See Reichard, 'Early Returns . . .'.

  66   John Orman, *Comparing Presidential Behavior* (New York: Greenwood, 1987); R. C. Thornton, *The Carter Years* (Washington DC: Washington Institute Press, 1991).

  67   Hargrove, *Jimmy Carter as President*; Charles O. Jones *The Trusteeship Presidency: Jimmy Carter and the United States Congress* (Baton Rouge: Louisiana State University Press, 1988).

  68   Hargrove, *Jimmy Carter as President*, p. 192. See also W. F. Grover and J. G. Peschek, 'The Rehabilitation of Jimmy Carter and the Limits of Mainstream Analysis', *Polity*, 23, 1990, pp. 139–52.

  69   See, e.g., Thomas E. Cronin, *The State of the Presidency* (Boston: Little, Brown, 1980).

  70   *The Listener*, 1 July 1976 (p. 826).

  71   See R. S. Hirschfield, ed., *The Power of the Presidency* (Chicago: Aldine, 1973), pp. 128–33.

  72   Jimmy Carter, *Why Not the Best?* (Eastbourne: Kingsway, 1977), p. 161.

  73   Remarks of Presidential aides, cited in Hargrove, *Jimmy Carter as President*, p. 17.

74   *Why Not the Best?*, p. 178.

75   *National Journal*, 28 Aug. 1979, p. 1239.

76   *Why Not the Best?*, p. 178.

77   L. Thurow, *The Zero Sum Society* (London: Penguin, 1981).

78   See Robert Dahl, *Dilemmas of Pluralist Democracy* (New Haven: Yale University Press, 1982; M. Crozier, S. P. Huntington and S. Watanuki, *The Crisis of Democracy: Report to the Trilateral Commission on the Governability of Liberal Democracies* (New York: New York University Press, 1975); Patrick Dunleavy and Brendan O'Leary, *Theories of the State: The Politics of Liberal Democracy* (London: Macmillan, 1987), pp. 66–8.

79   T. J. Lowi, *The End of Liberalism* (New York: Norton, 1969), pp. 86–9.

80   *CQ Almanac*, 1979, 46-E.

81   Daniel Bell, *The Cultural Contradictions of Capitalism* (New York: Basic Books, 1976).

82   Cited in Elizabeth Drew, *American Journal: The Events of 1976* (New York: Random House, 1977), p. 108.

83   Speech of 10 Oct. 1979, cited in J. M. Burns, *The Power to Lead* (New York: Simon and Schuster, 1984), pp. 23–4.

84   Hargrove, *Jimmy Carter as President*, p. 36.

85   *The Listener*, 1 July 1976, p. 827.

86   Michael Charlton, *The Star Wars History* (London: BBC Publications, 1986), p. 92.

87   *Why Not the Best?*, p. 104.

88   Cited in John Osborne, *White House Watch: The Ford Years* (Washington DC: New Republic Books, 1978), p. 396.

89   Carter, *Keeping Faith*, p. 74.

90   Carter cited in Miller, *Yankee From Georgia*, p. 220.

91   Glad, *In Search of the Great White House*, p. 484.

92   *Why Not the Best?*, p. 12.

93   See Elizabeth Drew, 'A Reporter at Large: Human Rights', *The New Yorker*, 18 July 1977.

94   D. H. Wrong, 'Stumbling Along with Carter', *Dissent*, 25, 1978, pp. 3–6, at 6.

95   R. Plant, *Modern Political Thought* (Oxford: Blackwell, 1991), p. 77.

96   See R. Dworkin, *Taking Rights Seriously* (London: Duckworth, 1977); B. Ackerman, *Social Justice in the Liberal State* (New Haven: Yale University Press, 1980).

97   See J. Donnelly, *The Concept of Human Rights* (London: Croom Helm, 1985); David Miller, *et al.*, eds, *The Blackwell Encyclopaedia of Political Thought* (Oxford: Blackwell, 1991), pp. 222–5.

98   See Michael Freeden, *Rights* (Milton Keynes: Open University Press, 1991), p. 1.

99   D. Bonafede, 'Presidential Mythology', *National Journal*, 12 Jan. 1980, p. 61.

100   See *National Journal*, 8 Sept. 1979, p. 1478; Godfrey Hodgson, *All Things to All Men* (London: Weidenfeld and Nicolson, 1980); Alan Ware, *The Breakdown of Democratic Party Organisation, 1940–1980* (Oxford: Clarendon Press, 1985); Paul Light, *The President's Agenda* (Baltimore: Johns Hopkins University Press, 1982).

101   See Hedrick Smith, *The Power Game: How Washington Works* (London: Collins, 1988) p. 37; Graham K. Wilson, *Interest Groups in the United States*

(Oxford: Clarendon Press, 1981); Hugh Hedo, 'One Executive Branch or Many?', in Anthony King, ed., *Both Ends of the Avenue: The Presidency, the Executive Branch and Congress in the 1980s* (Washington DC: American Enterprise Institute, 1983), pp. 26–58, at 37.

   102 *Keeping Faith*, p. 73.

   103 *Ibid.*, p. 99. On Congressional assertiveness and fragmentation, see T. E. Mann and N. J. Ornstein, eds., *The New Congress* (Washington DC: American Enterprise Institute, 1981); Smith, *The Power Game*, ch. 7; T. M. Franck and E. Weisband, *Foreign Policy by Congress* (New York: Oxford University Press, 1979).

   104 See *National Journal*, 19 Jan. 1980, p. 112.

   105 *National Journal*, 14 Jan. 1978, p. 44.

   106 Powell, *The Other Side of the Story*, pp. 172–3.

2

Competence? Washington from the outside

In September 1978, Gerald Rafshoon, recently appointed White House Director of Communications, advised the President of the centrality to his public reputation and popularity of 'the competence issue'.[1] Charges of incompetence had a special resonance for a Presidency supposedly wedded to technocratic values. As the 1980 election approached, 'the competence issue' loomed ever larger. Alonzo McDonald was brought in from McKinsey and Company to clarify the administrative practices of the White House. He commented in August 1980: 'The issue of competence is a major perception problem that must be addressed if we are to build positive, enthusiastic support. Too many people think Jimmy Carter has done a marginal to poor job.'[2] Too many people thought, McDonald might have added, that White House business was being conducted by a coterie of brash, inexperienced Georgians.

The present chapter considers 'the competence issue': firstly, in terms of the central White House staff and its relations with domestic policy Cabinet officers. (Carter's foreign policy advice structrue will be discussed in Chapter 7.) It also examines White House relations with Congress, press, party and public, and with the federal bureaucracy.

The Carter White House, the 'Georgia Mafia' and Cabinet government

Carter's original blueprint for the organisation of his Presidency centred on two key ideas, both of which were abandoned by 1979: the 'spokes-in-the-wheel' arrangement for the White House staff and the commitment to Cabinet government. Both ideas derived from Carter's advocacy of an open Presidency, of collegiality, of procedural efficiency and from a desire to distance the new Administration from the 'palace guard' operations of the later Nixon years. Carter was also influenced by Stephen Hess's study of Presidential organisation. Hess advocated a Cabinet which would assume the focal point of the White House machinery and which the President would consistently support.[3] Looking back beyond Nixon, to the Eisenhower years, Carter also determined that his White House would not contain 'a Sherman Adams'.[4] As operationalised between 1977 and 1979, both concepts – 'spokes-in-the-wheel' and Cabinet government – proved defective.

Between January 1977 and July 1979, the White House Office operated with no chief of staff. The Office's top personnel – the 'spokes-in-the-wheel' revolving around the President – consisted essentially of the 1976 campaign team: Assistant to the President Hamilton Jordan; Assistant for Domestic Affairs Stuart Eizenstat; Assistant for Intergovernmental Affairs and Cabinet Secretary Jack Watson; Congressional Liaison Assistant, Frank Moore; and Counsel, Robert Lipshutz. In addition, 'Midge' Costanza, the 1976 New York campaign director, served as Public Liaison Officer.

In the early months, the staff concentrated on organisational issues. A June 1977 study from the President's Reorganisation Project, written by Harrison Wellford and A. D. Frazier, recommended significant staff cuts. Numbers were reduced from 534 in 1976 to 381 in 1978. By October 1977, however, Frazier was recommending that the White House Office should adopt a more centralised structure, with a chief of staff. In a memorandum to Hamilton Jordan from the Office of Management and Budget, Frazier commented:

The public and various constituent groups are forming an impression of the Carter Presidency. This impression is based not only on what position he takes on the issues, but also on how well he is perceived to be going about his tasks. Has he mastered the intricacies of dealing with the Congress? Is his Administration working together as a well-coordinated unit or are they making procedural mistakes? Can 'those Georgians' run the Government?

Without 'an orderly process for prioritizing issues' there was a danger that the efforts of the 'very bright, hard-working and dedicated staff' would degenerate into 'fuzziness'.[5]

Yet Jordan was not appointed chief of staff until after the 1979 'crisis-of-confidence' speech, by which time the Administration's priorities had switched from open government to political survival. From mid-1977 onwards, however, there were moves towards greater centralisation. These were provoked by stories of poor staff co-ordination, notably in connection with the Bert Lance affair,[6] and by growing Presidential appreciation of the virtues of concerted, politicised advice. Eizenstat's Domestic Policy Staff (DPS) was expanded in July 1977 to forty-three full-time positions. It remained relatively unstructured, certainly in comparison with the National Security Council staff; yet the President, in the words of E. C. Hargrove, increasingly came 'to use the DPS as a coordinator of policy' as well as 'for his own political tutelage'.[7] Eizenstat, the only original inner staffer with Washington experience – he had been a speech-writer for LBJ – was far more than a domestic policy 'honest broker'. He acted as a policy advocate as well as centraliser of advice and information. He also urged greater formal White

House co-ordination, calling early on for the appointment of a chief.[8]

By the early part of 1978, it appeared that the 'spokes-in-the-wheel' system was combining with Carter's habitual work practices to produce a situation not of incompetence but of Presidential over-extension. With people drifting in and out of the Oval Office, the President found himself repeating conversations and duplicating effort.[9] Vice-President Mondale later compared the President in this period to a 'quarterback running all the plays to the center of the line'.[10] Carter's personal work practices involved extreme thoroughness, a search for comprehensive understanding and a determination (derived in part from the memory of his mentor, Admiral Rickover) to master detail as a prerequisite to such understandings. Such an approach led to the familiar view that Carter could not see the wood for the trees: that he was, in Brzezinski's phrase, like a sculptor who could not stop chiselling.[11] (Carter's associates tended later to see the immersion in detail as both a strength and a weakness. Bert Lance, for example, held that the President's attention to detail was occasionally excessive, but that this did not in any sense prevent him from making effective decisions. Shirley Hufstedler later testified that Carter certainly did his homework, but that this did not lead him to try to do other people's jobs. He was not the kind of obsessive leader who cannot delegate.)[12] However, it seems reasonable to argue that Carter's style – and public perceptions of it – were better served by a structured rather than an unstructured staff system. White House aide Tim Kraft estimated in April 1978 that the President was spending thirty hours a week on reading. At the same time, opinion polls were showing only about 50 per cent public approval of the President's job performance. Many saw Carter as floundering. Reforms made in April 1978 involved a strengthening of staff *vis-à-vis* Cabinet authority, greater staff centralisation and elevation of 'political' staffers (like Kraft). New emphasis was placed on the White House Executive Management Committee, headed by Mondale. This was intended to strengthen Administration priority-setting. Jody Powell later described this story of developing White House management styles as one of gradual improvement:

We found that we needed a greater degree of centralization than we thought at the outset . . . No system works perfectly all the time, but to the extent that you can have one that works pretty well in most cases, I think we had arrived at one in which there was enough centralization to keep things from slipping through the cracks . . . but which did not block access to the president.[13]

Jordan's designation as chief of staff was overly delayed. Carter probably should have paid more attention to his predecessor's experience. President Ford had abandoned the 'spokes-in-the-wheel' system after about six months. Richard Cheney, Ford's chief of staff, actually warned the incomers against resurrecting it.[14] Carter underestimated the centrifugal political and administrative forces which had led earlier Presidents to centralise. Yet his attitude was neither egregiously pigheaded nor ill informed. Past Presidents *had* become stranded and out of touch, metaphorically incarcerated within a centralised staff core. The choice between staff organisation patterns involved trade-offs: between enhanced 'multiple advocacy' and free information flow on the one hand and enhanced coherence on the other.[15]

There was also the question of how best to use Hamilton Jordan. Carter later stated that Jordan's reluctance to serve as chief was a factor. (If Charles Kirbo had been willing to work in Washington, Carter's lawyer friend might also have been appointed as chief quite early in the Administration.)[16] Along with Jody Powell, Jordan clearly enjoyed the President's complete confidence. (Brzezinski later referred to Powell and Jordan as Carter's 'vicarious sons').[17] It had, after all, been Jordan who, in 1972, had presented Carter with what was to become the blueprint for the 1976 nomination bid. Yet when Jordan was eventually named as chief, Richard Moe, from Mondale's office, wrote to him:

One of the greatest dangers of your new role is that it will tend to consume you in the day-to-day affairs of the White House and that you will have little or no time to do what you do best – be the President's chief strategist.[18]

Jordan himself saw his 1979 designation as belated recognition of the need for political advice to be injected into policy deliberation at all levels.[19] He remained as chief until mid-1980 when, amid criticism about alleged misuse of staff for re-election purposes, he left to direct the 1980 campaign. David Rubinstein of the DPS later expressed doubt as to whether Jordan ever really performed the chief of staff role in anything but name. According to Rubinstein, Jordan 'had no administrative abilities', and the White House had an effective chief only when Jack Watson was appointed in mid-1980.[20] To some extent, the problems of Jordan as chief were alleviated through the appointment of Alonzo McDonald. Yet there seems little question that Jack Watson's tenure as chief in the last months of the Presidency represented the high point of its organisational effectiveness.[21]

Alongside the demise of the 'spokes-in-the-wheel' went the transcendence of Cabinet government. Early in 1977 Carter had promised that there would 'never be an instance while I am President' when White House staffers 'dominate or act in a superior position' to Cabinet members.[22]

Yet Carter's staff were soon furnishing him with accounts of breakdown in the Cabinet government system. In an undated memo from early 1977, Hamilton Jordan declared that part of the problem was a failure to 'depomp' the Presidency radically enough: 'very few of your staff or Cabinet members are as direct and frank with you as you would like. *The institution of the Presidency is still a powerful and awesome thing.*' He went on, however, to suggest that perhaps part of the problem was Cabinet government itself. Discussing the operations of the Economic Policy Group, Jordan suggested that the individual sectional interests of the group members – 'small but very powerful constituencies' – were inhibiting cohesion. (The Economic Policy Group included several top Cabinet people. Treasury Secretary Blumenthal and Council of Economic Advisers chairman Charles Schultze tended to lead discussion.) According to Jordan: 'Each cabinet officer is pursuing programs and goals independent of one another and oblivious to the political inter-relationships of their programs.'[23] In the early period, Cabinet members chose their own immediate subordinates. David Rubinstein later spoke of Carter's mistake in 'giving the government away to the Cabinet officers'.[24] Things changed, however, as complaints about this reached the Oval Office. In April 1978, Tim Kraft was designated Assistant for Political Affairs and Personnel and given the job of clearing departmental appointments. By this time, staffers, and even Cabinet members like Commerce Secretary Juanita Kreps, were becoming openly critical of the frequent, long, often agenda-free, Cabinet meetings. Brzezinski read newspapers under the Cabinet table.[25] Jordan called the meetings a 'waste of time', and another staffer was later quoted to the effect that Cabinet government was always doomed: 'you can't run a government ... from 10 different locations'.[26] The 1979 reorganisation essentially obliterated the commitment to Cabinet government. Jordan was given authority to adjudicate disputes between the White House and the departments. He would decide whether or not the President should be brought in.[27]

Part of the problem was indeed the difficulty of running a government from ten different locations. This was illustrated in the early attempts to achieve a comprehensive, trans-departmental urban policy. In the urban report of December 1977, 'Cabinet government' produced (in the words of B. H. Patterson) 'not an integrated policy but a set of departmental wish lists stapled together'.[28] The urban initiative of May 1978 was characterised by inter-departmental and inter-agency squabbling. (The Office of Management and Budget (OMB), the Housing and Urban Development department (HUD) were, along with the DPS, the main contenders.) Attempts to form 'Cabinet clusters' – inter-agency and inter-departmental task forces to examine problems – did not succeed in dismantling vested bureaucratic interests. In October 1978, for example, Gerald Rafshoon reminded the President that opposition to Presidential anti-inflation initiatives would come not only from 'outside', but 'just as much' from 'our own people' whose 'turf' was threatened.[29]

More obviously, the situation was aggravated, and the crisis of 1979 precipitated, by endemic and debilitating bickering between staff and Cabinet officers. At one level, this was a highly personal issue. HEW Secretary Joseph Califano, for example, was patently contemptuous of the White House Georgians. They, in turn (including Rosalynn Carter) saw him as 'disloyal'.[30] At another level, it was a matter of substantive policy differences, and competing (departmental versus White House) perspectives. In June 1977, Jody Powell deplored the practice whereby Cabinet members publicly assumed 'an advocacy role' without ascertaining what constituted Adminis-tration policy in the relevant area.[31] Califano earned White House enmity, for example, by attempting to mobilise Congressional support for an anti-smoking bill, which Carter opposed. The President later complained that Califano had been 'operating his own shop'.[32] Treasury Secretary Blumenthal and the DPS frequently clashed, notably in 1978 over tax policy. The former saw the DPS as economically illiterate and as arrogant turf-invaders. The DPS saw Blumenthal as 'disloyal' and blind to Carter's electoral need for individual tax cuts. The DPS apparently also detected Blumenthal's hand behind the leaking to the *Washington Post* in early 1979 of an unfavourable story about Eizenstat.[33] The supposed Cabinet uncon-cern for electoral consequences was a constant irritant. Even after the 1979 reorganisation, Jordan was complaining to the President that the Cabinet 'generally regards' the re-election 'campaign as "somebody else's busi-ness" '.[34] Such differences of perspective underpinned the well known con-flicts not only with Califano and Blumenthal but also with Secretary of Transportation Brock Adams, Agriculture Secretary Bob Bergland and even Attorney General Griffin Bell.[35]

As with the commitment to a decentralised staff system, the experiment in Cabinet government was not simply a product of Carter's naive belief in the smooth functioning of collegial bodies. It was based in the commitment to open government, and in an attempt – ironic as it turned out – to avoid the bureaucratic disorder that had characterised past Administrations. The argu-ments for Cabinet government were consistently rehearsed for Carter's benefit by Judge Bell, who saw the Cabinet system as one of the essential checks and balances in American government.[36] The President did, however, overestimate the ability of White House and departmental officers to arrive at a shared perspective. He also made some bad appointments. Califano was appointed primarily to appease the liberal, Great Society wing of the Demo-cratic party. The HEW Secretary made little effort to respect the principle of Administration collegiality. It may also be argued that Carter suffered from the American Presidency's relative lack of institutional memory. The Carter–Mondale transition team's preparation to take over from Ford was exceptionally thorough, especially regarding personnel and the budget; attempts were made to learn from past mistakes. Yet there was a tendency to write off the Republican years as an era of corruption, imperialism and hubris. Closer study of the Nixon period might have yielded valuable lessons about Cabinet government. Richard Nixon, after all, had trodden a similar path. (It was also cruelly ironic that the 1979 mass resignations so closely resembled Nixon's action in 1972.)[37]

To what extent was Califano justified in portraying the core of Carter's staff as inept and arrogant? Numerous quotations may be assembled to support his view of the 'Georgia mafia'. For House Speaker O'Neill, for example, Carter's people were like some of John Kennedy's staff in 1961.

They 'assumed that because they had succeeded in capturing the White House, they had Washington all figured out'. (Nevertheless, O'Neill recorded his respect for Eizenstat, felt that Lance 'really knew the score', and dubbed Carter himself 'the smartest public official I've ever known'.) The Bostonian saw the problem as having an important regional dimension. The Southerners 'just didn't understand Irish or Jewish politicians' and were unhappy with the 'blunt and rambunctious' style of Northern Democrats.[38] Ben Bradlee, on his retirement as editor of the *Washington Post* in 1991, reminisced: 'I was thrilled by Carter at the beginning, but he was so anti-Washington, so hostile to anyone not part of the Georgia mafia. He became very tiresome . . . although I've yearned for him since.'[39] Hedley Donovan, former *Time* editor-in-chief who was brought into the White House (as a 'non-Georgian with gray hair') in 1979 precisely to meet these criticisms, also commented upon Carter's continuing over-reliance on the Georgians.[40]

There is no question that the Georgians served Carter loyally and enthusiastically. Also, as Lloyd Cutler (another 'non-Georgian with gray hair' introduced in 1979) later testified, it is a tendency of *any* set of President staff to become protective of their boss's time, and therefore of access to him.[41] Generally, however, as Jim Fallows and many others have pointed out, Carter was too ready to assume that his campaign team could be painlessly translated to the White House.[42] Carter must accept a degree of blame for foisting upon political Washington what was by any standards a brash and inexperienced team. According to David Rubinstein, the Georgians' 'cockiness' caused unnecessary waves.[43] Southern defensiveness, contempt for what were seen as empty Washingtonian courtesies and overprotectiveness of Carter all played a part. Yet Carter was not the first President to have his staff perceived in this way. O'Neill's invocation of JFK in 1961 was apt. Carter himself saw the Georgians' inexperience as compensated for by the appointment – and integration into White House staffing mechanisms – of Mondale and the various Cabinet appointees.[44] It is also possible to argue that Charles Kirbo's reluctance to serve in Washington, along with the early disappearance of Bert Lance, robbed the Georgian contingent of two of its potentially weightier members. More importantly, however, it should be recognised that, in Carter's case, the 'outsider' persona was no mere election gimmick. The President did genuinely wish to make a clean break with what he saw as the compromised 'special interest' – dominated politics of Washington, as well as with the entire Vietnam-Watergate era. His was, in Agriculture Secretary Robert Bergland's phrase, a 'zero-based presidency'.[45] He saw his new team as a means of accomplishing the break. He eventually realised that their inexperience and style was causing problems. The Donovan and Cutler appointments, and the growing influence of Robert Strauss, were signs of this realisation. (Indeed, sections of the Washington press corps seized on the appointment of Lloyd Cutler, by anyone's standards a Washington 'insider', as a sign of the President's capitulation to the capital's wicked ways.)[46]

Some of the statements of, in particular, Hamilton Jordan unquestionably gave unnecessary hostages to fortune. His pre-election remark about resigning if Vance became Secretary of State and Brzezinski became National Security Adviser was a case in point.[47] Similarly, his assertion that the political dynamics of Georgia and Washington were 'not that different'[48] was ill-judged. Yet he was at least under no illusion about how political Washington regarded him. Looking forward to the chief of staff job in 1979, he told Carter: 'I embody a lot of the criticisms that people direct at you and your staff: that we are all from Georgia, that we don't go out socially enough, that we have disdain for Congress, so forth.'[49]

The Georgia loyalists did their best to present a united front. Tim Kraft, Jordan and Pat Cadell, the President's personal pollster, shared a house in Georgetown for some time. Yet there were tensions, notably between Jordan and Jack Watson. Neither did the Georgians form an ideologically coherent group. Especially if one includes the conservative Kirbo, Carter's 'irregular' adviser, the group represented a wide range of the political spectrum.[50] In actuality, the Administration was accused simultaneously of harbouring an excessive multiplicity of views – the famous 'fuzziness' – and of being dominated by a cohesive 'mafia'. To some extent, Carter's close associates seemed 'fuzzy' precisely because of the cross-cutting nature of many of the post-liberal issues – energy, tax reform, human rights – with which the Administration concerned itself. It should also be stressed that Carter, while not necessarily appointing people with opposing views in order to stimulate 'creative conflict', did not overvalue consensus. His favoured advice structrue might be termed 'collegial countervaillance'.[51] Within such a system, disputes – such as that between the DPS and the fiscally conservative OMB (especially under James McIntyre, Lance's successor) – were inevitable.

Carter's management of domestic policy-making represented a potentially creative hybrid: between, on the one hand, the Domestic Council and, on the other, the White House-monitored interagency task force models.[52] He actually abolished the Domestic Council in 1977, but retained its staff structure (the DPS), upgrading its importance. As originally proposed by the 1970 Advisory Commission on Executive Organization, headed by Roy Ash, the Domestic Council was designed to channel domestic policy proposals in an orderly way from the departments. It was particularly to concentrate on proposals which transgressed departmental boundaries. Under Nixon, it had performed poorly and had become immersed in Watergate. As it developed under Carter, however, the DPS actually began to perform the functions ascribed to Ash's Council. One DPS staffer later declared: 'We were the President's fingers out there in the government . . .'[53] The DPS developed a method – the Presidential Review Memoranda system, adapted from

National Security Council staff practice – for examining complex issues with inputs from a variety of public and private sources. Youth unemployment, solar energy and Vietnam veterans' issues were all examined in this way. Even unsympathetic observers of the Carter Presidency have awarded the DPS high marks.[54] Problems associated with this (Domestic Council/DPS) approach tend to be those of excessive centralisation and over-simplification of problems. As a way of meeting such drawbacks, the Carter White House developed another, parallel, approach to domestic policy-making: the 'cluster' system. Interagency task forces were designed to recruit relevant personnel from across the Administration, and to structure decisional and informational flows in a decentralised fashion. Differing clusters of bureaucratic players would form around different issues. The 'cluster' system probably did contribute to the Administration's reputation for incoherence; yet it is important to appreciate that it was adopted as a conscious counter to the more centralised Domestic Council/DPS system.

Another potential force for presentational incoherence was Carter's developing tendency to appoint to his staff 'special pleaders': people either designated as or in effect performing the role of conduits to particular social groups. Female and Jewish groups, blacks, Hispanics and the elderly all had such institutionalised White House 'special pleaders' by 1979. They were appointed for a combination of electoral and information-gathering reasons. They provided the Administration with much needed channels of communication to different sectors of the Democratic party coalition. David Rubinstein later testified to the degree to which the 'special pleaders' beneficially broadened the staff input. Several of them undoubtedly performed well. Nevertheless, their appointment fitted awkwardly with the Administration's hostility to 'special interests'. There was also the danger of the 'special pleaders' becoming co-opted by their own lobby and, in effect, quitting the Administration's reservation. As we will see in Chapter 3, this is essentially what happened in the case of Margaret Costanza. On one notorious occasion, Nelson Cruikshank, the Presidential counsellor on ageing, went so far as to testify in Congress against the Administration's social security changes.[55]

Carter's domestic policy staff system was neither an anarchic mess nor a streamlined, well-tuned machine. Other Presidencies, after all, had experienced bureaucratic 'turf wars'. Carter's loyalty to his Georgian campaign team was not always well placed. But the 'Georgia mafia' hardly constituted an ominous 'palace guard' on the Nixon model. Carter was also always ready to experiment with new bureaucratic procedures. The Carter Administration had its personality clashes, but again it was scarcely the first Presidency to experience this problem. According to those who worked in it, the Carter White House was actually a happy environment in which to be employed. Carter did not give the same job to different people in order to see them compete. He encouraged frankness. Hedley Donovan was impressed by the young Georgians' frankness towards their boss and by their 'fervent desire' to serve.[56] According to Bertram Carp of the DPS: 'A member of the senior staff could lose an argument in front of Carter and not be weakened in terms of the next argument.'[57] The problem with the Carter White House was not one of incompetence. It was rather one of public perception, rooted in the intrinsic complexities of the post-liberal political and institutional environment. Secretary Blumenthal articulated this in a 1979 memorandum on the working of the Economic Policy Group:

Like it or not, we have failed to convince the public that the President is a strong economic brief, leading and influencing events rather than reacting to them. That's why he gets little credit for the positive and more blame than he deserves for the problems.[58]

In at least one positive facet of White House operations, the Carter Presidency stands apart from other Administrations: the creative utilisation of the Vice-Presidency. In 1979, Mondale reviewed the 'grim' history of US Vice-Presidents: 'Almost every President begins by saying, 'This is going to be different'. But I think this is the first President who has really delivered on that pledge.'[59] The Carter–Mondale relationship really does seem to have been devoid of that mutual suspicion and distrust – often a holdover from the nomination race – which often relegates the Vice-President to the policy-making sidelines. Mondale was not the nation's chief mourner and was worth far more to Carter than a pitcher of warm spit. The Minnesotan's liberal credentials, and former association with Hubert Humphrey, proved valuable. His personal intercession with auto-workers' president Douglas Fraser, for example, was crucial to the White House's plan to bail out Chrysler in 1979. He operated as a conduit to labour, black and Jewish groups. Mondale occupied an office close to the President's; he enjoyed the right to participate in any conference unless requested to leave; he lunched every Monday with Carter and was a vocal contributor to the Friday morning foreign policy breakfast. His staff became integrated with other elements of the White House staff to an unprecedented degree. Bert Carp of the DPS and David Aaron (Brzezinski's deputy) kept Mondale informed on domestic and foreign issues respectively. Of course, Mondale's liberal stance – which arguably became somewhat softer as the Presidency developed – brought him into conflict: with, for example, Charles Schultze and James McIntyre over the federal budget in 1978–9. Mondale unsuccessfully argued against Carter's decision to drop the $50 tax rebate in 1977, and he had severe doubts about the wisdom of the 'crisis-of-confidence' address. He disagreed with Administration policy on farm price support. Yet, especially after the resignation of Bert Lance, Mondale's Vice-Presidency matured into one of the major operational successes of the entire Administration.[60]

Congressional relations

The context for President Carter's relations with Congress was set by the assertive and fragmented legislative environment described in Chapter 1. It is true that the removal of the entrenched power of committee chairmen also removed some potential obstacles to Presidential leadership. Countervailing developments, however, more than compensated for any gains which the White House might have gained from the new environment. Assertiveness; fragmentation; individualism; localism; low levels of party discipline; decline in committee cohesion; expanding numbers of recorded votes; the tendency for laws increasingly to be written on the floor rather than in committee; the proliferation of subcommittees; power shifts among Congressional Republicans (towards the conservative South and West): in all these ways Carter's ability to lead Congress effectively was severely inhibited.

Congress had become exceptionally complex and also exceptionally busy. Some fifteen thousand bills and joint resolutions were introduced between 1977 and 1979 (compared to approximately eight thousand in Reagan's first two years). The legislature's restless activism was bolstered by the revolution in staffing levels. During the Carter years, the White House legislative liaison office received somewhere in the region of fifteen hundred telephone calls per day from Capitol Hill. High membership turnover rates and senior retirements also contributed to the new atmosphere of change and restiveness. (Carter had the particular misfortune to lose to retirement three senior Georgians, Representatives R. F. Stephens, Philip Landrum and W. S. Stuckey.)[61]

Most commentators on the Carter record acknowledge that dealing with the 'new', 'open' Congress was never going to be easy. Eizenstat declared in 1979 that Moses would have problems getting the Ten Commandments through Congress unscathed. However, many commentators also contend that the Carter team's insensitivity, high-handedness and inexperience made things immeasurably worse.[62] Certainly, it does appear that the new President was poorly prepared for the situation he encountered on Capitol Hill in 1977. Carter later confessed that he had never realised before how fragmented the Congress had become. He was also shocked to discover that committee leaders frequently did not 'have the slightest idea' what was in the bills for which they were supposedly responsible.[63] The President seemed out of sympathy with the culture of Capitol Hill and tended, at least in the early period, to lecture Members. Mark Nimitz, a lawyer who served in Carter's State Department, recalled in 1985 that Carter never understood that Members did not come to the White House to hear 'logical argument'; they sought rather the opportunity to extract personal and political kudos from contact with the Chief.[64] As governor in Georgia, Carter had tended to present legislators with technocratic arguments. He had been little bothered about traditional courtesies.[65] When transferred to Washington, this approach did, to some degree unnecessarily, ruffle Congressional feathers.

The choice of Frank Moore to head the legislative liaison operation sent the alarms ringing. From Carter's viewpoint, Moore seemed an ideal embodiment of the Administration's desire to stand aloof from 'special interests'. Moore's weekly legislative reports were diligently researched and intelligently prioritised.[66] However, to many on Capitol Hill, the choice of the inexperienced Moore appeared to epitomise the new regime's contempt for political Washington. House Speaker O'Neill called the new liaison head 'just plain dumb'.[67] Madeleine Albright (of Carter's National Security Council staff) later remembered how distant was Moore from the way 'Washington lobbyists usually look and talk and act'.[68] Veteran liaison operator Larry O'Brien had advised Moore on his appointment to 'maintain full-time vigilance' in the case of Members. This was not done. The early Carter liaison operation was organised along issue lines and was not geared to the need-servicing of individual Members. Early blunders included the failure to consult Senate Majority Leader Robert Byrd over the nomination of Sorensen to the CIA, and the parallel offence given to O'Neill by the unexpected announcement of the appointment of Republicans to the jobs of White House protocol chief and ambassador to the Law of the Sea conference. More importantly, many top Democrats felt excluded from the 1977 energy package. They saw it as a White House effort, arrogantly dropped into the legislative arena for approval. The abandonment of the $50 tax rebate also angered those Democrats who had supported the original proposal, and now found the ground taken from under them.[69]

The most public altercation with Congress in 1977 concerned the President's attempt to eliminate $5 billion worth of water projects from the 1978 budget. To Carter the issue was quite clear. The projects were wasteful pork barrel boondoggles. They reminded him, according to Bert Lance, of his campaign against the Squirrel Buff dam project in Georgia.[70] Here was a good opportunity to educate the nation and the Congress in the need to observe budgetary discipline as part of the war against inflation. The problem, of course, was that many Members had come to regard such projects as a means of enhancing their re-election constituency service profile. To a seasoned Congressional hand like Vice-President Mondale the assault on the water projects was politically naive. It threatened to alienate important figures like Russell Long of Louisiana, whose goodwill as chairman of the Senate Finance Committee the White House needed. Given the geographical spread of the projects, it also looked too much like a 'war on the West'.[71] In 1977 Carter was prepared to compromise on some of the projects, but in October 1978 he actually issued a veto of the Energy and Water Development Authorization bill, containing the projects. Carter later admitted that the battle left 'deep scars'. White House lobbyist Robert Beckel remembered how, when attempting to persuade one Senator of the virtues of a foreign aid bill, he was reminded that the bill included a dam for Pakistan. 'Once I get my dam', declared the Senator, 'you can have your dam.'[72]

On the water projects issue, the President appears to have favoured confrontation, with Moore, Mondale and Eizenstat urging caution and compromise.[73] On many occasions, the Administration was caught between its desire to educate Congress and the public – to take a stand against 'special interests' – and a growing awareness of the claims of political expediency. Carter always preferred direct talking to ego stroking. In September 1979, for example, he treated his audience at a Congressional breakfast to the following speech on the need for energy deregulation:

I . . . know that the special interests, particularly the oil interests, are . . . determined to block the kind of action I believe is absolutely crucial for our nation's energy future. I have been fighting them and I will continue to fight them across the country. And to the degree that the Congress fails to act, I am going to see to it that the American people hold those responsible to account.[74]

Carter's forthrightness on these occasions generally proceeded from rational argument, and was by no means always entirely politically counter productive. Administration lobbying, however, was certainly not always of the 'take-it-or-leave-it' variety. Despite the President's distaste, logical argument was often backed up by traditional 'oiling and stroking' of Members. In September 1978, for example, Frank Moore informed the President that Congressman Dan Rostenkowski had been flattered by Carter having taken time to have his photograph taken with Rostenkowski's daughters. The Illinois Congressman subsequently indicated his 'willingness to help' over the water projects.[75] In the same month it was reported that Senator Paul Hatfield of Montana had been offered a judgeship in return for supporting the President's compromise bill on natural gas pricing. As Brzezinski later testified, there was also no lack of 'stroking' of Senators in the Administration's 1979 efforts to have the SALT treaty ratified.[76]

A combination of rational argument and cajoling could, on occasion, produce very impressive results. The Panama Canal treaties, civil service reform, the 1978 foreign aid bill, extension of the deadline for the Equal Rights Amendment, trucking and airline deregulation: in all these areas the Administration lobbied effectively, diligently and successfully. It is also clear that the White House was continually refining and attempting to improve its liaison operation. The issue-lines organisation was soon abandoned in favour of more traditional servicing. By late 1978 William H. Cable, an experienced Congressional lobbyist, had organised a complex House operation whereby every Member was allocated to a liaison staffer.[77] Following her May 1978 appointment as head of the Public Liaison Office, Anne Wexler, working through task forces, took on directly the task of piecing together coalitions of interests to back Administration proposals in Congress. (This, essentially, represented the White House's response to charges that proposals had been sent 'naked' to Capitol Hill.)[78] In February 1979, *Congressional Quarterly* reported that a change of attitude regarding liaison had taken place. The Administration was now taking a deliberately softer line on sensitive issues, such as Congressional election funding reform. Compromise and horse-trading were now practised openly, with Carter's team even being criticised for cynicism in this area! House lobbyist Cable and Senate liaison head Danny Tate now enjoyed direct access to the President.[79]

By 1978 there was clearly a greater and more conscious stress on consultation and partnership with Democrats in Congress. Even in 1977 the supposed reluctance to consult had been exaggerated. (In spring of that year, for example, the Administration embarked upon a detailed consultation process with relevant Senators regarding the future of the Tennessee Valley Authority.)[80] By the following year's end, Congressional consultation in legislation preparation had been institutionalised in a liaison office operation headed by Les France and J. M. Copeland.[81] The 1980 anti-inflation package was adopted only after intense and prolonged consultation.[82] By late 1978 the Administration was clearly focusing and prioritising its legislative programme in a far more meticulous fashion than in 1977. (According to Mondale some first-year proposals had suffered from 'fratricide', defined by the Vice-President as a 'concept in missilry where you fire too many missiles too close together', each killing off its neighbour.)[83]

As the 1978 mid-term elections approached, the Administration decided to make a virtue of its flexibility and to admit to earlier errors: 'submitting too much legislation', 'expecting Congress to handle "comprehensive" packages', and 'not paying enough attention to the needs of individual Members'.[84] There was a danger here, however, as Jerry Rafshoon realised, of throwing the baby out with the bathwater. The Carter team wished to retain its reputation for moral integrity and for taking on vested interests. Rafshoon advised Moore in December 1978 to adopt the following line in media interviews:

Jimmy Carter has taken a very different approach toward Congress. He is willing to stand up to the special interests as his public works and defense vetoes showed. He has a close relationship with the leadership, based on a mutual trust and respect, but realize that there cannot always be perfect harmony.[85]

Relations did improve with Byrd and O'Neill. (One can only guess at the latter's reaction to a joke, relating to O'Neill's Massachusetts constituency, written for Carter at a 1978 Democratic Study Group function: 'Tip and I had our troubles at the start, I'll have to admit. But that all cleared up when I agreed to relocate the Central Arizona water project in Cambridge.')[86] Carter himself made the following remarks about his Congressional performance during a 1980 stump speech: 'If I had to do it all over again, I would not be on the Hill lobbying excessively, but I would have a few relationships in Congress that would allow me to have a better understanding of our problems there.'[87] Clearly, it would be absurd to argue that Carter had the legislative relations skills of a Lyndon Johnson. The Georgian did radiate a degree of aloofness and moral superiority which many Members resented. O'Neill, for example, simply could not understand Carter's reluctance to speed along government road improvement grants in his Cambridge district.[88] Yet it should also be observed not only that the legislative environment had changed significantly since Johnson's day but also that there is significant scholarly agreement that the importance of Presidential legislative skills tends to be exaggerated, and that they operate only at the margins of the executive's success with Congress.[89] It is not clear that, given the institutional and policy context of the late 1970s, greater mastery of 'dickering, bluffing, arm twisting' and 'wire pulling'[90] would have given Carter a higher rate of legislative success.

This leads on to the final question of this section. How well, comparatively speaking, *did* Carter do in terms of success on Capitol Hill?

In *Keeping Faith*, Carter wrote that his overall success rate in Congressional votes (the *Congressional Quarterly* box-score) was, at approximately 75 per cent, only slightly below Lyndon Johnson's score of 82 per cent.[91] Given Carter's reputation for ineptitude and LBJ's for supreme legislative skill, these figures, which reflect Presidential victories in roll-call votes where the White House has taken a clear position, should cause us to ponder the question of Presidential reputations. (Also, given Carter's reputation for having overloaded the system with an avalanche of proposals, it is worth recalling that the Georgian submitted far fewer domestic proposals to Congress than either LBJ or John Kennedy.)[92] However, the Congressional box-scores do not tell the full story. For example, the Administration claimed credit for most of the 223 bills enacted in 1977. Yet many of its highest priorities, notably the energy and hospital cost containment measures, remained on the table when Congress adjourned at the year's end. Many of the 223 bills essentially represented the Congressional Democratic agenda, held over from the Republican years. In many cases the White House simply added its approval to bills that were destined for easy passage in any case.[93]

Sophisticated analyses of Presidential success in Congress have, naturally, to take account of whether or not White House and Capitol Hill are controlled by the same party. Account also needs to be taken of characteristics of the Presidential proposals: whether their scope is wide or narrow, whether they are concerned to reduce or extend the scope of governmental action. Carter's agenda was wide and innovative, although, in its deregulatory thrust, it was by no means entirely geared towards extending government. Carter's agenda, however, certainly required a high degree of positive action by Congress. As Jeff Fishel has pointed out, it relied comparatively little on purely administrative options.[94]

The most relevant Presidents with whom Carter's performance may be compared are Kennedy and Johnson, Democratic Presidents facing Democratic Congresses. Regarding these comparisons, it is also important to consider a range of factors; some capable of quantification, others not. These include: the changing institutional context; particular policy and political circumstances affecting Presidential performance (for example, Kennedy's problem with Southern Democrats or the post-liberal policy environment of the Carter years); the economic context (especially the relatively high inflation and unemployment of the late 1970s); the success rate regarding votes on which significant White House effort was expended; and the success rate on close, conflictual and highly publicised votes.[95]

Jon Bond and Richard Fleischer have attempted to incorporate such considerations into a quantitative comparative analysis of Presidential success rates. They identify 'conflictual' votes as those on which at least 20 per cent opposed the White House position. On such votes, Carter performed less well than LBJ or JFK, although his failures were disproportionately in the House of Representatives. (Carter's score was 66.6 per cent average in the House, 73.5 in the Senate; JFK scored 78.2 and 80.2, LBJ 78 and 75.2.) They also analyse 'important' votes (based on a combination of the *Congressional Quarterly* identification of 'key votes' and an account being taken of turnout and closeness of the vote). Here, Carter did slightly better than Kennedy and Johnson in the House, and slightly worse in the Senate. A third measure, based on three major variables (partisan control of Congress, public approval rating and time in office), reveals Carter performing approximately as well as this model would predict. His performance according to this measure also improved over time.[96] A fourth measure, offered by Mark Petersen, relates to legislative initiatives to which the President devoted considerable effort, mentioning them frequently in speeches. On this measure, Carter scored poorly with a 28 per cent success rate (LBJ's score was over 80 per cent).[97]

Clearly, Carter did leave high-profile measure unenacted; leading examples would include tax reform, health insurance, consumer protection, no-fault auto insurance, and welfare reform. It should be emphasised, however, that the most high-profile bill of all – the energy bill – did pass eventually, albeit not entirely in a form which the White House approved. As Bond and Fleischer argue, it seems, in view of the powerful coalition of interests opposing it, excessively harsh to record the energy bill as a 'failure'.[98]

Finally, it should be noted that Carter suffered two veto overrides (on the oil import fee and on a Veterans Administration bill which the President held to be poorly targeted) both in 1980. Neither Kennedy nor Johnson suffered any overrides.[99]

In general terms, especially if we take into account the changing legislative and policy environment since 1968, Carter seems to have performed surprisingly well compared with his Democratic predecessors. The Bond and Fleischer measures yield some extraordinary conclusions. For example, in 'important' House votes, we find Carter beating both LBJ and JFK, as well as all the modern Republicans (including Eisenhower).[100] Carter's problem, like Kennedy's, was with the high-profile, high-effort measures. Yet Carter's problem went deeper still. His legislative victories were rarely acknowledged as such. The energy bill was a case in point. The Georgian received little credit for his exceptional success – far greater than LBJ's – in getting government reorganisation legislation through Congress.[101] A similar fate befell even the Panama Canal treaty victory, an obviously high-profile, high-effort measure, and one in a more clearly newsworthy area than the reorganisation bills. In fact, the Panama Canal lobbying was widely regarded in Washington and the press as a dissipation of energy on what really should have been a second-term issue.[102] The Panama Canal vote lobbying was effective, sophisticated and imaginative.[103] Yet it failed to shift the early image of the Administration as amateurish and aloof. Public and media perceptions of White House incompetence proved extraordinarily resilient.

Press, public and party relations

Reviewing press secretary Jody Powell's memoir, *The Other Side of the Story*, Lester Bernstein, a former *Newsweek* editor, wrote:

The fact is that Jimmy Carter as a national figure was almost invented by the media. He owed more to the engines of publicity for his emergence from obscurity to a Presidential nomination than any politician since Wendell Willkie in 1940. If Mr. Powell takes that as a norm, small wonder he has felt shortchanged ever since.[104]

Powell himself put the blame for deteriorating press treatment of the Administration on the 'residue of cynicism'[105] from Watergate. In remarks made in January 1992 he described a kind of collective guilt syndrome which was held over from the Nixon years. Having left the Watergate story to be broken by the metro staff, the White House press corps was determined to be unrelenting in its attitude towards the new Administration, to some degree precisely because the 'outsider' Georgians had been boosted by press and television in 1976. Carter also, according to Powell, was held to higher standards than his predecessors. Elected to cleanse the Augean stables in Washington, Carter was hurt excessively by the few, unsensational ethics problems (notably the Lance and Billy Carter affairs) which did emerge. There was also 'the Southern factor' – what Walt Wurfel, Powell's deputy, called the 'Civil War legacy':[106] the combination of elite journalistic patronisation and Georgian defensiveness.[107]

An unmistakable antipathy to the Washington press corps, and particularly to columnists like Jack Anderson and Joseph Kraft, emerges from the Powell memoir. Carter himself was quite frank about his dislike of such people. Occasionally this attitude was leavened with humour. In May 1979, the President told White House correspondents:

I would like to say in all sincerity that you . . . are some of my first and closest friends. We have a wonderful, almost unprecedentedly personal relationship. I am proud of you. As a group, I consider you one of our nation's treasures. And I am working to develop for you a permanent and suitable homeland.[108]

In January 1981, Carter was quoted in *Newsweek* as having remarked early in the Administration: 'If being President means I have to be nice to people like Joe Kraft, I'd rather not be President.'[109] In *Keeping Faith*, he remarked, *a propos* the Middle East peace process, that he had been 'disgusted' to find that the press was 'so negative'.[110]

Yet the Carter team had been taken up by influential sections of the media in 1976. The new Administration had even enjoyed a brief press honeymoon, when Carter was praised by columnists like David Broder for his skilled communications techniques and use of 'common man' symbolism.[111] His increasingly negative press treatment was, to some degree, connected to his reluctance to massage journalistic egos and to his prioritisation of substance over style. It was also related to the inherent difficulties of the policy areas highlighted by the Administration, the complexities of post-liberal politics and the (understandable) inability of journalists clearly to locate Carter on the liberal–conservative spectrum.[112]

While acknowledging all these problems, and also the dangerous potency of the Watergate legacy, Mark Rozell none the less has criticised Carter for not doing more 'to manage press expectations'.[113] There is substance to this charge. Carter saw himself as an educator-President, who would teach America the ways of post-liberal, post-imperial politics. Yet he was not able to alter press expectations of Presidential leadership. Press criticisms of his relations with Congress, for example, largely revolved around the assertion that he was failing to act as Franklin Roosevelt or Lyndon Johnson would have done. Moreover, where he did change expectations, as in the 1976 'honesty in government' theme, he tended to give too many hostages to fortune. Carter *was* held to a higher standard than other Presidents, and in a sense this was due to his own promises and undertakings to behave in a particularly exalted fashion. When, for example, he fired the Republican US Attorney David Marston in 1978, he was criticised for breaking his own promise not to let 'political' considerations affect policy towards the Justice Department.[114] Press treatment of Billy Carter's Libyan links – a matter almost entirely beyond the President's control – seriously damaged the re-election campaign. (A White House post-mortem identified 'Billygate' as one of eight main causes of defeat.)[115]

According to Jody Powell, many of the Administration's problems with the press derived from the relative lack of internal discipline in the White House, together with a generally 'excessively candid' attitude.[116] Powell's importance within the Carter Administration, of course, extended far beyond his press duties. He was an important adviser on substantive issues. He has been praised as a highly skilled press secretary.[117] He tended, however, to be almost entirely taken up, as press secretary, with the Washington press corps.

There was little, especially in the early days, in the way of long-range communications planning. No effort was made, for example, to set a 'line-of-the-day' for Administration spokespersons, or to develop consistent themes. Powell enjoyed only limited control over the departmental public information officers. White House speech-writers and communications officers tended to perceive their contribution to the Administration as undervalued and poorly supported.[118]

Gerald Rafshoon's 1978 appointment to head a revived White House Office of Communications signalled a new determination to prioritise and professionalise media relations. At his appointment, Rafshoon found the President's public approval rating standing at 38 per cent. He sought to revive the energy and purpose that had attended his Atlanta advertising agency's part in the 1976 campaign. In particular, Rafshoon moved to increase the White House's technical efficiency in media matters, to develop coherent themes, to prioritise television exposure and to instruct the President in the virtues of style and professional packaging.

Rafshoon's suggestion regarding a coherent theme for the Administration was 'getting control'. In a December 1978 memo to Carter, he linked this theme to the general tenor of the times. Outlining suggestions for the upcoming State of the Union address, Rafshoon and his deputies noted:

We have not fully recovered from the two decades of turmoil, dissension, war, tragedy and scandal . . . Our people feel alienated and cynical . . . The lack of participation by the disaffected leaves a vacuum that is being filled by ever more powerful interests at the expense of the national interest.

Echoing Walter Lippmann's theme of drift and mastery, Rafshoon suggested that the Administration should present itself as 'getting control' of all this.[119] A year after his appointment, Rafshoon lectured his boss on the proposition, 'style is everything'. Carter needed to learn from his 1980 opponents:

Consider the major challengers: Kennedy, Brown, Reagan, Connally. They cover the entire spectrum from liberal to conservative (Brown does this by himself). They have only one thing in common – style. They look like leaders.

Carter's failure, according to Rafshoon, was not in failing to provide leadership. Rather, the problem was that 'you don't *look* like you're providing leadership'.

Your natural style – low-key, soft spoken, gentleness – was perfect for 1976. People were looking for the antithesis of Richard Nixon – a non-politician. In 1980 they're looking for a leader . . . You're going to have to start looking, talking and acting more like a leader if you're to be successful – even if it's artificial. Look at it this way: changing your position on issues to get votes is wrong; changing your style (like the part in your hair) in order to be effective is just smart and, in the long run, morally good. I know you think it's phony and that you're fine the way you are but that pride is, by far, your greatest political danger.

The President should stop 'trying to please everybody'. He should 'fire some people'. He should abandon 'waffling' on television and 'present everything firmly'. Carter's 'soft' television 'speaking style' was 'the single greatest reason (under our control) why your Presidency has not been more successful . . .'. He should learn from Margaret Thatcher, who sharpened up her style prior to the 1979 British General Election. She accepted and responded to 'professional help', and Carter should do the same. 'Just being yourself' was not enough.[120]

There were dangers in Rafshoon's approach. As with the revamped post-1978 legislative relations operation, some felt that the post-imperial baby was being thrown out with the bathwater of amateurism. In a scenario of which Joseph Heller would have been proud, 'Rafshoonery' became a synonym for an over-slick media blitz. Barry Jagoda, television adviser to Carter before Rafshoon, indeed felt that his successor had gone too far and had largely killed off the 'open Presidency'.[121] Moreover, 'Rafshoonery' manifestly did not save the Presidency. His advice to 'fire some people' was taken. Carter's reaction to the Soviet invasion of Afghanistan could hardly have been more strong and decisive. Yet the President retained his reputation for dithering. In truth, the Carter experience appears to show not that Rafshoon's analysis was wrong but rather that reversing public perceptions of leaders is extraordinarily difficult. As Greg Schneiders, Rafshoon's deputy, pointed out in a 1979 memo on the 'crisis-of-confidence' address: 'People listen to Presidential speeches the way they listen to rock music. If they heard the same speech a hundred times they still wouldn't know any of the words. But they 'receive' the tone, the beat, the rhythm.' Against the backdrop of the events of 1979–80, Carter was not able to reverse the perception developed by his television audiences and encapsulated in three words used by Schneiders: 'uncertainty', 'softness', 'bemoaning'.[122]

Education Secretary Shirley Hufstedler later pointed out that Carter had failed to 'capture' the media. He failed the test whereby if a leader 'looks fine on TV he will be perceived as doing well'.[123] Significant public relations blunders did occur. The whole 'crisis-of-confidence' episode was something of a debacle. (Other instances may be cited. Attorney General Bell, for example, has suggested that a grave public relations error was made in not turning back the Mariel refugees expelled from Cuba in 1980.)[124] In the last resort, however, Jimmy Carter had too many poor, and poorly managed, television performances. While never relishing the public side of his Presidency, the thirty-ninth President performed consistently well in town meetings and Q and A sessions. Beyond that, there were problems. It was not simply a matter of specific blunders, nor of media hostility.

'Rafshoonery' represented a positive response to the President's difficulties. Improvements were made. (Some of Rafshoon's technical innovations, such as the provision of radio actuality services and of an interview video system were highly impressive. According to John Anthony

Maltese, the latter was a 'precursor to modern-day satellite hook-ups'.)[126] Too often, however, Carter's team showed a reluctance to admit mistakes, and a tendency to blame the media messengers. When Hedley Donovan joined the Administration in 1979 he detected an almost Nixonian hostility to the media: 'the danger sign is a reflex that blames the press first, and then asks only later – or maybe never – was there some Administration mistake here, and is there something that needs correcting'[127] It was exactly this kind of attitude which Rafshoon attempted to eradicate. He was not able, however, to control the President's television image. Such control was exercised, to a significant degree, by Carter's successor. This is not to suggest that Reagan's television operation, organised around highly structured media events, would have suited Carter. It represented the antithesis of the 'open Presidency'. Nevertheless, superficial and trivialising as the Reagan approach undoubtedly was, it did succeed in promoting positive images.[128]

In a 1989 interview, Jimmy Carter explained his problems with the press as follows:

When the president is riding high and has 50 or 55 percent favorable reaction in the public opinion polls, he's also treated with kid gloves and deference by the press. If he starts going down, though, then he's condemned by the press.[129]

The contrast between press treatment of Carter and of Reagan has frequently been commented upon. Rewarding behaviour they affect to despise, journalists preferred Reagan's simple messages. Key figures in the new team, notably James Baker, also took care to cultivate friendly media relations. (Donald Regan, Reagan's White House chief, has acknowledged that the press soft-pedalled on the 'Debategate' controversy in 1980–1. The issue centred on the alleged theft of confidential briefing materials from the Carter camp. According to Regan, the press, liking Baker, gave him the 'benefit of the doubt'.)[130] It may also be argued that the cycle of press hostility and guilt which followed Watergate had run its course by 1981. Above all, however, there was Reagan's apparent popularity. Media treatment and performance are not determined by poll ratings, but exist in a kind of cybernetic symbiosis alongside them. Yet Jimmy Carter's 1989 comment was essentially correct. By 1979 he found himself trapped within a vicious circle, wherein negative press and public reactions reinforced each other.[131]

In attempting to account for Carter's poor poll performance, it is important not to exaggerate the aberrance of these years. The average level of support for all Presidents has declined since the early 1960s. As noted in Chapter 1, the Vietnam and Watergate years witnessed a marked decrease in public confidence in governmental institutions. Carter actually had a higher level of Gallup poll approval at the end of his second year than did Reagan at the same stage in his Presidency. Both Presidents ended their third year with a 54 per cent approval score. Carter's average approval rating was 47 per cent, compared to Lyndon Johnson's 56 per cent. The Georgian did, however,

experience some disastrous dips. After nineteen months, Carter's approval
rate dropped below 40 per cent. This was lower than anyone since Truman at
this stage of the Administration. (Pat Cadell, the President's in-house pollster,
commented: 'He wouldn't have taken on issues like energy or Panama if he
just wanted to be popular')[132] His slide in the Autumn of 1979, after the
'crisis-of-confidence' address reached levels approaching (and even, according to some surveys, exceeding) Nixon's 1974 low. After forty-five months in
office, Carter's approval was 31 per cent; Reagan's equivalent score was 54
and Nixon's 62 per cent.[133] The most obvious explanation for Carter's
problems lies with the economy. As a general rule, Presidential popularity
tracks economic indicators. However, Democratic Presidents seem to suffer
more than Republicans from increases in inflation. Carter experienced a
generally rising 'misery index'; and a rising inflation rate for seven (out of
sixteen) quarters. He also faced, and indeed contributed to, real public doubts
about economic growth prospects. In general, according to Zukin and
Carter, it appears that economic issues dominated perceptions of the Presidential performance until the Iranian hostage crisis appeared in 1979.[134] Too
often Jimmy Carter appeared to the American people as the bearer of bad
news, both regarding the economy and concerning American power in the
world. Even more than in other Presidencies, crisis appeared the norm:
energy, the Middle East, inflation, nuclear weapons, spiritual malaise, Iran,
Afghanistan, Poland.[135]

Pat Cadell later remarked: 'Truth is the enemy of anyone presiding over a
nation in decline. Anyone who acknowledges the truth is out, because it is an
acknowledgement of failure.[136] However, part of the problem was presentational. Invocation of crisis is subject to the law of diminishing returns. The
energy policy was, especially early on, sold to the public as a choice between
competing evils. The crisis language did not hit home. Carter seemed, in
Schneiders's word, to be again 'bemoaning'. Only later did the Administration begin to argue that changes in energy consumptions might actually lead
to lifestyle improvements.[137]

A helpful, if over-simplified, way of looking at the Carter Administration is
to see it as torn between two orientations, each of which had potentially
negative implications for public relations. On the one hand was the comprehensive problem-solving orientation, of which Eizenstat emerged as the main
proponent. Conscientious, mature and responsible though it was, this
orientation offered difficult 'solutions'. It tended, in Roy Strong's words, to
neglect 'gestures or rhetoric designed to promote public support'.[138] On the
other hand, there was the populist 'outsider' symbolism which had
triumphed in 1976. Some key figures in the Administration, notably Pat
Cadell, attempted to prolong this orientation after Carter's election. The
'crisis-of-confidence' address represented a largely disastrous attempt to
revive Carter's 'outsider' status. It revealed that the Carter team had failed to
develop a new symbolic, populist language appropriate to a President in

office.[139] Neither the comprehensive problem-solving nor the populist, 'outsider' orientation managed to establish for Carter what Bruce Buchanan has called a 'privileged cushion': the kind of self-sustaining public support which gives some Presidents (notably Reagan) an extended honeymoon – 'assuming the best, softening critical scrutiny, and suspending skepticism and disbelief'.[140]

Jimmy Carter's vulnerability to swings in popularity was accentuated by his shallow basis of support within his own party. As will be discussed in the following chapter, he owed his 1976 nomination to new forces and new rules within the Democratic party. Traditional centres of power within the party meant little to Carter's personal organisation in 1976. Political scientist and Democratic 'insider', Austin Ranney remarked in 1978: 'Carter and his people have no interest in building the Democratic Party. He is *par excellence* a loner. He feels he doesn't owe a damn thing to the Democratic party.'[141] To some extent Ranney was exaggerating. Carter had, for example, been chairman of the '74 Campaign Committee of the Democratic National Committee (DNC), which he used to launch his White House bid. As President, Carter relied not only on Hamilton Jordan and Tim Kraft for party liaison, but also on Mark Siegel, former executive director of the DNC. The growing prominence of Robert Strauss, a former DNC chairman, also evidenced some growing concern for the party and its organisation. White House relations to DNC chairman John C. White, who succeeded Kenneth Curtis at the end of 1977, were, ostensibly at least, very cordial. White's correspondence with the White House generally took the line that the President should be congratulated for tackling difficult issues but that greater attention should be given to presentation. In April 1978, for example, White told Carter:

Your leadership in taking on the tough issues and your dedication to doing what is right for the American people is a constant source of inspiration . . . but those of us who work with you and for you *must* simply do a better job of conveying your programs and accomplishments to the American people.[142]

Even Kenneth Curtis, whose resignation was widely interpreted as evidence of antipathy between the White House and the DNC, was reluctant openly to criticise Carter personally. Curtis made little secret of his hostility to the President's team, but declared that the major reason for his resignation related to the problem of managing the Democrats' $2.5 million debt.[143] Moreover, the White House was keen to show its backing for Democratic candidates in the 1978 mid-term elections. In September of that year, Tim Kraft and Frank Moore reported to the President: 'We have made at least one major appearance in each marginal race . . .' Particular attention was paid to candidates thought to be threatened by the 'anti-tax' 'conservative voter backlash'.[144]

All this is not to deny that there were significant tensions between the Carter team and party organisations. An early attempt to place Georgian Phil

Wise on the DNC chairman's staff caused difficulties. Many state party organisers found themselves unable to integrate 1976 'Peanut Brigaders' into the regular organisation. In January 1978, *Congressional Quarterly* reported three major complaints being voiced by state party leaders: that the White House preferred to deal with remnants of the 1976 Carter network at the local level, even appointing 'outsiders' to patronage jobs; that Carter aides arrogantly countermanded local decisions; and that the Administration was generally too generous towards Republicans. Democratic leaders in Chicago protested that the White House had deliberately ensured that Illinois patronage posts were given to individuals opposing the political machine of former mayor Richard Daley.[145] In 1980, particular party anger was directed at Carter for conceding defeat so early on election night, thus damaging the election prospects of Democratic candidates on the West coast.[146]

The Carter Presidency was a product of a party system in decline. Modern Presidents simply do not tend to regard their job as encompassing party strengthening and reinvigoration. Carter's attitude towards the party organisation represented a compromise between caution and the desire to confront corrupt, vested interest. (In Chicago, Mayor Jane Byrne, the inheritor of Daley's mantle, emerged in 1980 as a leading supporter of Edward Kennedy.) Carter's methods of dealing with his party did nothing to strengthen his political position. However, it makes little sense to blame Jimmy Carter, of all people, for failing to resist the centrifugal tendencies of the 1970s party system.

Governmental reorganisation

Carter's technocratic faith and concern with governmental process formed a major theme of the 1976 campaign. Who else but Jimmy Carter would have devoted a chapter of his campaign autobiography to the subject of zero-based budgeting? During the campaign, Carter promised to cut the number of governmental agencies from 1,900 to 200.[147]

Attacks on the 'mess in Washington' were partly rhetorical, partly a reflection of Carter's own technocratic and populist belief structure. He promised a 'bottom up' review of Washington and its programmes. Occasionally this veered towards a rather negative 'bash the bureaucrat' demagoguery.[148] When Rafshoon joined the Administration, he actually encouraged Carter's bureaucrat-bashing tendencies, feeling that it would please public opinion. The American people were convinced, Rafshoon advised the President, that federal employees were 'lazy, shiftless, crooked and overpaid'.[149]

Carter's stress on fighting governmental waste was not an outright attack on 'big government' *per se*. In this he differed from Democrat George Wallace and Republican Ronald Reagan, the other main anti-Washington candidates in 1976. (Another Democratic contender, Jerry Brown, had offered an anti-

Washington rhetoric of lowered expectations considerably more radical than Carter's.) The Georgian was not above exploiting public hostility to bureaucrats. Yet he did actually create two new Cabinet departments: Energy and Education. Though philosophically inclined to distrust regulation, he was by no means entirely opposed to it.[150] The (failed) hospital cost containment plan would have significantly extended the scope of federal regulation, as would the early energy proposals. Rather than a simplistic assault on 'big government', Carter's policies involved a strong commitment to the public administration dictum that organisation matters. The policies also represented another effort to cut the Gordian knot of post-liberal politics. Attempting to alleviate waste was an obvious response to diminished economic growth prospects. Government reorganisation was also a potentially painless way to respond to powerful lobbies. The creation of the Education Department provides a good example. The Administration was anxious to upgrade education in the Washington context for its own sake. It also, however, despite its antipathy to 'special interests', was keen to retain the support of the National Education Association. The NEA, the main teachers' union, had endorsed the Democrats in 1976 for the first time in its 114-year history. The NEA, with about 1.8 million members spread evenly across the country, also represented a formidable force in the reformed Democratic party. Against this background, Hamilton Jordan informed Carter in late 1977 that establishing the new department '*is one of the few things that we can do for the teachers' organizations in the next few years as additional funds for education will be difficult with our goal of balancing the budget*'.[151] Despite public antagonism towards 'horrible, bloated bureaucracy' – Carter's phrase – governmental reorganisation is not the stuff of which Presidential heroics are made. As Griffin Bell later commented, the Administration was not able to sustain public interest in reorganisation.[152] The relative intractability, complexity and infinite tedium of administrative reform tend inevitably to remove these issues from the political centre-stage. Carter actually did extremely well to avoid the whole effort becoming bogged down in interminable 'turf wars'.

Several agencies and jurisdictions were consolidated, though nowhere near the 1,700 promised in 1976. A press release of July 1978 claimed that the Administration had achieved a 10 per cent reduction in paperwork in the government departments, and that the battle against excessive regulation was being won (notably regarding the administration of the 1970 Occupational Safety and Health Act, and the Civil Aeronautics Board).[153] Campaigns were undertaken to have regulations written in 'plain English' and for them to be reviewed from 'bottom up'. In April 1978, the President issued the following directive to all heads of agencies and departments:

One of the Administration's principal goals is to ensure that each agency of the Federal Government adequately responds to consumer needs in its development of policy and provides adequate opportunities for consumer participation in its decision-making processes.[154]

The Carter Administration generally encouraged the pre-existing moves towards 'government in the sunshine', notably in the context of greater agency openness and accountability.[155]

The commitment to 'bottom up' reviews underpinned Carter's pet reform: zero-based budgeting. Previously confined to state and local budgeting, the Georgian introduced ZBB to the federal arena. The idea was to subject every programme and agency to an annual base-level review. Nothing would be assumed; incrementalism and inexorable budgetary growth would be halted. In fact, Carter's enthusiasm for ZBB was rather overheated. ZBB, as mere process, could not bring comprehensive rationality to the budget, whose political dimension remained stubborn. ZBB also had no impact on the federal budget's uncontrollable element: the portion deriving from past commitments and entitlements. (In fiscal year 1979, some 89 per cent of Health, Education and Welfare's budget was 'uncontrollable'.) The willingness and ability of leading budgetary actors to unpack past bargains and compromises on an annual basis must also be questioned. In the event, ZBB had, by the early 1980s, merged (at least at the federal level) into old-fashioned incrementalism.[156]

In March 1978, the *New York Times* described Carter's civil service reform plan as 'the most sweeping the Civil Service has faced since its inception in 1883'. Two writers in the *Review of Public Personnel Administration* in 1980 described the reforms as probably 'the most impressive domestic achievement of Jimmy Carter's Presidency'.[157] The 1978 Civil Service Reform Act established a Senior Executive Service (SES) for top managers; it created a performance evaluation system, linking performance and pay; it abolished the Civil Service Commission, creating in its stead an Office of Personnel Management and the Merit Systems Protection Board; it codified the role of the Federal Labor Relations Authority; it extended protection to 'whistleblowers', who reported on waste or corruption; and it embodied commitments to equal employment opportunities and affirmative action.

The Act was skilfully guided through Congress, with necessary compromises being made over labour relations and veterans' benefits. The philosophy behind the Act was not entirely consistent. There was some ambivalence, for example, between the commitments to efficiency and to responsiveness. Thus the provisions to eliminate 'featherbedding' for employees sat rather awkwardly with the protection for 'whistleblowers'.[158] The SES did not develop, as Carter intended, into an administrative elite on the British model. The larger number of political appointments made possible by the reform was something of a bonus for Reagan. The ethics provisions also – embodied in a separate 1978 act – proved difficult to enforce in the political atmosphere of the 1980s. (Several commentators pointed to the eagerness of former Carter employees in 1980 and 1981 to seek lucrative posts in the private sector. This appeared to violate at least the spirit of the 1978 ethics legislation, with its attempts to stall the 'revolving door' between public and private.)[159] However, there is no question that Carter's civil service reforms represented a coherent and measured attempt to answer widely accepted criticisms of the civil service.[160]

Notes

1 Memo to the President from G. Rafshoon, 22 Sept. 1978, box 103, PHF (folder, '9/25/78 (1)').

2 Memo to the President from A. McDonald, 29 Aug. 1980, box 203, PHF (folder, '8/29/80'). See also J. G. Benze, *Presidential Power and Management Technique* (New York: Greenwood, 1987), ch. 4.

3 S. Hess, *Organizing the Presidency* (Washington DC: Brookings, 1976).

4 Carter, MC transcript, p. 8.

5 Report to H. Jordan from A. D. Frazier, 19 Oct. 1977, box 57, SO: Chief of Staff Jordan (folder, 'White House Staff Reorganisation').

6 See R. E. Neustadt, *Presidential Power: The Politics of Leadership from FDR to Carter* (New York: Wiley, 1980), pp. 225–228; also Colin Campbell, *Governments under Stress* (Toronto: University of Toronto Press, 1983), pp. 43–4.

7 E. C. Hargrove, *Jimmy Carter as President* (Baton Rouge: Louisiana State University Press, 1988), pp. 42–4; also, Colin Campbell, *Managing the Presidency: Carter, Reagan and the Search for Executive Harmony* (Pittsburgh: University of Pittsburgh Press, 1986), p. 87.

8 See D. Bonafede, 'Stuart Eizenstat', *National Journal*, 9 June 1979, pp. 944–8; J. H. Kessel, 'The Structures of the Carter White House', *American Journal of Political Science*, 27, 1983, pp. 431–63, at 437; Bradley H. Patterson, *The Ring of Power: The White House Staff and its Expanding Role in Government* (New York: Basic Books, 1988), p. 302.

9 Carp and Rubinstein, MC transcript, p. 61 (Rubinstein).

10 Kenneth W. Thompson, ed., *The Carter Presidency: Fourteen Intimate Perspectives* (Lanham: University Press of America, 1990), p. 246.

11 Brzezinski saw Carter as over-punctilious regarding detail, but not as indecisive. See Brzezinski, MC transcript, p. 84; Z. Brzezinski, *Power and Principle* (London: Weidenfeld and Nicolson, 1983), p. 522.

12 Bert Lance, *The Truth of the Matter* (New York: Summit, 1991), p. 126; Lance MC transcript, p. 78; Thompson, ed., *The Carter Presidency*, p. 35 (Hufstedler); Hargrove, *Jimmy Carter as President*, p. 28; Sol M. Linowitz, *The Making of a Public Man: A Memoir* (Boston: Little, Brown, 1985), p. 210.

13 Cited in Kessel, 'The Structures . . .', p. 461.

14 See J. P. Pfiffner, 'White House Staff versus the Cabinet', *Presidential Studies Quarterly*, 16, 1988, pp. 666–89, 671; Samuel Kernell and S. I. Popkin, eds, *Chief of Staff: 25 Years of Managing the Presidency* (Berkeley: University of California Press, 1986), pp. 229–30.

15 See, e.g., M. S. Weatherford, 'The Interplay of Ideology and Advice in Economic Policy-making', *Journal of Politics*, 49, 1987, pp. 925–52.

16   See Carter, MC transcript, p. 8; Kirbo, MC transcript, p. 18.

17   Brzezinski, MC transcript, p. 81. See also Bruce Mazlich and Edwin Diamond, *Jimmy Carter: A Character Portrait* (New York: Simon and Schuster, 1979), p. 172.

18   Memo to H. Jordan from R. Moe, 8 Aug. 1979, box 57, SO: Chief of Staff Jordan (folder, 'White House Staff Reorganization').

19   See memo to the President from H. Jordan (undated, 1979), box 34, SO: Chief of Staff Jordan (folder, 'Image Analysis and Changes').

20   Carp and Rubinstein, MC transcript, p. 63.

21   See Kessel, 'The Structures . . .', p. 461.

22   Cited in James P. Pfiffner, *The Strategic Presidency: Hitting the Ground Running* (Chicago: Dorsey Press, 1988), p. 55.

23   Memo to the President from H. Jordan (undated, 1977), box 34, SO: Chief of Staff Jordan (folder, 'Early Months Performance').

24   Carp and Rubinstein, MC transcript, p. 61.

25   Brzezinski, MC transcript, p. 64.

26   See Robert Shogun, *Promises to Keep* (New York: Crowell, 1977), p. 192; Pfiffner, *The Strategic Presidency*, p. 56; J. Califano, *Governing America* (New York: Simon and Schuster, 1981), p. 410.

27   See Shirley Warshaw, 'The Carter Experience with Cabinet Government', paper presented to the Eighth Presidential Conference, Hofstra University, Nov. 1990.

28   Patterson, *The Ring of Power*, p. 135. See also David McKay, *Domestic Policy and Ideology* (Cambridge: Cambridge University Press, 1989), pp. 120–7.

29   Memo to the President from G. Rafshoon, 18 Oct. 1978, box 28, SO: Rafshoon (folder, 'Memoranda').

30   See Campbell, *Managing the Presidency*, p. 89; Rosalynn Carter, *First Lady from Plains* (Boston: Houghton Mifflin, 1984), p. 164.

31   Memo to G. Schneiders from J. Powell, 1 June 1977, box 28, SO: Rafshoon (folder, 'Memoranda').

32   Carter, MC transcript, p. 13; Califano, *Governing America*, p. 188.

33   *National Journal*, 9 June 1979, p. 946.

34   Memo to the President from H. Jordan, 5 Nov. 1979, box 77, SO: Chief of Staff Jordan (folder, 'Cabinet Meetings').

35   See Warshaw, 'The Carter Experience . . .'; *CQ Almanac*, 1977, pp. 417, 530; Griffin Bell, *Taking Care of The Law* (New York: Morrow, 1982), p. 46.

36   *Taking Care of the Law*, p. 47.

37   See Warshaw, 'The Carter Experience . . .'; Pfiffner, *The Strategic Presidency*, p. 117; J. Sundquist, 'Jimmy Carter as Public Administrator', *Public Administration Review*, 39, 1979, pp. 3–11; Carl M. Brauer, *Presidential Transitions* (New York: Oxford University Press, 1986), ch. 4.

38   Tip O'Neill, *Man of the House* (New York: St Martin's, 1987), pp. 355, 364, 368–71.

39   *The Observer*, 14 July 1991.

40   H. Donovan, Exit Interview, 14 Aug. 1980 (Carter Library). See also Hedley Donovan, *Roosevelt to Reagan* (New York: Harper and Row, 1985), p. 212; G. W. Ayres, 'The Carter White House Staff', in M. G. Abernathy, D. M. Hill and P. Williams, eds., *The Carter Years* (London: Pinter, 1984), pp. 144–63, at 156; Michael Medved, *The Shadow Presidents* (New York: Times Books, 1979), pp. 348–52.

41 Cutler, MC transcript, p. 21.

42 See, e.g., Richard Rose, 'Governments against Sub-governments', in R. Rose and E. N. Suleiman, eds, *Presidents and Prime Ministers* (Washington DC: American Enterprise Institute, 1980), pp. 321–43, at 335.

43 Carp and Rubinstein, MC transcript, p. 61.

44 Carter, MC transcript, p. 9.

45 Bergland, MC transcript, p. 17.

46 See *National Journal*, 22 Dec. 1979, p. 2139.

47 *Playboy*, Nov. 1976.

48 *National Journal*, 14 Jan. 1978, p. 49.

49 Memo to the President from H. Jordan (undated, 1979), box 34, SO: Chief of Staff Jordan (folder, 'Image Analysis and Changes'). See also Jordan's remarks on his 'outsider' status and on the drugs charges against him and Kraft, *New York Times*, 4 Dec. 1980.

50 See Hargrove, *Jimmy Carter as President*, pp. 18–19; O'Neill, *Man of the House*, p. 370; Kessel, 'The Structure . . .', p. 437.

51 See Brzezinski, MC transcript, p. 70; Carp and Rubinstein, MC transcript, p. 13; Campbell, *Managing the Presidency*, p. 177 and *Governments under Stress*, p. 38.

52 See L. M. Salamon, 'The Presidency and Domestic Policy Formulation', in Hugh Heclo and L. M. Salamon, eds, *The Illusion of Presidential Government* (Boulder: Westview, 1981), pp. 177–202. Also J. P. Burke, *The Institutional Presidency* (Baltimore: Johns Hopkins University Press, 1992), ch. 5.

53 Cited in C. O. Jones, *The Trusteeship Presidency* (Baton Rouge: Louisiana State University Press, 1988), p. 86; also, *National Journal*, 9 June 1979, p. 948.

54 See Jones, *The Trusteeship Presidency*, pp. 84–6.

55 See Carp and Rubinstein, MC transcript, p. 61; *National Journal*, 24 Feb. 1979, p. 296.

56 Donovan, *Roosevelt to Reagan*, p. 212.

57 Carp and Rubinstein, MC transcript, pp. 12–13, 60.

58 Memo to the President from M. Blumenthal, 14 March 1979, box 34, SO: Chief of Staff Jordan (folder, 'Economics, 1978–79').

59 *National Journal*, 1 Dec. 1979, p. 2014.

60 See *National Journal*, 3 Feb. 1979, p. 189; Joel K. Goldstein, *The Modern American Vice-Presidency* (Princeton: Princeton University Press, 1982), pp. 172–81; Paul C. Light, *Vice-Presidential Power* (Baltimore: Johns Hopkins University Press, 1984), pp. 208–21; Thompson, ed., *The Carter Presidency*, pp. 239–47; Jules Witcover, *Crapshoot* (New York: Crown, 1992), ch. 6.

61 See Jones, *The Trusteeship Presidency*, ch. 3; Norman J. Ornstein, 'The Open Congress meets the President', in Anthony King, ed., *Both Ends of the Avenue* (Washington DC: American Enterprise Institute, 1983), pp. 185–211; Dean Rusk, *As I Saw It: A Secretary of State's Memoirs* (London: Tauris, 1990), p. 356; Christopher J. Bailey, *The Republican Party in the US Senate* (Manchester: Manchester University Press, 1988), ch. 6.

62 See, e.g., Nigel Bowles, *The White House and Capitol Hill* (Oxford: Clarendon Press, 1987), ch. 8; T. E. Yarborough, 'Carter and the Congress', in Abernathy *et al.*, eds., *The Carter Years*, pp. 165–91. Eizenstat remark: *CQWR*, 6 Oct. 1979, p. 2199.

63 Carter, MC transcript, pp. 25–7.

64   Hedrick Smith, *The Power Game* (London: Collins, 1988), p. 461.

65   See Gary Fink, *Prelude to the Presidency* (Westport: Greenwood, 1980), pp. 163–80.

66   See, e.g., Memo to the President from F. Moore, 7 Mar. 1979, 'Weekly Legislative Report', box 122, PHF (folder, '3/8/79 (1)').

67   Remark reported in *New York Times*, 18 Feb. 1977.

68   Brzezinski (including Albright), MC transcript, p. 22.

69   See *CQWR*, 8 Jan. 1977, p. 55 and 26 Feb. 1977, p. 301; Eric L. Davis, 'Legislative Liaison in the Carter Administration', *Political Science Quarterly*, 95, 1979, pp. 287–302; Michael J. Malbin, 'Rhetoric and Leadership: A Look Backward at the Carter National Energy Plan', in King, ed., *Both Ends of the Avenue*, pp. 212–45.

70   Lance, MC transcript, p. 34.

71   Thompson, ed., *The Carter Presidency*, p. 243.

72   Beckel, MC transcript, p. 5; J. Carter, *Keeping Faith* (London: Collins, 1982), p. 79.

73   See Memo to the President from the Vice-President, S. Eizenstat and F. Moore, 4 May 1977, box 26, PHF (folder, '5/23/77 (3)').

74   'Congressional Breakfast Themes', 4 Sept. 1979, box 4, SO: Speech-writers: SF (folder, 'Congressional Breakfast Themes').

75   Memo to the President from F. Moore, 26 Sept. 1978, box 103, PHF (folder, '9/26/78 (2)').

76   *Christian Science Monitor*, 5 Sept. 1978 (Hatfield). Brzezinski, MC transcript, p. 20.

77   See D. Bonafede, 'The Tough Job of Normalizing Relations with Capitol Hill', *National Journal*, 13 Jan. 1979, pp. 54–7.

78   See Jones, *The Trusteeship Presidency*, pp. 93–8; Amitai Etzioni, 'The Lack of Leadership', *National Journal*, 23 Feb. 1980, pp. 334–7.

79   Larry Light, 'White House Lobby gets its Act Together', *CQWR*, 3 Feb. 1979, pp. 195–200; Jones, *The Trusteeship Presidency*, at pp. 118, 188; James McGregor Burns, 'Jimmy Carter's Strategy for 1980', *Atlantic Monthly*, Mar. 1979, pp. 41–6; Mark A. Petersen, *Legislating Together: The White House and Capitol Hill from Eisenhower to Reagan* (Cambridge (Massachusetts): Harvard University Press, 1990), p. 73.

80   See box 26, PHF (folder, '5/26/77') (on meeting with Senators from TVA states).

81   See Campbell, *Managing the Presidency*, p. 87.

82   See *National Journal*, 22 Mar. 1980, p. 482.

83   Cited in Bailey, *The Republican Party in the US Senate*, p. 112.

84   Memo to F. Moore from G. Rafshoon and G. Schneiders, 12 Oct. 1978, box 28, SO: Rafshoon (folder, 'Memoranda').

85   Memo to F. Moore from G. Rafshoon, 21 Dec. 1978, box 28, SO: Rafshoon (folder, 'Memoranda to F. Moore').

86   Memo to the President from J. Fallows and J. Doolittle, 7 Feb. 1978, box 13, SO: Speech-writers: SF (folder, 'Jokes').

87   Box 5, SO: Speechwriters: SF (folder, 'Core stump').

88   O'Neill, *Man of the House*, p. 369.

89   See George C. Edwards, *At the Margins: Presidential Leadership of Congress*

(New Haven: Yale University Press, 1989) and Jon R. Bond and Richard Fleischer, *The President in the Legislative Arena* (London: University of Chicago Press, 1990).

90 Burns, 'Jimmy Carter's Strategy for 1980', p. 44.

91 *Keeping Faith*, p. 88. Carter's scores were 75. 4 (1977), 78. 3 (1978), 76. 8 (1979) and 75. 1 (1980).

92 See Petersen, *Legislating Together*, p. 220.

93 See D. Bonafede, 'A Report Card on Carter', *National Journal*, 14 Jan. 1978, pp. 44–9.

94 Jeff Fishel, *Presidents and Promises* (Washington DC: Congressional Quarterly, 1985), pp. 38–41. See also Edwards, *At The Margins*, p. 216.

95 See Bond and Fleischer, *The President in the Legislative Arena*, pp. 71–80.

96 *Ibid.* But see also P. C. Light, *The President's Agenda* (Baltimore: Johns Hopkins University Press, 1983), p. 38.

97 Petersen, *Legislating Together*, p. 259.

98 See Jon R. Bond and Richard Fleischer, 'Carter and Congress: Presidential Style, Party Politics, and Legislative Success', paper presented at the Eighth Presidential Conference, Hofstra University, Nov. 1990, pp. 4–6; also Eric Uslaner, *Shale Barrel Politics: Energy and Legislative Leadership* (Palo Alto: Stanford University Press, 1989).

99 See *CQWR*, 7 Jan. 1989, p. 7. Also, Samuel B. Hoff, 'Veto Policy and Use by the Carter Administration', paper presented at the Eighth Presidential Conference, Hofstra University, Nov. 1990.

100 *The President in the Legislative Arena*, p. 79.

101 See Carter, *Keeping Faith*, p. 70.

102 See Linowitz, *The Making of a Public Man* p. 205.

103 *Ibid.*, pp. 189–204.

104 Cited in John Tebbel and Sarah M. Watts, *The Press and the Presidency* (New York: Oxford University Press, 1985), p. 531.

105 Jody Powell, *The Other Side of the Story* (New York: Morrow, 1984), p. 104. For a questioning of this legacy of Watergate, see Brigitte L. Nacos, *The Press, Presidents and Crises* (New York: Columbia University Press, 1990).

106 Cited in John A. Maltese, *Spin Control: The White House Office of Communications and the Management of Presidential News* (Chapel Hill: University of North Carolina Press, 1992), p. 167. (There were a few other minor allegations of corruption – e.g., concerning Robert Vesco: see *New York Times*, 20 Aug. 1980.)

107 Remarks made by Jody Powell, 7 Jan. 1992, Jimmy Carter Presidential Centre (session attended by the author). See also John Orman, *Comparing Presidential Behavior* (New York: Greenwood, 1987), ch. 5.

108 *National Journal*, 5 May 1979, p. 751.

109 *Newsweek*, 19 Jan. 1981, p. 27.

110 *Keeping Faith*, p. 426.

111 See Mark J. Rozell, 'President Carter and the Press: Perspectives from White House Communications Advisers', *Political Science Quarterly*, 105, 1990, pp. 419–34, at 419. Also, M. J. Rozell, *The Press and the Carter Presidency* (Boulder: Westview, 1989), p. 7.

112 See Rozell, 'President Carter and the Press', p. 420.

113 Rozell, *The Press and the Carter Presidency*, p. 233.

114 *Ibid.*, p. 106.

115   The other causes were: Carter's poor performance in the pre-election debate; the 1980 'Rose Garden strategy'; the bungled March 1980 United Nations vote against Israel; Carter's over-strident attacks on Reagan; his unsuccessful attempt to depict Reagan as a warmonger; 'absence of vision'; and efforts to keep discussion of 'real issues' out of the campaign (*New York Times*, 9 Nov. 1980). See also Barbara Kellerman, *All the President's Kin* (New York: New York University Press, 1981), pp. 223–31, and Larry J. Sabato, *Feeding Frenzy* (New York: Free Press, 1991).

116   Powell remarks, 7 Jan. 1992.

117   See Robert Locander, 'Carter and the Press: The First Two Years', *Presidential Studies Quarterly*, 10, 1980, pp. 101–15.

118   See Rozell, 'President Carter and the Press'; Maltese, *Spin Control*, pp. 149–52.

119   Memo to the President from G. Rafshoon, G. Schneiders and B. Aronson, 19 Dec. 1978, box 114, PHF (folder, '1/3/79'). See also Michael Link, 'Perception, Style, and Theme in the Carter–Rafshoon White House', *Proceedings and Papers of the Georgia Association of Historians*, 10, 1989, pp. 131–43.

120   Memo to the President from G. Rafshoon, 'Style', undated, box 28, SO: Rafshoon (folder, 'Memoranda') (probably Aug. 1979).

121   Cited in Maltese, *Spin Control*, p. 171.

122   Memo to G. Rafshoon from G. Schneiders, 10 July 1979, box 28, SO: Rafshoon (folder, 'Memoranda').

123   Thompson, ed., *The Carter Presidency*, p. 35.

124   *Ibid.*, p. 79.

125   Carp and Rubinstein, MC transcript, p. 80 (Carp).

126   Maltese, *Spin Control*, p. 158.

127   Memo to the President from H. Donovan, 24 Oct. 1979, box 2, SO: Donovan (folder, 'Memos to the President').

128   See Frederic T. Smoller, *The Six O'Clock Presidency* (New York: Praeger, 1990), chs. 7–8.

129   Cited in Maltese, *Spin Control*, p. 167.

130   Donald T. Regan, *For the Record* (London: Arrow, 1988), p. 255.

131   See Michael B. Grossman and Martha J. Kumar, 'The Refracting Lens', in Doris A. Graber, ed., *Media Power in Politics* (Washington DC: Congressional Quarterly, 1984), pp. 184–203, at 198; Mark Hertsgaard, *On Bended Knee: The Press and the Reagan Presidency* (New York: Farrar, Straus, Giroux, 1988); Samuel M. Kernell, *Going Public: New Strategies of Presidential Leadership* (Washington DC: Congressional Quarterly, 1986); John K. White, *The New Politics of Old Values* (Hanover: University Press of New England, 1990).

132   *National Journal*, 19 Aug. 1978, p. 1312.

133   See Bruce Buchanan, *The Citizen's Presidency: Standards of Choice and Judgement* (Washington DC: Congressional Quarterly, 1987), p. 91; Barbara Hinckley, *The Symbolic Presidency* (New York: Routledge, 1990), p. 31; Edwards, *At the Margins*, p. 178.

134   See David J. Lanoue, *From Camelot to the Teflon Presidency: Economics and Presidential Popularity since 1960* (New York: Greenwood, 1987), pp. 89, 109–10; Richard A. Brody, *Assessing the President* (Stanford: Stanford University Press, 1991), p. 99; Alan Wolfe, 'Presidential Power and the Crisis of Modernization', *democracy*, 1, 1981, pp. 27–36; Cliff Zukin and J. R. Carter, 'The Measurement of

Presidential Popularity', in Doris A. Graber, ed., *The President and the Public* (Philadelphia: Institute for the Study of Human Issues, 1982), pp. 207–41, at 230.

135 See Dick Kirschten, 'Government by Crisis', *National Journal*, 5 Apr. 1980, p. 570.

136 Cited in Hertsgaard, *On Bended Knee*, p. 299.

137 See Malbin, 'Rhetoric and Leadership', at 238.

138 Roy A. Strong, 'Recapturing Leadership: The Carter Administration and the Crisis of Confidence', *Presidential Studies Quarterly*, 16, 1986, pp. 636–50, p. 649.

139 See Stephen Skowronek, 'Presidential Leadership in Political Time', in Michael Nelson, ed., *The Presidency and the Political System* (Washington DC: Congressional Quarterly, 1984), pp. 87–131, at 123.

140 Buchanan, *The Citizen's Presidency*, p. 89.

141 Rhodes Cook, 'Carter and the Democrats: Benign Neglect?', *CQWR*, 14 Jan. 1978, pp. 57–63, at 57.

142 Memo to the President from J. C. White, 14 Apr. 1978, box 82, PHF (folder, '4/21/78').

143 *CQWR*, 14 Jan. 1978, p. 58. See also H.F. Bass, 'The President and the National Party Organisation', in Robert Harmel, ed., *Presidents and their Parties* (New York: Praeger, 1984), pp. 59–89, at 75; Hal Bruno, 'Democrats in Disarray', *Newsweek*, 17 Dec. 1977; *New York Times*, 9 Dec. 1977 (Terence Smith). Carter has denied any rift with Curtis (MC transcript, p. 44).

144 Memo to the President from F. Moore and T. Kraft, 22 Sept. 1978, box 2, SO: Rafshoon (folder, 'Memoranda'). See also Howard Reiter, 'The Gavels of August', in Harmel, ed., *Presidents and their Parties*, pp. 96–121, at 107.

145 *CQWR*, 14 Jan. 1978, p. 59. See also Thomas E. Cronin, 'The Presidency and the Parties', in Gerald M. Pomper, ed., *Party Renewal in America* (New York: Praeger, 1980), pp. 176–93, at 180.

146 See Raymond Wolfinger and Peter Linquiti, 'Tuning In and Turning Out', *Public Opinion*, 4, 1981, pp. 56–60.

147 Jimmy Carter, *Why Not the Best?* (Eastbourne: Kingsway, 1977), p. 11; pamphlet, 'President's Reorganization Authority', box 44, SO: Counsel: Lipshutz (folder, 'Reorganization of Government').

148 See Sundquist, 'Jimmy Carter as Public Administrator', p. 9.

149 Memo to the President from G. Rafshoon, undated, box 28, SO: Rafshoon (folder, 'Memoranda March/April/May 1979'). See also National Commission on the Public Service (Volcker Commission), *Leadership for America* (Lexington: Heath, 1989), p. 63.

150 See Michael Malbin, 'Big Government or Small Government – The Candidates Give Their Views', *National Journal*, 26 Jan. 1980, pp. 136–7.

151 Memo to the President from H. Jordan, undated, box 34, SO: Chief of Staff Jordan (folder, 'Education, Dept. of'); David Stephens, 'President Carter, the Congress, and NEA', *Political Science Quarterly*, 98, 1983–4, pp. 641–63.

152 *National Journal*, 4 Mar. 1978, p. 354; Bell, *Taking Care of the Law*, p. 75.

153 'What the Press Overlooks in their Criticism of Carter', 31 Aug. 1978, box 28, SO: Rafshoon (folder, 'Memoranda'). On occupational safety and health, see William F. Grover, *The President as Prisoner* (Albany: State University of New York, 1989), ch. 3.

154 Memo to heads of departments and agencies, undated, box 82, PHF (folder,

'4/25/78').

155   See J. D. Lees, 'Open Government in the U.S.A.', *Public Administration*, 57, 1979, pp. 333–78.

156   See Frank D. Draper and Bernard T. Pitsvada, 'ZBB – Looking Back After Ten Years', *Public Administration Review*, 41, 1981, pp. 76–83; T. H. Hammond and J. H. Knott, eds, *A Zero-Based Look at Zero-Based Budgeting* (New Brunswick: Transaction, 1980), at p. 102.

157   *New York Times*, 8 March 1978; P. W. Colby and P. W. Ingraham, 'Civil Service Reform: The Views of the Senior Executive Service', *Review of Public Personnel Administration*, 1, 1980, pp. 75–89, at 75.

158   See P. W. Ingraham and John White, 'The Design of Civil Service Reform: Lessons in Politics and Rationality', *Policy Studies Journal*, 17, 1988–9, pp. 315–30. See also Benze, *Presidential Power and Management Techniques*, pp. 63–6.

159   See S. Taylor, 'Those Job-hopping Carter people', *New York Times*, 10 May 1981; Mark Huddleston, 'Is the SES a Higher Civil Service?', *Policy Studies Journal*, 17, 1988–9, pp. 406–19.

160   See essays in *Policy Studies Journal*, 17, 1988–9; also, P. W. Ingraham, 'The Civil Service Reform Act of 1978', in P. W. Ingraham and Carolyn Ban, eds, *Legislating Bureaucratic Change* (Albany: State University of New York Press, 1984), pp. 13–28; G. E. Caiden, *Administrative Reform Comes of Age* (Berlin: de Gruyter, 1991), p. 137.

3

Human rights in domestic context: the case of women's rights

The domestic side of human rights

Despite its more frequent articulation in the context of foreign policy, the Carter Administration's commitment to human rights was not designed to begin at the water's edge. During the 1976 campaign, Carter promised an audience at the University of Notre Dame a 'renewed commitment to civil rights, human rights, domestic and around the world . . .'. At a pre-election rally in Harlem, New York City, Carter evoked the Democrats' determination 'to seek out basic human rights and basic civil rights', a determination which American Presidents had abandoned 'when Lyndon Johnson left the White House and Richard Nixon came in . . .'[1]

The interconnection between the domestic and foreign faces of human rights was evidenced in the appointment of Patricia Derian as, first, co-ordinator and subsequently (in August 1977) Assistant Secretary of State for Human Rights. Appointed to the State Department without prior foreign policy experience, Derian undertook to apply the lessons gleaned from her background as a Mississippi civil rights activist. She saw the Administration's commitment to human rights as transcending the domestic/foreign divide, and wrote in March 1978 of the possibility of establishing 'a domestic human rights coordinating office of some kind'.[2] Deeply affected by the civil rights revolution in the South, Jimmy Carter too saw its values as replicable and transferable. A national re-commitment to human rights values would, as the President put it in his 'crisis-of-confidence' address (15 July 1979) remind Americans that they were 'part of a great movement of humanity' and help restore that sense of national purpose that had been so badly impeded during the Vietnam and Watergate years.[3]

At a less exalted level, Administration spokesmen frequently found themselves forced, because of the high-profile stance on human rights abroad, on to the defensive regarding the record at home. A television interview of April 1978 included the following question to President Carter: 'Many people feel that the President of the United States is more concerned about human rights outside of the United States and not enough concerned about human rights at home. What is your reaction to that?' Carter's defensive reply involved a characteristic subsummation of 'civil' (political/citizenship) rights under the more general category of 'human rights':

I don't think that is an accurate assessment.\ I think that our whole international emphasis on human rights would be undercut and fruitless if we didn't set an example in our country of being very insistent that human rights be protected here. Also, it is important for us to acknowledge that we still have a long way to go in giving our people genuine human rights, not just political rights, but also that right . . . to an education, to health care, to good housing, good clothing, good place to live. [*sic*].[4]

Such a broad commitment to human rights at home – economic as well as political – constituted, in effect, a promise to take up the flame of reform from the ashes of the Great Society. Indeed, Carter saw his domestic policy in terms of 'a continuum of what had been initiated under Lyndon Johnson and talked about under President Kennedy . . .'.[5] The Administration's financial prudence, however, together with the post-liberal political climate in which the Carter Presidency operated, made this wide-ranging commitment to human rights at home little more than merely rhetorical.

Jimmy Carter was not the first Cold War President to suffer the discomfort which accrues to those who hurl stones from glasshouses. Several of his predecessors had found the denial of civil rights to Southern blacks a severe diplomatic embarrassment. Lectures on the US federal system and the inability of the White House to dictate to the governments of Mississippi or Arkansas had cut little ice with sceptical world opinion in the 1950s and 1960s. For the Carter Administration, however, the embracing of human rights raised special difficulties. United Nations Ambassador Andrew Young's remarks about poverty and the denial of human rights in the US exemplified the explosively unpredictable domestic overspill of the new foreign policy.

It became something of a commonplace, observable at both extremes of the political spectrum, to accuse the Administration of hypocrisy. Even Anastasio Somoza, the Nicaraguan dictator, saw his opportunity, remarking in April 1977 that the US government, which had 'been discriminating against dark-skinned people for years', could have 'nothing to tell me about human rights'.[6] In 1978, radical feminist writer Andrea Dworkin criticised Carter's failure to condemn the treatment of women in Saudi Arabia. She added:

Disbelief leads me to wonder why the plight of male dissidents in Russia overtakes Mr. Carter's not very empathetic imagination when women in this country are in mental institutions or lobotomized or simply beaten to death . . . by men who do not like the way they have done the laundry or prepared dinner.[7]

Sections of the American public began to draw out implications from the highly publicised human rights commitment in foreign policy. In July 1977, for example, Carter found in his in-box the following analysis (by White House staff secretary Rick Hutcheson) of incoming mail:

People have seized the words 'human rights' and are applying them to every argument, cause and issue imaginable. Domestic concerns, including gay rights, inflation and the Wilmington Ten, have taken precedence over foreign affairs in the minds of many writers. 'If you (the President) are so concerned about the violation of human rights in other countries, why don't you do anything about the abuse of human rights here (in the U.S.)?'[8]

Despite its genuine, 'good faith' commitment to domestic human rights, the Carter Administration was hardly in a position to meet the variety of demands described by Hutcheson. In the remainder of this chapter, and in the subsequent one, the focus will be on two central domestic human/civil rights areas: women's rights and black civil rights. In both instances the Administration took steps to respond to demands articulated by key sectors within the Democratic party coalition. It attempted conscientiously to meet these demands, though always within the limits imposed by its post-liberal, financially cautious and (to some degree) socially conservative ethos. The focus in these two chapters is on female and black rights. However, if we bear in mind Carter's definition of human rights in the April 1978 television interview, it is clear that the President's entire domestic programme – from health care reform to inflation control – impacted on 'human rights' as defined by the Administration. Even in the narrower context of 'civil rights', it should be emphasised that the Carter Presidency took important (and often very successful) initiatives in areas other than female and black issues. When Hamilton Jordan began to compile a list of 'civil rights achievements' in preparation for the 1980 campaign, for example, he laid stress on the fact that this was the first Administration to issue guidelines prohibiting discrimination against the handicapped. (His list also included the Administration's record in appointing women, blacks and Hispanics; its success in obtaining an extension from Congress for the Equal Rights Amendment ratification deadline; and passage through Congress of a constitutional amendment to grant full voting rights to citizens of the District of Columbia.)[9] In similar vein, Stuart Eizenstat, looking back on the Administration's record from the vantage point of 1981, laid stress on Carter's support for the 1977 Protection of Children Against Sexual Exploitation Act and the 1978 Child Abuse Prevention Act.[10] Other domestic civil/human rights initiatives which bore fruit included legislation on privacy protection and civil justice reform.[11] Human rights commitments also influenced refugee admittance. The Administration eventually ran into controversy over its apparent reluctance to admit black Haitian refugees. However, it did preside over a general relaxation in policy, which culminated in the 1980 Refugee Act. In July 1977, Brzezinski himself advised Carter that the Administration had 'a moral obligation' regarding the admittance of Indochinese refugees: 'our human rights stand requires us to admit some of those who flee tyranny.'[12]

The women's movement, Jimmy Carter and the Democrats

Somewhere near the heart of the 'quiet revolution' in the Democratic party, which set the scene for both the McGovern nomination in 1972 and Carter's success in 1976, lay the forces of organised feminism.[13] The McGovern–Fraser Commission, set up to purge the Democratic party of the kinds of delegate selection and party management abuses associated with the 1964 and 1968 conventions, created what has been called a ' "nationalized" party of amateurs',[14] in which both liberal and militant feminists played a prominent role. Among other blows at the power of the party regulars, the Commission directed the states to take 'affirmative steps' in delegate selection to ensure representation of women, blacks and young people in 'reasonable relationship to the group's presence in the population of the state'.[15] Consequently, 40 per cent of the delegates to the Democrats' 1972 Miami convention were female, compared with 13 per cent at Chicago in 1968. The 1972 platform was strongly influenced by the National Women's Political Caucus (founded in 1971 and already hugely successful in pushing for strict enforcement of the McGovern-Fraser Commission's recommendations on female delegate selection). The platform outlined a broad commitment to women's rights: from Equal Rights Amendment (ERA) ratification to elimination of tax inequities and the appointment of women to top government jobs. George McGovern did manage to smother demands for a pro-choice plank on abortion, and some radical feminists condemned him as a phoney. Yet there was no denying the advances that had been made since 1968.[16]

As Byron Shafer has written, 'the Carter campaign was every bit as independent of the regular party as that of George McGovern'. It was also 'every bit as *dependent* on reformed institutions . . .'.[17] Carter loyalists on the Democratic National Committee largely opposed the post-1976 efforts of the Winograd Commission to restore power to party regulars.[18] Yet Carter was manifestly not 'Southern fried McGovern',[19] as George Wallace attempted to label him. Certainly, Carter was very concerned to win the support of the party's new Presidential elite, with its strong feminist commitments. The Mikulski Commission, set up to draft delegate selection rules for 1976, continued the commitment to 'affirmative action' in female delegate selection. At the 1976 convention in New York City, Carter won the support of women's leaders – notably of (then) Congresswoman Bella Abzug – by energetic lobbying and by pledging to support the ERA.[20] Yet Carter was also concerned (in 1976 as well as in 1980) to avoid that association with militant radicalism that had destroyed McGovern. Carter aides worked successfully in 1976 to moderate platform commitments to abortion choice and homosexual rights.[21] During the campaign he managed, unlike McGovern, to hold together with forces of the New Politics and those of Democratic traditionalists, notably organised labour.

Preservation of this alliance between new and old Democratic coalitions proved increasingly tricky. On the one hand, the women's rights wing of the party continued to consolidate its position. It was noticeable that the Winograd Commission (set up to draft rules for the 1980 convention), although it urged a limited turn back of power to party regulars in many areas, continued to affirm the position of women in the delegate selection process. (In the event, 49 per cent of delegates to the 1980 New York City convention were women, compared to 33 per cent in 1976.) The problems of managing the newly powerful women's groups within the Democratic coalition were made apparent when Carter fired Bella Abzug from her position as co-chair of the National Advisory Committee on Women in January 1979. Eleanor Holmes Norton, head of the Equal Employment Opportunities Commission, warned of the dangers ahead. Women's organisations, wrote Norton:

will have a greatly disproportionate effect on such critical matters as which women will become delegates to the 1980 convention, where half the delegates must be women. Even if they ultimately support the President, it would be wasteful to have them feel they must test him during that period.[22]

On the other hand, the Carter years also witnessed an enormous strengthening of organised anti-feminism, rooted in an apparent resurgence of social conservatism. Phyllis Schlafly and the New Right pro-family lobby were only the most prominent manifestations of the new temper. Its effect was soon felt within feminist circles, especially when it became apparent that ERA ratification was no longer a foregone conclusion. Radicals condemned false friends like McGovern and Carter, while others urged that support for Carter be redoubled in order to keep out Ronald Reagan. Mildred Marcy, mainstream feminist activist (as well as State Department employee) in this period, later recalled: 'We began to change from our rather naive idealistic belief in inevitable progress – into realizing that we were hitting where people lived, and it was endangering the status quo and family life as they knew it.'[23] The firing of Abzug represented the most public and bitter breach between the Carter Administration and the women's movement, and undoubtedly reflected the Administration's perception of a need to accommodate itself to the 'new' social conservatism. The relationship between Carter and organised feminism had, in fact, started very promisingly. At the time of Carter's inauguration, women's organisations were in the process of organising state conventions as a prelude to the First National Women's Conference, to be held in Houston in November 1977. The work was being carried out by the secretariat (under Mildred Marcy) of the National Commission on the Observance of International Women's Year. (This Commission had been set up by President Ford following the United Nations designation of 1975 as

International Women's Year.) In a dramatic demonstration of his commitment, Carter enlarged the Commission and appointed Abzug to replace
Elizabeth Athanasakos, Ford's choice as chairwoman. Although a great
success in its own terms, the Houston conference, along with the preceding
state conventions, witnessed significant pro-life, anti-ERA and anti-feminist
demonstrations. By this time, some cracks had already begun to appear in the
new President's alliance with feminist forces in his own party. In March 1977,
for example, Margaret Costanza, Carter's senior assistant for public liaison
and – in effect – his first White House women's rights officer, reported on the
dissatisfaction of the National Women's Political Caucus with the Administration's early performance. Though 'happy with the caliber of women
named to top positions within government' the NWPC felt 'that not enough
has been done in this area'. It also 'voiced dismay over omission of specific
reference to women in the economic stimulus package' and demanded
specific 'women's impact statements' related to economic and welfare
policies.[24]

Even more revealing of the developing tension was the growing isolation of
Costanza herself within the White House. A former vice-mayor of Rochester
(New York), and co-chair of Carter's 1976 New York campaign, 'Midge'
Costanza was appointed in 1977 as Carter's highest ranking female aide,
with an office just down the hall from the President. She was the only
non-Georgian among Carter's top seven White House aides. A classic
struggle over Presidential propinquity with the Georgian loyalists saw her
removal to a basement office, before she resigned in August 1978.

Costanza's high-profile support for feminist causes displeased the Carter
loyalists. In July 1978, she criticised the President for not prioritising ERA to
the same degree as the Panama Canal treaties. (Robert Beckel, a White House
lobbyist for the treaties, later ridiculed Costanza's supposed preoccupation
with 'some constituency of left-handed Nicaraguan refugees'.)[25]

White House speech-writers frequently tried to use humour to defuse
possible sources of tension and embarrassment for the President. Jerry
Doolittle, for example, wrote a joke for the President to the effect that Billy
Carter was writing an autobiography entitled 'Why Not the Pabst?'. He also
wrote the following for Costanza: 'The President calls me in frequently for
advice. "Midge", he asked me just the other day, "what do you think of this
color for the drapes?".' Jokes could not, however, camouflage the bitterness
which characterised the relationship between Costanza and the Georgian
loyalists. In July 1978, for example, 'an administration woman' attacked,
through the *Washington Post*, 'that Southern boy network that sent Midge to
the basement'.[26]

Hamilton Jordan's attitude was made clear in a memo written to the
President shortly before the resignation. Especially irksome to Jordan was
Costanza's use of her position and her staff to publicise and promote the
pro-choice side of the abortion debate: '*for a group of women who are in high*

position because of Jimmy Carter to question publicly one of his positions that has been known for over a year after he simply restates it borders on disloyalty'. He continued:

> *to the extent that she serves as a conduit to outside groups and organizations, the perception here is that she listens to persons espousing liberal positions and causes and not to others.*
>
> I told Midge that she should think . . . how she would have reacted *if several days after you had announced your decision not to build the B-1, a member of the staff had hosted a meeting of generals at the White House who opposed his decision and made public statements in opposition and circulated a memorandum stating that.*[27]

On 15 July 1977, Costanza had organised at the White House a meeting of pro-choice women in the Administration, including some senior personnel from the Department of Health, Education and Welfare (HEW). When Jody Powell put to Eileen Shanahan of HEW the point about these women owing their jobs to Jimmy Carter, Shanahan replied: 'These women left damn good jobs to join the administration. Most are better qualified than men who got jobs of the same rank.'[28]

Costanza was succeeded as head of the White House Office of Public Liaison by Anne Wexler, herself a prominent Democratic party feminist and key figure in the intra-party debates of the early 1970s over the delegate selection issue. Wexler, however, operated as liaison to the burgeoning constituency of single issue groups, rather than as a women's rights officer *per se*. The latter role fell to Sarah Weddington, who found herself translated to the White House from the Agriculture Department upon Costanza's departure. Weddington's brief was to advise the President on issues with a particular significance for women, and generally to oversee the inclusion of women and women's perspectives in all aspects of the Administration's work. Working closely with Stuart Eizenstat, Weddington was able to avoid the kind of controversy that surrounded Costanza and Bella Abzug. A strong Carter loyalist, she took on a more 'political', campaign-oriented role in the latter part of 1979.[29]

Aside from the position of White House women's rights officer, the Carter Administration created two bodies to further policy in this area: the Inter-departmental Task Force on Women's Rights and the National Advisory Committee on Women. The former body, technically within the Department of Labour, was designed to monitor and promote women's rights issues across the Administration. The National Advisory Committee essentially followed the tradition of President Kennedy's Commission on the Status of Women. Composed of individuals prominent in the field of women's rights outside the Administration, the Committee was designed to enshrine Carter's commitment and good faith, as well as to provide post-Houston continuity with the International Women's Year Commission. Tensions emerged even before Abzug's appointment as chairwoman in June 1978. On 9 May 1978,

White House aide Beth Abramowitz reported to Eizenstat on the bureaucratic battles taking place over staffing levels both for the Task Force and for the Committee. Gloria Steinem of the Committee was 'threatening to hold a press conference' and 'accuse the President of dragging his feet on making his commitments to women'.[30] The Committee cancelled a meeting with Carter in November 1978 on hearing that the President had allotted it only fifteen minutes in his schedule.

The dismissal of Abzug, and consequent resignation of half the Committee's membership, followed public sniping by the Committee at Administration policy. In particular, it criticised military spending increases, a cutback in Comprehensive Employment and Training Act (CETA) programmes, as well as Carter's stance on abortion. Press reports described the Administration's growing exasperation with Abzug: over her putative domineering of the Committee, her open breach with and attempted undermining of Weddington, and her (unsuccessful) attempts to orchestrate a women's walk-out from the Democrats' 1978 mid-term conference at Memphis. A 'White House official' was quoted to the effect that Abzug 'had attempted to lecture the President . . .'. During an explosive interchange, White House Counsel Robert Lipshutz berated Abzug: 'The next thing I know you'll be saying you were fired because you're a Jew.'[31] Carter simply commented: 'It saps our joint strength to be confrontational'. Further press reports suggested that Carter had been highly sceptical about Abzug's original appointment, and that Rosalynn Carter had actively opposed it. In fact, Rosalynn had agreed to withdraw her veto in the face of arguments presented on Abzug's behalf by Eizenstat, Wexler and Powell. The trio informed the President in April 1978:

If we appoint her, we will have a strong card to play in 1980 when we need the support of the group she represents. Although she is a controversial person, she understands politics and the nature of such commitments. Her leadership on your behalf in 1980 will be significant since she represents an activist constituency who can be counted on for strong grass roots support.[32]

In a trenchant piece in the *Washington Post*, David Broder related both the Costanza and Abzug affairs to Carter's slightly desperate attempt to accommodate himself to new forces in the Democratic party. Broder pointed to the Carter team's palpable unease with militant feminism. (The President himself later described himself as 'never . . . quite compatible' with feminist organisations.) According to Broder, Costanza and Abzug:

were hired in an effort to placate, through Government patronage, a force within the Democratic party that Carter finds, frankly, threatening . . . In a system overly porous to interest-group influence, it is a mistake to placate interest groups with symbolic presidential appointments. But Carter has done that, not only with women's groups, but with ethnic, religious and other groups as well, and each time he does so, he invites more trouble.[33]

Marcus Raskin of the Institute for Policy Studies interpreted the dismissal as an early shot in the Carter re-election campaign:

It means that Carter is calculating that Ronald Reagan is going to be the Republican candidate. He is positioning himself to the right, assuming there will be no liberal Democratic challenger and that the liberals will have no place to go.[34]

Soon after the firing, a further row developed over the White House's refusal to allow Weddington to testify before a Congressional committee considering women's education and job-training. Women's groups condemned it as a Nixonism – the phrase 'executive privilege' was used by the Administration in the course of its refusal – designed to camouflage spending cutbacks. Carol Burris of Women's Lobby commented: 'If Sarah hasn't seen the handwriting on the wall and decided to resign, then she can't expect those of us who helped get her the job in the first place to be supportive.'[35] The Administration's relationship with Abzug's successor, Marjorie Chambers, remained testy. On 30 March 1979, Chambers voiced her worries about Carter's anti-inflation policy. She pointed out that the 'benefits of controlling inflation' might, owing to low unionisation levels and low wage positions, 'largely pass women by'.[36] However, after Abzug's departure, the Committee was largely content to interpret its 'women's rights' brief relatively narrowly and not to embark upon swingeing critiques of Presidential policy.[37] By the end of 1979, Committee leadership had passed to Lynda Robb (with Carter's daughter-in-law Judy as honorary chair). Meanwhile, Carter forces prepared themselves for possible conflicts with women's rights activists at the 1980 convention.

Abortion

Although attacked for 'fuzziness' on the abortion issue, Carter's position here was made abundantly clear during the 1976 campaign and did not alter during his tenure at the White House. His stance was outlined in a February 1976 letter to Karen Mulhauser of the National Abortion Action League:

I am personally opposed to abortion. I favor strong and accessible family planning services. My record in Georgia shows that. I am aware that abortion is the treatment for failed contraception, but I believe that the need for abortion services can be minimized by improved family planning services. I am opposed to a constitutional amendment to alter the Supreme Court's decision by prohibiting abortion or giving states local option authority . . .

. . . I am personally opposed to government spending for abortion services. However, as President, I will be guided and bound by the courts . . .[38]

This basic line was reaffirmed time and again, even in the notorious *Playboy* interview published in September 1976.[39] During the Iowa caucuses campaign – and also at a meeting with Catholic bishops in Washington DC in August – Carter did seem to equivocate over support for a constitutional amendment. He was always anxious to use his pro-life views to shore up his appeal to Catholic voters. (Though viewing the abortion issue as largely marginal to the voting decisions of a majority of voters, Carter seems to have regarded Gerald Ford's ambivalence – and Betty Ford's clear pro-choice position – as having harmed the Republicans in 1976.)[40]

Accusations of 'fuzziness' came not so much from odd campaign trail hints but rather from the spectacle of Carter, the pro-life Baptist, promising to uphold the Supreme Court's *Roe v. Wade* decision while also opposing the action – a constitutional amendment – thought by many pro-lifers to be necessary to reverse it. The 1973 decision (*Roe v. Wade*, 410 US 113) had been strongly influenced both by the rise of the concept of privacy in American constitutional law and by an increasing concern for women's rights. Under the decision, states could not prohibit abortions during the first six months of pregnancy. (Sarah Weddington acted for 'Jane Roe' in *Roe v. Wade*.)

Carter's position was logically and constitutionally sound. It satisfied his strong religious beliefs. It allowed Congress and the Court to lead policy in this most sensitive of areas. It also gave no encouragement to those pro-lifers who were calling for a national constitutional convention (under Article V) on the issue. (Any call for a national constitutional convention has traditionally been opposed by the federal government, because of the uncontrollable and unpredictable character of any such gathering. In September 1977, White House aide Beth Abramowitz wrote to Eizenstat concerning the 'nightmarish implications of holding the first and only constitutional convention' held on a national basis since 1787.)[41]

In 1976, Congress passed the Hyde amendment, disallowing the use of federal funds to finance abortions for poor women. This was upheld in the Court's 1980 McRae decision. Between 1977 and 1980, various HEW appropriations bills had language appended to them, setting down conditions under which federally funded abortions could be performed. Generally speaking, Congressional language became increasingly restrictive. A December 1977 compromise allowed federal money to be used in the case of threats to the mother's life or 'long-lasting physical health', incest and rape, if 'reported promptly'. By the time it pronounced on the appropriation for fiscal year 1981, Congress had narrowed the conditions to threats to the mother's life, incest and rape reported within seventy-two hours.[42]

Potentially, Carter's position was quite popular.[43] Yet it failed to appease pro-life activists, while severely displeasing those on the pro-choice side of the debate. In particular, pro-choicers resented his opposition to federal funding for poor women's abortions ('Medicaid abortions'). In July 1977, both Costanza and Eizenstat urged him to soften his line. A memo from Costanza expressed concern at remarks made by the President during a 12 July news conference. Pressed on the issue of 'Medicaid abortions', Carter had replied: 'there are many things in life that are not fair, that wealthy people can afford and poor people can't.'[44] During the same news conference, Carter had stressed that federal funds were not to be used for abortions: 'except when the woman's life is threatened, or when the pregnancy was a result of rape or incest . . . it ought to be interpreted very strictly'.He added that he did not believe that 'either States or the Federal government' should fund abortions. Costanza's protest elicited some unusually direct margin comments in the President's handwriting. Asked simply to avow support for federal funding when 'medically necessary', Carter added the word 'no' in the margin. To the allegation that he had 'interfered in a State process in an unfair way' in his remark about state funding, Carter appended: 'If I had this much influence on state legis [*sic*] ERA would have passed.' His final marginal comment to Costanza's memo ran: 'My opinion was well defined to U.S. during campaign. My statement is actually more liberal than I feel personally.'[45] Eizenstat also tried unsuccessfully to convince Carter of the political desirability of amending his position and looking more favourably on federal funding for abortions in the case of 'unmarried girls'. (Eizenstat attempted to persuade Carter that such a move would not contravene the President's oft-stated opposition to 'accepting abortion as a routine contraceptive').[46]

In line with Presidential preference and legislative enactment, federal money for abortion during the Carter years was severely restricted – essentially to cases of rape, incest and threats to the mother's life. Women's groups pointed out that abortion policy had been considerably more liberal under Carter's Republican predecessor. After August 1977 – when a federal court injunction on operation of the Hyde amendment was lifted – federally funded abortions averaged (according to HEW secretary Joseph Califano, himself a pro-life Catholic) between 1,000 and 1,500 annually. This compared with possibly as many as 300,000 per annum (about a third of all legal abortions) before 1977.[47] The responsibility for the decrease rested primarily with Congress. The President, however, consistently urged Califano to interpret the law very strictly, especially regarding arrangements for reporting in cases of rape: 'I want rules that will prevent abortion mills from simply filling out forms and encouraging women to lie.'[48] The White House's response to charges of illiberalism was to point to the Administration's strong commitment to family planning and counselling. During the 1976 campaign, Carter boasted that, under his governorship, each of Georgia's 150 county health departments had an operating family planning clinic.[49] A survey of policy on women's issues published by Sarah Weddington's office in 1980 noted Presidential support for increasing funding to the Community Health Center Programs, which particularly emphasised family planning. Funding increased from $219 million in 1977 to $374 million in fiscal year 1981. The survey spotlighted the counselling and education available under the Department of Health and Human Services' new Adolescent Pregnancy Prevention and Services project and the allocation of $2.4 million in CETA funds for the Labour Department's Women's Bureau to raise consciousness about 'the teen pregnancy issue'. Further significant budget increases had taken place regarding the Health Services Administration's provision of family planning and family planning research. More controversially, Califano suggested that the federal government might subsidise the adoption of unwanted children by 'minority and rural families who might want to adopt children but can't afford to'.[50]

It was sensible for Carter to try to leave it to the legislative and judicial branches to fight out the debate over abortion. He once told a reporter that abortion was an 'impossible political' issue; people would 'still be arguing about it' fifty years hence.[51] Yet a combination of strong personal belief, political opportunism and his special relationship with the Democratic party feminists prevented him from standing entirely aloof. As Laurence Tribe puts it:

Although President Ford had not favored federal funding, he never stressed the issue, nor had he sought to initiate a funding cutoff. By sending approving signals on the Hyde Amendment, the Supreme Court and the Carter White House together did much to legitimize what had not previously been established as a legitimate political position.[52]

The Equal Rights Amendment to the Constitution

'Equality of rights under the law shall not be denied or abridged by the United States or by any State on account of sex.' Originally drafted in 1923, and passed by Congress in 1972, the ERA initially enjoyed spectacular success at the state ratification stage. It was accepted by thirty states within a year of Congressional passage. The rise of oppositional sentiment soon put this process into reverse. The ERA eventually failed when the time available for ratification expired on 30 June 1982.

ERA ratification formed the centrepiece of the agenda promoted by the National Organization of Women (NOW) and other mainstream feminists in the late 1970s. Aware of the dissatisfaction of many Democratic party feminists with his stance on abortion, Carter sought to win them over with a vigorous commitment to the ERA. As early as February 1977, the conservative journal *Human Events* recalled how ERA opponents had resented Betty Ford's utilisation of White House prestige to promote the amendment: 'Betty Ford lives in the White House and his name is Jimmy Carter.'[53]

Carter was anxious to establish his long-standing support for the ERA. In fact, as governor, he had first made his position known only after the 1973 Georgia legislative session. Even then, he had not lobbied enthusiastically, seeing the issue essentially as one 'between the individual legislator and his hometown women'.[54] Nevertheless, despite the fact that one of his rivals for the Democratic nomination in 1976 – Senator Birch Bayh of Indiana – was one of ERA's chief sponsors, Carter made a number of effective campaign commitments to the cause.[55] Characteristically, throughout his career,

Carter's declarations of support tended to come in a context of modulated social conservatism and suspicion of feminist militancy:

I'm from Georgia, and I understand Georgia, South Carolina, Alabama and North Carolina – states that didn't ratify the Equal Rights Amendment. And for these brassiere-burning firebrands to come down here and try to ram the Equal Rights Amendment down the throats of a conservative Georgia Senate was the worst possible thing they could have done.[56]

(Speaking in support of ERA in a vote in the Georgia House of Representatives in January 1974, Carter had mistakenly declared that his wife actually opposed the ERA. He had, according to Rosalynn Carter, 'misinterpreted' her opposition to a pro-ERA march in Georgia led by Gloria Steinem.)[57] Mrs Carter also typically couched her enthusiasm for the ERA in terms of a strong prior commitment to traditional values:

I feel that it is especially important to explain that women like me support the ERA. I am a relatively traditional person. I enjoy my roles as wife, mother, partner and businesswoman. I care how I look – and what I think. I am not threatened by ERA. I feel freed by it.[58]

Carter's Presidential lobbying for ERA was far more activist than anything he had attempted as Georgia's governor. Indeed, his record in this area runs counter to any view of the Carter Presidency as standing aloof from legislative arm-twisting and as innocent of the ways of Washington. Although the final battle was lost, a significant victory was achieved in the fall of 1978 when Congress extended the deadline for state ratification from March 1979 to June 1982. In March 1978, Eizenstat urged caution, suggesting that there was little Congressional support for extension.[59] However, from at least July 1978, Carter and Frank Moore organised a detailed programme of personal contacts with Members on behalf of the extension.[60] In the event, extensive lobbying by the Carters, as well as by Walter and Joan Mondale, helped swing seven crucial votes.[61] North Carolina Congressman Lamar Gudger's switch was followed by the release of $1.6 million in federal funds for Asheville Airport.[62]

At the state level, Carter's enthusiastic lobbying elicited frequent shouts of 'foul!' from ERA's opponents. At his 'ERA summit', held at the White House for eight hundred pro-ERA activists and for officials from unratified states, the President reminded the latter (as the *New York Times* put it) 'of the need for the Equal Rights Amendment every time federal grants . . . are made'.[63] According to Phyllis Schlafly: 'During the week Iran was going down the tube, President Carter was sitting in the Oval Office telephoning North Carolina senators begging them to vote for ERA.'[64] At a press conference in May 1978, Schlafly alleged that Carter had blatantly threatened to cut off federal funds to Mayor Michael Bilandic's Administration in Chicago unless it pressured more local legislators to support the ERA. According to Schlafly,

Mondale had been sent to Chicago: 'to reinforce the threat that the Carter administration would make Bilandic's life miserable unless he used his power to force Chicago-area legislators against their will to vote yes on ERA.'[65] Naturally, Schlafly's hyperbolic descriptions should be treated cautiously. However, there is no question as to the enthusiasm with which the Carters (Jimmy, Rosalynn and Judy) waded into the increasingly acrimonious state ratification battles.[66]

May 1980 saw the Illinois state legislature refusing to ratify for the eighth time. On 20 January 1981, the Georgia House defeated ERA by a two to one margin, despite a personal plea from the (just) ex-President. The forces represented by Phyllis Schlafly and by Ronald Reagan – the 1980 Republican platform dropped an ERA commitment which had been there for forty years – were in the ascendant. By this time, ERA opponents had added to their traditional invocation of a threat to family values a new emphasis upon the ERA's implications for women in the military.

During the Carter years, the American military was moving, with the Commander-in-Chief's approval, towards a blurring of some traditional distinctions between male and female military roles. The process would lead eventually, during the Panamanian invasion of 1989 and the Gulf conflict of 1991, to virtual female participation in combat. Sarah Weddington's 1980 survey of Administration policy noted approvingly how the Army had modified its definition of 'combat and combat support' to open up 94 per cent of its jobs to women. Army recruiting qualifications were put on an equal basis for both sexes. Carter himself made some highly publicised appointments of women to high military posts. The controversial nature of such changes was revealed in November 1979 when the House of Representatives opened hearings on the Administration's proposal to alter the legal position regarding women in combat. (The proposal was simply to bring the Air Force, Navy and Marines into line with the Army by subjecting the issue of women in combat to internal military, rather than statutory, ruling.)[68] Carter's decision to re-introduce draft registration, this time for both sexes, further stoked the flames. As Sarah Weddington noted on 30 January 1980: 'Opponents of the ERA will undoubtedly again use the registration issue as a reason to oppose the Amendment. We have long believed equal rights carry equal responsibilities.'[69] Carter took pains to explain that there was no intention to assign women – much less drafted women – to close combat positions; however, there was: 'no distinction possible, on the basis of ability or performance, that would allow me to exclude women from an obligation to register.'[70] Carter's proposal was defeated in Congress, and men alone were subjected to draft registration. It was widely felt, however, that ERA ratification would have necessitated a gender-neutral registration and would lead to women participating in combat.[71] On the pro-ERA side, the draft issue served to undermine old certainties. NOW followed its commitment to equal treatment and supported female registration. Many (especially) young feminists, of course, were self-conscious opponents of American militarism. The prospect of being drafted into military service, as a result of the federal government's commitment to equal treatment, alerted them to the ambivalence of the ERA as a progressive cause.

Honouring a commitment

Apart from ERA, the most obvious way in which the Carter Administration sought to honour its commitment to women's rights was in the use of the Presidential appointment power. Even before the 1976 Presidential election, the National Women's Political Caucus organised a coalition of over sixty women's groups to pressure the new Administration into appointing women to important posts. After November, the coalition developed a close relationship with Carter's transition staff, furnishing lists of qualified women for a vast range of positions.[72] Carter's response was positive. In *First Lady from Plains*, Rosalynn Carter points out that, by 1981, her husband had appointed three of the six females to have served as full Cabinet members in all American history. (The three were: Juanita Kreps, Secretary of Commerce (1977–9); Patricia Harris, Housing and Urban Development Secretary (1977–9) and Health Education and Welfare/Health and Human Services Secretary (1979–80); and Shirley Hufstedler, Education Secretary (1979–81).) Jimmy Carter appointed three of the five women ever appointed as undersecretaries, as well as 80 per cent of pre-1981 female assistant secretaries. Of the forty-six women serving as judges on the federal bench at the end of his term, Jimmy Carter appointed forty-one. (According to Rosalynn Carter, he would also have appointed a woman to the Supreme Court had he had the opportunity. This may have been the case, although the favourite candidate for such a vacancy would have been Charles Kirbo, South Georgia lawyer and senior adviser to the President.) Carter also appointed sixteen women to ambassadorships, compared to twenty-five in all previous Administrations.[73]

That the Carter Administration was exceptionally well disposed to the appointment of women – far more so than any of its predecessors or its successor – is not in question. In the field of judicial appointments, for example, White House Counsel Robert Lipshutz saw himself as practising 'affirmative action', defined not in terms of quotas but of a conscious policy of seeking out, where possible, well qualified female candidates.[74] This policy also had a ripple effect, as female appointees sought to ensure that it did not degenerate into mere tokenism. In July 1977, Patricia Harris wrote to inform Carter of progress at Housing and Urban Development:

Since January 20, we have filled a total of 116 non-career positions in this Department. Of these, 43 per cent have been filled by women and 26 per cent by members of minority groups. 92.5 per cent of the women in the group were appointed at the level of GS-11 or above.[75]

Some qualifications do need to be made. Although significant female appointments were made to the National Security Council staff, it still remained the
case that the top foreign/defence policy elite remained a male province. It was
Jeane Kirkpatrick (appointed as Ambassador to the United Nations in 1981
by Reagan) who declared: 'I was the only woman in our history, I think, who
ever sat in regularly at top-level foreign policy meetings.'[76] Perhaps the best
known of Carter's foreign policy appointments of a woman – that of Pat
Derian – was significantly to the putatively 'soft' area of human rights. There
is also some evidence that Carter's early activism had subsided by mid-term.
He initially appointed women to 16.3 per cent of subcabinet posts, but
appointed females to only 10.5 per cent of mid-term replacement
vacancies.[77] Regarding White House appointments, it may also be observed
that Carter's inner circle of Georgian loyalists essentially constituted a male
enclave,[78] culturally at odds with the feminism represented by Midge
Costanza or even Anne Wexler.

In connection with the influence of women in the White House, mention
should be made of the role of Rosalynn Carter. As with Nancy Reagan –
though not in so lurid a fashion – the question of 'improper' ('steel magnolia')
influence was raised by the press. Her assumption of the Vice-President's
chair at an August 1978 Cabinet meeting scarcely helped to quash these
stories. Her importance in forming and reinforcing Carter's view was manifest. However, the best judgement on her role appears to be that offered by
Winifred Wandersee: she acted as a kind of 'seventies' style Eleanor
Roosevelt', but one who was more concerned to perform as an advocate for
her husband than to set off in her own direction.[79]

Besides its appointments policy, the Carter Administration supported a
host of policies and legislative initiatives designed to further its commitment
to women's rights. Among many others, these included: goals set by the
Office of Federal Procurement Policy for the award of government contracts
to women-owned firms; Farmer's Home Administration funding ($50
million in financial year 1980) for rural women's projects; the establishment
of a new Office on Domestic Violence within the new Department of Health
and Human Services; support for legislation designed to help states and
localities combat domestic violence; support for the Privacy Protection for
Rape Victims Act; support for the development of non-sexist educational
material and sexual equality in education under the 1978 Educational
Amendments; implementation under CETA of training schemes for displaced
homemakers;[80] reorganisation of the Equal Employment Opportunity Commission (EEOC) to enforce anti-discrimination legislation, with a 40 per cent
budget increase and significant improvement in efficiency; successful spon-
sorship of legislation to amend the 1964 Civil Rights Act to protect women
from occupational discrimination based on pregnancy; budget requests for
child care funds under the Social Security Act; and the establishment of the
principle that older women who remarried should not lose social security

benefits.[81]

The record was impressive. But it is also important to retain a degree of scepticism. On the one hand, anti-discrimination practices can easily slide over into zealotry. In *Governing America*, for example, Califano described his efforts to curb the excesses of HEW's Office of Civil Rights. At one stage the Office threatened to withdraw federal funding from two schools: one because it had a boys' choir, and one because it had an annual father–daughter dinner. HEW spent an inordinate amount of effort attempting to develop acceptable regulations, under Title IX of the 1972 Educational Amendments Act, regarding non-discrimination in intercollegiate athletics.[82] On the other hand, Bella Abzug was perfectly correct to point out that Administration spending on women's rights issues was minute compared to the cost of the 1979–80 military build-up. Nevertheless, if one compares the actual record with Carter's 1976 'Position Paper on Women's Rights',[83] it is clear that the commitments were – within the limits set by the Administration's fiscal restraint – honoured.

As the 1980 election approached, the Administration found itself in the unenviable position of having simultaneously to appease two vastly different constituencies. Firstly, there were the forces of organised feminism at the Madison Square Garden convention. Secondly, there was the electorate as a whole, widely felt to be feeling the influence of the new tide of social conservatism, especially in those sectors which had traditionally supported the Democrats: notably lower-income whites, Catholics and union families.[84]

Carter's early attempts to square this circle involved the embracing of a 'family' policy, which the Administration attempted to sell as part of its commitment to women's rights. In May 1978, the President included 'Family' among a list of seven priorities he jotted down on a sheet of paper. (The others were: 'Peace', 'Strong Defense', 'Human Rights', 'Inflation', 'Bureaucracy' and 'Partnership').[85] The original concept behind the 'family' policy was to hold a Family Conference at the White House in 1980. This derived from a campaign promise. However, the cavilling of lesbian activists at the Administration's definition of the word 'family' caused the conference to be de-prioritised. Regional meetings eventually took place at Baltimore, Minneapolis and Los Angeles. When the meetings eventually convened, non-traditional families (including homosexual couples) were represented.[86]

Prior to the 1980 convention, Carter forces sought to keep the platform deliberations as low-key as possible. Initial meetings were held as early as June to avoid the kind of immediate pre-convention publicity ('acid, amnesty, abortion') which had attended McGovern's platform drafting meeting in 1972. Tensions in the White House over this strategy led to women's liaison deputy Linda Tarr-Whelan leaving her job. The 'human needs' task force of the June 1980 platform committee was dominated by issue activists: primarily feminist and gay rights activists. As Michael Malbin put it: 'a number of the Carter delegates acted as issue activists first and as Carter delegates second'.[87] The President agreed to add the phrase 'sexual orientation' to the party's civil rights plank. The task force succeeded in sending two minority reports to the New York convention: the first declared that party funding would be withheld from candidates who did not support ERA; the second supported federal funding for Medicaid abortions. At the convention, NOW President Eleanor Smeal threatened to support independent candidate John Anderson unless both recommendations were accepted: 'We do not feel the commitment level of the past three and a half years has been strong enough to guarantee our support.'[88] Sarah Weddington attempted to secure compromises on Carter's behalf. However, Carter was defeated on both issues, though he continued strongly to voice his personal opposition to federally funded abortions.

Women's issues appear to have affected the 1980 election result in a number of apparently contradictory, cross-cutting ways. Unsurprisingly, the 1980 Democratic platform was considerably stronger on these issues than its 1976 equivalent. Where the 1976 platform referred to the need to eliminate 'discrimination against women in all federal programs', the 1980 women's plank advocated 'strong steps to close the wage gap' between the sexes. The 1980 platform clearly supported federal funding to extend the 'constitutionally guaranteed right of privacy' to 'poor women' (i.e., abortion rights).[89] On the face of it, the vast gulf between Republican and Democratic platforms – far greater in 1980 than in 1976 – might seem to account for the 'gender gap' in voting which appeared in 1980. (In that year, 44 per cent of women voters supported Carter, compared to 38 per cent of men; the corresponding 1976 figures were 48 and 53 per cent.) Reagan's anti-ERA stance undoubtedly hurt his appeal to female voters. (However, those *men* who supported women's rights were far less likely than women to take this as their voting cue.)[90] In fact, many academic studies of the post-1980 'liberal' women's vote tend to play down the importance of women's issues as such. More crucial to the persistence of the 'gender gap' appears to be the tendency of women to take more liberal positions on foreign and defence issues, environmental and general 'welfare' policy.[91] Studies of the 1980 election conclude that perceptions of Carter's performance, notably in economic management, swayed far more votes than did social issues. In fact, had the election been decided on women's issues alone, Carter would have won. Election year polls showed a substantial majority for ERA and against a constitutional ban on abortions. Few voters, however, supported Carter purely on the basis of these issues.[92] Indeed, as we have seen, Carter was not even able to look to the enthusiastic support of feminists as a compensation for the relative coolness of more traditional Democratic voters towards the feminist position. In contrast, Reagan's opposition to both abortion and ERA guaranteed his hold on evangelical and anti-feminist opinion. He, rather than the Southern Baptist, had become the 'conviction' candidate.

Notes

1 *The Presidential Campaign 1976: Vol. I: Part 2* (Washington DC: US Government Printing Office, 1978), p. 998 (Notre Dame, 10 Oct. 1976), p. 1048 (Harlem, 19 Oct. 1976).

2 Letter, P. Derian to B. W. von Zellen, 3 Mar. 1978, box 22, SO: DPS: Gutierrez (folder, 'Human Rights').

3 *CQ Almanac* 1979, p. 46-E.

4 Interview transcript, 'Black Perspectives on the News', 5 Apr. 1978, box 5, SO: DPS: Neustadt (folder, 'Blacks').

5 1983 interview with Carter, cited in M. Glenn Abernathy, 'The Carter Administration and Domestic Civil Rights', in M. G. Abernathy, D. M. Hill and P. Williams, eds, *The Carter Years*: (London: Pinter, 1984), pp. 106–22, 106.

6 Robert A. Pastor, *Condemned to Repetition: The United States and Nicaragua* (Princeton: Princeton University Press, 1987), p. 49.

7 Andrea Dworkin, 'A Feminist Looks at Saudi Arabia', in A. Dworkin, *Letters From a War Zone* (London: Secker and Warburg, 1988), pp. 97–9, at 97.

8 Rick Hutcheson, 'Weekly Mail Report', 18 July 1977, box 38, PHF (folder, '7/18/77 (2)'). The Wilmington Ten were a group of (nine black and one white) civil rights activists convicted in North Carolina of arson and assault.

9 'Record on civil rights', undated, box 77, SO: Chief of Staff: Jordan (folder, 'Campaign'). On regulations for the handicapped, see Joseph A. Califano, *Governing America* (New York: Simon and Schuster, 1981), pp. 221–2.

10 The former Act established federal penalties for inter-state transport of pornographic material involving children. The latter provided funds for child abuse prevention and treatment programmes.

11 See Abernathy, 'The Carter Administration . . .', pp. 108–12, 115–17. Carter successfully supported legislation to safeguard the confidentiality of customer records held by banks, to protect the privacy of rape victims and to ease access to the civil justice system.

12 Memo to the President from Z. Brzezinski, undated, box 38, PHF (folder, '7/15/77 (3)'). See Michael C. LeMay, *From Open Door to Dutch Door* (New York: Praeger, 1987), pp. 114–16. On the operation of the 1980 Act, see Norman L. Zucker and Naomi Flink Zucker, *The Guarded Gate: The Reality of American Refugee Policy* (San Diego: Harcourt, Brace, Jovanovich, 1987).

13 See Byron E. Shafer, *Quiet Revolution: The Struggle for the Democratic Party and the Shaping of Post-Reform Politics* (New York: Russell Sage Foundation, 1983), especially ch. 17; also, Winifred D. Wandersee, *On The Move: American Women in the 1970s* (Boston: Twayne, 1988), p. 24.

14 Caroline Arden, *Getting the Donkey out of the Ditch: The Democratic Party in Search of Itself* (New York: Greenwood, 1988), p. 5.

15 *Ibid.*, p. 4.

16 See Wandersee, *On The Move*, p. 31; also, William Crotty, *Party Reform* (New York: Longmans, 1983), p. 137.

17 *Quiet Revolution*, p. 534. See also Howard L. Reiter, *Parties and Elections in Corporate America* (New York: St Martin's, 1987), pp. 115–28.

18 See X. Kayden and E. Mahle, *The Party Goes On* (New York: Basic Books, 1985), p. 64; also Carol F. Casey, 'The National Democratic Party', in Gerald M.

Pomper, ed., *Party Renewal in America* (New York: Praeger, 1981), pp. 71–103, at 91.

19 Shafer, *Quiet Revolution*, p. 534.

20 See Jules Witcover, *Marathon* (New York: Viking Press, 1977), pp. 358–9.

21 On the 1976 platform, see *National Party Conventions, 1831–1984* (Washington DC: Congressional Quarterly, 1987), pp. 126–8.

22 Letter, E. H. Norton to H. Jordan, 19 Jan. 1979, box FG-221, WHCF: SF: Federal Government Organization.

23 Wandersee, *On The Move*, p. 191. See also Jane Dehort-Mathews and Donald Mathews, 'The Cultural Politics of the ERA's Defeat', in Joan Hoff-Wilson, *Rights of Passage: The Past and Future of the ERA* (Bloomington: Indiana University Press, 1986), pp. 44–53, at 45.

24 'Report on the 10 March National Women's Political Caucus Reception', from M. Costanza, 29 Mar. 1977, box 323, SO: DPS: Eizenstat (folder, 'Women's Issues'); see also Sara M. Evans, *Born For Liberty: A History of Women in America* (New York: Free Press, 1989), p. 306.

25 See Judy Bachrach, 'Midge Costanza: The View from the White House Third Floor', *Washington Post*, 26 July 1978; R. Beckel, MC transcript, p. 13.

26 Bachrach, 'Midge Costanza', memo to H. Jordan from J. Doolittle, undated, box 13, SO: Speechwriters: SF (folder, 'Jokes').

27 Memo to the President from H. Jordan, undated ('Re Midge Costanza'), box 34, SO: Chief of Staff: Jordan (folder, 'Midge Costanza').

28 Cited in Califano, *Governing America*, p. 66. (Costanza had also been criticised in the press for campaign funding irregularities: see Betty Glad, *Jimmy Carter: In Search of the Great White House* (New York: Norton, 1980), p. 440.)

29 Sarah Weddington, Exit Interview, 2 Jan. 1981 (Carter Library).

30 Memo to S. Eizenstat and D. Rubinstein from B. Abramowitz, 9 May 1978, box FG-221, WHCF: SF: Federal Government Organization.

31 See *New York Times*, 13 and 14 Jan. 1979; *Washington Star*, 13 Jan. 1979; *Atlanta Constitution*, 16 Jan. 1979.

32 Memo to the President from S. Eizenstat, J. Powell and A. Wexler, 24 Apr. 1978, box 82, PHF (folder, '4/24/78 (2)'). Carter's comment is in *New York Times*, 14 Jan. 1979.

33 *Washington Post*, 17 Jan. 1979; Carter, MC transcript, p. 46.

34 *Washington Star*, 16 Jan. 1979. See also D. Bonafede, 'Billy and Bella', *National Journal*, 20 Jan. 1979, p. 105.

35 *New York Times*, 1 Feb. 1979.

36 Letter, M. Chambers to the President, 30 Mar. 1979, box FG-221, WHCF: SF: Federal Government Organization.

37 Wandersee, *On The Move*, p. 195.

38 *The Presidential Campaign 1976: Vol. I: Part 1* (Washington DC: US Government Printing Office, 1978), pp. 92–3.

39 See Witcover, *Marathon*, pp. 561–6. This was the interview where Carter stated: 'I've looked on a lot of women with lust. I've committed adultery in my heart many times. This is something that God recognizes I will do . . . and God forgives me for it.'

40 See Witcover, *Marathon*, pp. 206–7; Califano, *Governing America*, pp. 50–1; James Wooten, *Dasher: The Roots and Rising of Jimmy Carter* (London: Weidenfeld and Nicolson, 1978), pp. 349–50; Laurence H. Tribe, *Abortion: The Clash of Absolutes* (New York: Norton, 1990), p. 148.

41   Memo to S. Eizenstat from B. Abramowitz, 12 Sept. 1977, box 323, SO: DPS: Eizenstat (folder, 'Women's Issues'). By this time thirteen states (of the required two-thirds) had called for a constitutional convention. See Tribe, *Abortion*, p. 151.

42   *Harris v. McRae*, 448 US 297 (1980). Two 1977 decisions held that no state was required to provide public funds for abortion. See Califano, *Governing America*, pp. 71–86; Tribe, *Abortion*, pp. 151–9.

43   See E. J. Dionne, *Why Americans Hate Politics* (New York: Simon and Schuster, 1991), p. 226; *Congressional Quarterly Weekly Report*, 5 Nov. 1977, p. 2351.

44   HEW Secretary Joseph Califano later commented on this remark: 'At worst, it was an on-the-spot, clumsy attempt to appeal to fiscal conservatives and right-to-lifers; at best it was an inept, off-the-top-of-his-head answer to a question for which he was not prepared'. (*Governing America*, p. 70).

45   Memo ('Staff and Interest Group Reactions to President's Abortion Statements') from M. Costanza to the President, 13 July 1977, box 38, PHF (folder, '7/15/77 (3)').

46   Memo ('House/Senate Conference on Abortion') to the President from S. Eizenstat, 20 July 1977, box 323, SO: DPS: Eizenstat (folder, 'Women's Issues').

47   Califano, *Governing America*, pp. 85–6.

48   *Ibid.*, p. 85.

49   *The Presidential Campaign 1976: Vol. I: Part 1*, p. 97.

50   Cited in Abernathy, 'The Carter Administration . . .', p. 117; also, *Honoring a Commitment to the People of America* (From the Office of Sarah Weddington, The White House, 1980), pp. 22–3.

51   Wooten, *Dasher*, p. 351.

52   Tribe, *Abortion*, p. 155.

53   *Human Events*, 19 Feb. 1977.

54   See Janet K. Boles, *The Politics of the Equal Rights Amendment* (New York: Longmans, 1979), p. 91; see also Carol Felsenthal, *The Sweetheart of the Silent Majority: The Biography of Phyllis Schlafly* (Garden City, NY: Doubleday, 1981), p. 247 (Carter's 1975 remarks to the Oklahoma Senate).

55   See Witcover, *Marathon*, p. 358; *The Presidential Campaign 1976: Vol. I, Part 2*, pp. 874–8.

56   Cited in Abernathy, 'The Carter Administration . . .', p. 116; see also Boles, *The Politics of the Equal Rights Amendment*, pp. 77–8.

57   Rosalynn Carter, *First Lady from Plains* (Boston: Houghton Mifflin, 1984), p. 101.

58   *Honoring a Commitment to the People of America*, p. 20.

59   Memo to the President from S. Eizenstat, 22 Mar. 1978, box 323, SO: DPS: Eizenstat (folder, 'Women's Issues').

60   Memo to the President from F. Moore, 12 July 1978, box HU-14, WHCF: SF: Human Rights.

61   See R. Carter, *First Lady from Plains*, p. 286; *Honoring a Commitment to the People of America*, p. 19.

62   Felsenthal, *The Sweetheart of the Silent Majority*, p. 247.

63   Cited *ibid.*, p. 248.

64   *Ibid.*

65   *Ibid.*, p. 249.

66   See, e.g., 'League of Women Voters Q and A', 5 May 1980, *Public Papers of the Presidents of the United States: Jimmy Carter, 1980–81* (Washington DC: US Government Printing Office, 1981), p. 833.

67   *Honoring a Commitment to the People of America*, p. 29.

68   See Jane J. Mansbridge, *Why We Lost the ERA* (Chicago: University of Chicago Press, 1986), p. 73.

69   'Meeting with Presidents of Women's Organizations', report from S. Weddington, 30 Jan. 1980, box 168, PHF (folder, '1/30/80 (1)').

70   Cited in Mansbridge, *Why We Lost the ERA*, p. 267.

71   See Mary Frances Berry, *Why ERA Failed* (Bloomington: Indiana University Press, 1986), p. 74.

72   See G. Calvin Mackenzie, *The Politics of Presidential Appointments* (New York: Free Press, 1981), p. 210. Nelson W. Polsby ('Interest Groups and the Presidency', in W. D. Burnham and M. W. Weinberg, eds, *American Politics and Public Policy* (Cambridge (Massachusetts): MIT Press, 1978), pp. 41–54, at p. 46) speculates that the women's coalition may have effectively vetoed some appointments, notably that of John Dunlop as Labour Secretary. See also B. Adams and K. Kavanagh-Baran, *Promise and Performance: Carter Builds a New Administration* (Lexington (Massachusetts): Heath, 1979), pp. 77–9.

73   R. Carter, *First Lady from Plains*, pp. 289–90. See also *Women: A Documentary of Progress During the Administration of Jimmy Carter, 1977 to 1981* (From the Office of Sarah Weddington, The White House, 1981); *US News and World Report*, 21 Feb. 1977 (Kirbo).

74   Lipshutz, Exit interview, 29 Sept. 1979 (Carter Library).

75   Memo ('Weekly Reports of Major Departmental Activities') to the President from P. Harris, undated, box 38, PHF (folder, '7/18/77 (1)'). See also Susan Faludi, *Backlash: The Undeclared War Against Women* (London: Chatto and Windus, 1992), p. 404 (on Federal Communications Commission appointments under Carter).

76   See Joan Hoff-Wilson, 'Of Mice and Men', in E. P. Crapol, ed., *Women and American Foreign Policy* (Westport: Greenwood, 1987), pp. 170–86, at 170.

77   See Janet M. Martin, 'The Recruitment of Women to Cabinet and Subcabinet Posts', *Western Political Quarterly*, 42, 1989, pp. 161–72, at 165.

78   Califano (*Governing America*, p. 230) comments: 'the house Carter lived in was made of glass'.

79   Wandersee, *On The Move*, pp. 159–62; R. Carter, *First Lady from Plains*, pp. 175–6. See also *Newsweek*, 5 Nov. 1979, pp. 36–47 ('The President's Partner'); F. L. Jensen, 'An Awesome Responsibility: Rosalynn Carter as First Lady', *Presidential Studies Quarterly*, 20, 1990, pp. 769–75.

80   'Displaced homemakers are women who, because of divorce, death of a spouse, or other unforeseen event, are economically unable to continue as full-time homemakers and must enter or reenter the work force': *Honoring a Commitment to the People of America*, p. 16.

81   *Honoring A Commitment . . ., passim.*

82   Califano, *Governing America*, p. 226, also pp. 223–4.

83   *The Presidential Campaign 1976, Vol. I: Part 1*, pp. 591–2.

84   See Dionne, *Why Americans Hate Politics*, pp. 107–9. Also, Kevin Phillips,

Post-Conservative America (New York: Random House, 1982), p. 189.

85 List in Carter's handwriting, 23 May 1978, box 31, SO: Rafshoon (folder, 'Priorities').

86 See Susan H. Van Horn, *Women, Work and Fertility* (New York: New York University Press, 1988), p. 152; *Honoring A Commitment . . .*, p. 21; A. H. Merton, *Enemies of Choice: The Right-to-Life Movement and its Threat to Abortion* (Boston: Beacon Press, 1981), p. 142.

87 M. J. Malbin, 'The Conventions, Platforms and Issue Activists', in Austin Ranney, ed., *The American Elections of 1980* (Washington DC: American Enterprise Institute, 1981), pp. 99–141, 120; *New York Times*, 26 June 1980 (L. Tarr-Whelan).

88 *Ibid.*, p. 129.

89 *National Party Conventions, 1831–1984*, pp. 128, 141–2.

90 See James Douglas, 'Was Reagan's Victory a Watershed in American Politics?', *The Political Quarterly*, 52, 1981, pp. 171–83, at 177; also, William Schneider, 'The November 4 Vote for President', in Ranney, ed., *The American Elections of 1980*, pp. 212–63, at 254; Ethel Klein, *Gender Politics: From Consciousness to Mass Politics* (Cambridge (Massachusetts): Harvard University Press, 1984), p. 163; Faludi, *Backlash*, p. 306.

91 See, e.g., Kathleen Frankovic, 'Sex and Politics – New Alignments, Old Issues', *PS*, 3, 1982, pp. 439–48; Daniel Wirls, 'Reinterpreting the Gender Gap', *Public Opinion Quarterly*, 50, 1986, pp. 316–30; Klein, *Gender Politics*, pp. 151–64.

92 See E. J. Dionne, 'Catholics and the Democrats', in S. M. Lipset, ed., *Party Coalitions in the 1980s* (San Francisco: Institute for Contemporary Studies, 1981), pp. 307–26, at 318; Schneider, 'The November 4 Vote . . .'; Dionne, *Why Americans Hate Politics*, p. 109.

4

Black civil rights

Jimmy Carter and black America

Jimmy Carter's attitudes towards race relations were profoundly shaped by his own experience of the Southern civil rights revolution of the 1960s. He habitually referred to this as 'the best thing that ever happened in the South'.[1] It was 'the good things and the bad things' in the South's race relations heritage that 'made the human rights issue . . . very vivid to me'. He frequently emphasised his own indebtedness, as a creature of the New South, to the civil rights changes:

I would not be here as President had it not been for the Civil Rights Act and for the courage of some leaders – and I don't claim to be one of them – who changed those bad aspects of the South to the present greatness of the South.[2]

The changes of the 1960s had not only brought about desegregation but had showed the South the way to modernisation, and made it possible for a rural Georgian to be elected President. Carter characteristically associated himself with the traditions of Southern populism and Southern liberalism, which he learned at his mother's knee. According to Patricia Derian, Carter's concern for human rights 'began in Plains' when his parents 'talked about how they felt about black people and . . . Jimmy decided his mother was right'. Andrew Young saw Carter's early imbibing of Southern liberalism as enabling him to avoid both the guilt of the 'converted redneck' or the 'paternalism' of the Northern white liberal.[3] To Southern audiences he was prepared to own up to a degree of 'embarrassment' over the region's history in 'the last fifteen to twenty years'.[4] However, to read Carter's account of the civil rights revolution in *Why Not the Best?* one might imagine the achievements of the 1960s to have been as much the product of white Southern liberalism and Southern adaptability as of the civil rights movement itself. An inveterate booster for his region, Carter occasionally allowed his local pride to lead him to the fringes of atavistic romanticisation. He invoked the 'courage' with which the South had met the challenge,[5] and in his campaign autobiography even ventured an upbeat account of the South's racial legacy: 'Both black and white Southerners, to a great extent, had a better understanding of each other, of attitudes and customs, than black and white Americans in other parts of the country.'[6] Yet Carter was nothing if not a representative of the New South. He frequently stressed his own refusal to join the local White Citizen's Council in the wake of the Supreme Court's 1954 school desegregation decision. In May 1974, he reminded an audience at the University of Georgia:

The first speech I ever made in the Georgian Senate, representing the most conservative district in Georgia, was concerning the abolition of thirty questions that we had so proudly evolved as a subterfuge to keep black citizens from voting ... questions that nobody could answer in this room.[7]

Rosalynn Carter portrayed herself and her husband as 'realists who knew that desegregation was a foregone conclusion ...'.[8] It would be wrong to imagine that either Jimmy or Rosalynn were in the vanguard of Southern civil rights; and, indeed, neither of them fell to the temptation of describing themselves in such terms. Jimmy did not, for example, use his appointment to the Sumter County Board of Education in 1955 to campaign vigorously against segregation. Much has been made of his putative courting, during his successful 1970 bid for the Georgian governorship, of the segregationist vote. The strategy of the Carter camp (Jordan, Powell, Kirbo, Rafshoon) was very definitely to run well to the right of Democratic primary opponent Carl Sanders. In *Why Not the Best?*, Carter made much of his active campaigning in black communities. Such campaigning was, in fact, far more characteristic of the more liberal 1966 campaign. (In the campaign autobiography, Carter also, while admitting his relative failure to attract votes in the contest against Sanders, stressed his black support in the general election. But, of course, in Georgia in 1970 the real election was the Democratic primary.)[9] In 1970 Jimmy secured the backing of key Georgia segregationists: Roy Harris, Marvin Griffin and Lester Maddox. However, his electioneering was essentially geared towards the 'little (white) guy' populism of the constituency bequeathed by outgoing governor Maddox and 1968 Presidential candidate George Wallace. Carter's 1971 Inaugural Address, which made page one of the *New York Times* and established him as a prominent exemplar of the New South, underlined his rejection of the racist base of the Maddox/Wallace tradition. In it Carter spoke eloquently of the South's transformation:

I say to you quite frankly that the time for racial discrimination is over. Our people have already made this major and difficult decision. No poor, rural, weak or black person shall ever have to bear the additional burden of being deprived of the opportunity for an education, a job, or simple justice.[10]

Carter's governorship with its strong orientation towards consolidation and New South technocratic values, did not live up to the promise of the

Inaugural. None the less, as Earl Black noted in 1976, Carter's 'explicit repudiation of racial discrimination' was – at that time – 'one of the few such statements made by southern politicians'; it was 'a far cry from the standard rhetoric of Georgia politics'.[11]

Carter's 1976 Presidential nomination campaign attracted strong backing from local black leaders: notably Representative Andrew Young, Atlanta mayor Maynard Jackson and the Reverend Martin 'Daddy' Luther King Sr. (The latter's convention speech – 'Surely the Lord sent Jimmy Carter to come on out and bring America back to where she belongs . . .' – was to be the emotional highlight of the New York City convention.) There was, however, little sign of other, national, black leaders rushing to board the Carter bandwagon. (An exception was Detroit mayor Coleman Young.) An address given by the candidate to an early May meeting of the Caucus of Black Democrats in Charlotte, North Carolina, appeared to elicit little enthusiasm.[12] The problem was not so much Carter's background, and supposed pursuit of the Maddox/Wallace vote in 1970; rather, it centred on his whole 'anti-Washington' orientation. As Senator Hubert Humphrey put it in March 1976: 'Candidates who make an attack on Washington are making an attack on government programs, on the poor, on blacks, on minorities, on the cities.'[13] Georgia state senator Julian Bond, an increasingly respected black Southern leader and sometime fringe candidate for the 1976 nomination himself, chided Carter for not supporting 'traditionally liberal principles . . .'.[14] Further problems arose over Carter's 'ethnic purity' gaffe on 2 April. (Declaring his opposition to 'racial integration of a neighbourhood by government action', the candidate said he saw 'nothing wrong with ethnic purity being maintained'. Six days later, Carter acknowledged his 'very serious mistake' in using language which, according to Andrew Young, 'summoned up memories of Hitler'. Hamilton Jordan later admitted that 'we had a little bit of a cultural problem' in using language appropriate to 'the politics of big cities'.)[15]

The final weekend before the General Election threw up another controversy which led straight back into the candidate's rural Southern background. This time it related to the racially exclusive membership practices of Carter's First Baptist Church of Plains. Carter was able to weather the storm, pointing to his own opposition to these policies and declaring: 'Now if it was a country club, I would have quit . . . But this is not my church, it is God's church.' He would work for change from within.[16]

When the votes were counted and exit polls taken, it was clear not only that blacks had overwhelmingly supported the Georgian (94 per cent of voting blacks) but also that in several states the black vote had made a crucial difference. With 64 per cent of registered blacks actually voting, victory margins in Ohio, Pennsylvania, Louisiana, Mississippi and North and South Carolina were widely attributed to the black vote. Carter was clearly more attractive to Southern blacks than to Southern whites. (In Louisiana, for example, he received 94 per cent of the black votes cast, compared to 41 per cent of the white.) Andrew Young recalled his feelings on election night: 'I heard that it may depend on how Mississippi went, and I thought "Lord have mercy". But when I heard that Mississippi had gone our way, I knew that the hands that picked cotton finally picked the president.'[17] The *New York Times* noted the irony of a 'south Georgia white man with a mint julep drawl' being sent to the White House by the 'grandchildren of slaves'.[18] Carter's success testified to the staunch black opposition to the Nixon–Ford economic and civil rights policies, as well as to the efficacy of his final campaign drive (especially 'Operation Big Vote', directed at the black urban vote).

As in the case of women's rights, black civil rights activists turned their attention during the transition period to the securing of appointments. Major black appointments included that of Andrew Young, Patricia Harris (to HUD) and Eleanor Norton (former head of New York City's Human Rights Commission, to the chair of the EEOC). Such goodwill as these appointments secured was partially dissipated by the controversy surrounding the confirmation of Griffin Bell as Attorney General. Bell (like Cyrus Vance and Harold Brown) belonged to private clubs that excluded blacks; he resigned his membership in December, 1976.[19] Two high-profile minority appointments to the Justice Department were intended to deflect criticism. Drew Days, a civil rights lawyer from the National Association for the Advancement of Colored People's Legal Defense Fund, was named Assistant Attorney General for Civil Rights; Wade McCree, a black appeals judge, became Solicitor General. Despite these appointments, in April 1977 Congresman Parren Mitchell, chair of the Congressional Black Caucus, declared that blacks under Carter were 'almost going through the same kind of tokenism as we had before'.[20] In fact, 14 per cent of Carter's judicial appointments related to African Americans. As in the case of women, the Administration practised a kind of *ad hoc* affirmative action, searching out qualified blacks across a whole range of appointments. Academic surveys of the appointment policy reveal the Carter Administration as the apex of the increase in black appointments which began with President Kennedy and tapered away under President Reagan. Overall, approximately 12 per cent of Carter's appointments were of African Americans, compared to 4 per cent of Reagan's.[21]

The Administration was naturally anxious to woo black leaders, in the hope that black votes could be retained for 1980. Black newspaper editor and Democratic National Committee deputy chairman Louis Martin was hired in 1978 as Special Assistant to liaise with African American groups. In September 1979, Martin recommended that leading black appointees be taken along on Presidential trips, and that the President should worship occasionally at black Baptist churches.[22] Before the 1978 mid-term elections, Frank Moore met Congressman John Conyers to discuss 'tactics for votes turnout in the black community'.[23] As the 1980 election approached, White

House aides worried whether the black vote would hold. Pat Cadell told Carter in August 1980: 'I fear that we could go into election day a winner but come out a loser as blacks, liberals, Hispanics, etc fail to turn out.'[24] By this time, several prominent black leaders – notably Vernon Jordan of the National Urban League – had publicly questioned the Administration's commitment to black causes. Symbols – appointments, actions like Carter's 1978 award to honour the (hitherto largely forgotten) war record of African Americans in the 761st Tank Battalion – were not enough. Bayard Rustin, the veteran civil rights leader, contended in 1979 that 'voters need a clear choice next year' between clearly defined 'sets of economic and social . . . philosophies':

Without this clear choice, Americans can expect yet another Administration afflicted with President Carter's most serious problem – widespread disappointment caused by unrealistically high expectations and an unclear even contradictory campaign program. Symbols, even when offered by a decent man like Carter, are simply no substitute for policy.[25]

Few black leaders were prepared openly to break with the Administration. At the very least, Carter was 'a decent man' and some members of the Administration – notably Andrew Young and Labour Secretary F. Ray Marshall[26] – could be trusted. Even Vernon Jordan was prepared to allow that the President had at least addressed important issues.[27] When 1980 came around, black leaders (including most of the Congressional Black Caucus) stood by the President.[28] In the primary races, it was notable that Carter was able to attract greater black support than his ostensibly more liberal challenger, Edward Kennedy. The latter did well among blacks in California; but Carter won 52 per cent of the black Democratic vote in New York, 68 per cent in Florida, 67 per cent in Alabama and 59 per cent in Illinois. (Attempts to explain Kennedy's relative failure to appeal to blacks focused on black scepticism as to his ability either to win the election or to deliver on his promises; on black disapproval of Kennedy personally; and on Carter's personal popularity).[29]

The black vote in the 1980 Presidential election was overwhelmingly pro-Carter, though somewhat less solid than in 1976. The 1980 figures also revealed the marked effect of the gender gap, and continuingly large black/white turnout differentials. (In 1980, 82 per cent of voting black males supported Carter, with 14 per cent going for Reagan and three for the independent, John Anderson; 88 per cent of voting black women backed Carter, with only 9 per cent for Reagan and three for Anderson. As in 1976, the differential in black/white turnout was over ten per cent). Carter's own 1982 remarks on his black support were broadly accurate, if a little disingenuous about the 1980 figures: 'blacks supported me with some trepidation in '76, but strong enough and staunchly all the way through 1980 and today.'[30] The Carter camp had reason to be disappointed with the 85 per cent black support figure for 1980. Pat Cadell had advised the President in August that Reagan 'has said or done things that not only displeases but should frighten' blacks.[31] Many African Americans undoubtedly felt aggrieved at the Administration's record in promoting economic initiatives for minorities, and shared the wider electorate's scepticism about Carter's leadership.

Growing tension between the Administration and black leaders and voters was partially attributable to specific incidents, such as the resignation/firing of Andrew Young and the 1980 disquiet over the treatment of Haitian refugees. (The – mainly black – Haitians were classed as 'economic migrants' and received significantly less favourable treatment than the Cubans who entered the US via the Mariel boat-lift.) Going deeper than this, however, was the familiar problem of heightened expectations and the post-liberal failure to meet them. At one level, as with women's rights, heightened expectations were stimulated by the human rights orientation in foreign policy. Assistant Attorney General Drew Days attempted to take on this issue directly in a November 1977 address to the Black Lawyers Association in Alabama, entitled 'Human Rights, Home Style'. Days acknowledged that 'this Administration's public utterances on human rights problems abroad' had 'raised very high expectations' among American blacks, and admitted that so far these expectations had been disappointed. He promised action in the case of specific domestic grievances, notably regarding the Wilmington Ten.[32]

Far more profoundly, however, black grievances centred around the question of economic redistribution. The post-liberal economic climate overshadowed the Administration's entire relationship with black opinion. As Parren Mitchell, of the Congressional Black Caucus, pointed out in May 1977: 'It's much more difficult now. When the caucus makes efforts to redistribute power, that's a different thing from civil rights.'[33] The term 'civil rights' was still in vogue. However, the debate was now shifting to a more explicit conflict over economic redistribution. Writing in June 1980, in the wake of the Miami riots and the shooting of Vernon Jordan, Special Assistant Louis Martin presented the President with a wide-ranging analysis of the explicit economic basis to inter-racial tension:

In the troubled 60s the paramount concerns of Blacks centered around some basic civil rights issues, notably public accommodations and voting rights. Civil rights issues are still on the Black agenda today but the greatest concern by far revolves around economic issues. Unemployment is the most critical issue today and it is generating an almost revolutionary spirit among Black leaders who heretofore have shown some moderation in their protests.

Blacks were generally well disposed to the Administration, but were increasingly sceptical about its economic initiatives:

Taken as a whole the administration's record is hailed by most Blacks as progressive. The Black appointments, especially to the federal judiciary, and most of the programs for the disadvantaged have won acclaim. It is the unemployment issue . . . that is becoming a rock upon which everything threatens to break.[34]

Affirmative action

The Carter Administration was consistently at pains to emphasise its strong commitment to affirmative action, defined in terms of the taking of special steps to compensate for past discrimination. We have already seen this process at work in the case of female and minority appointments. Government departments and agencies were regularly urged to develop target-led programmes for female and minority hiring. (The most celebrated of such initiatives was that devised by Civil Service Commission vice-chair Jule Sugarman. It provided for 'experimental personnel procedures' to be made available to federal agencies, allowing them – for example – to select less qualified minority applicants to serve as trainees, pending their gaining qualifications).[35]

Reviewing the Administration's affirmative action record in August 1979, Louis Martin noted that nine companies had been debarred from doing business with the federal government because of their failure to comply with minority hiring requirements. (Under Carter's appointee, Weldon Rougeau, the Office of Federal Contract Compliance (OFCC) significantly stepped up its enforcement of these requirements.) Martin stressed the Administration's commitment to 'minority set-aside' programmes (i.e., the reserving of fixed percentages of government business to minority-owned firms). Carter's budget for fiscal year 1979 directed $3.3 billion to minority firms (compared to 1.1 billion in fiscal year 1977). The 'set-aside' requirements included several 'showcase' projects, such as the North-east Railroad Corridor, built with a 15 per cent set-aside. The Administration consistently supported legislation, such as the 1978 Omnibus Minority Business Act, which followed the 'set-aside' principle. The Small Business Administration offered special management and technical assistance to black-owned firms, while minority-owned banks were encouraged by the deposit of (in 1979) $145 billion in government funds.[36] According to Martin's upbeat public pronouncements – significantly more optimistic than the private 1980 memo quoted above – this new commitment to black business enterprise constituted a rebirth of civil rights: 'Black businessmen by the hundreds are knocking on the doors of the Federal establishment for contracts with some of the same passion and concern that civil rights leaders exhibited a decade ago.'[37] As administered by the OFCC, the 'set-aside' programmes essentially involved numerical quotas rather than 'targets' or 'goals'. When applied to minority hiring or to the admission of students to college, however, quotas became – in the Administration's view – unacceptably controversial. Quotas were especially anathema to significant sections of Catholic and Jewish opinion, which recollected how quotas had been used to *restrict* the entry of these groups into higher education. Jewish opinion was outraged at Health Education and Welfare Secretary Joseph Califano's apparent support for quotas in early 1977; he subsequently withdrew his remarks, saying that 'quota' was a 'nerve-jangling word'.[38]

Carter himself regularly drew a clear 'distinction between flexible affirmative action programs using goals and inflexible racial quotas'.[39] This distinction stood at the heart of the controversy over the various drafts of the Administration's *amicus curiae* brief in the Bakke case. The latter involved white would-be student Allan Bakke's famous complaint against his non-admission to the University of California medical school at Davis. Attesting that his qualifications were higher than several minority students who were admitted, Bakke alleged 'reverse discrimination' contrary to Title VI of the 1964 Civil Rights Act and the Constitution's Fourteenth ('equal protection') amendment. The Justice Department's first draft of its brief leaned so far against quotas as to provoke black and liberal opinion severely. It failed to endorse even 'goals' or 'targets' and declared that 'racial classifications favorable to minority groups are presumptively unconstitutional'.[40]

The leaking of Justice's original draft of its Bakke brief unleashed a three-way bureaucratic battle between the Justice Department, Califano at HEW (supported by Andrew Young and Pat Harris at Housing and Urban Development) and the White House. As Stuart Eizenstat and Robert Lipshutz summarised it for Carter in September 1977, Justice believed 'that all racial classifications must be strictly scrutinized' and were 'presumptively unconstitutional'. Califano and HEW argued that 'classifications favorable to minorities should be judged on a lenient, rational basis'.[41] (According to Califano, Solicitor General Wade McCree, one of Carter's key black appointees at Justice, was 'carrying so much personal freight' that he found it difficult to argue clearly for his own positive orientation towards affirmative action.)[42] From the point of view of the President's close aides, any Administration involvement in the case was likely to be dangerous. Hamilton Jordan judged Bakke a 'very emotional and complex issue', requiring extreme caution. His words to the President were characteristically robust:

Because the Bakke case has taken on tremendous symbolic significance to the minorities of the country, we should realise that they are going to pay little attention to our eloquent language and focus almost exclusively on which side we support in our brief. Neither you nor I have been able to understand the legalisms in this case – how can we expect illiterate and disadvantaged people to understand when they are told by their leaders and the media that, 'Carter has ruled against the blacks and Hispanics of the country'.

According to Jordan, support for Allan Bakke would simply serve to 'discredit Days and McCree in their own community'. The bureaucratic battles were threatening to discredit the Administration. Carter had instructed Eizenstat and Lipshutz to 'jump into the drafting' but 'the people at Justice' were still not allowing them fully to participate.[43]

Califano made his position clear in Cabinet, in memos to Carter and to the Justice Department. Commenting on a second drafting of the brief, he declared it still 'not concerned enough with providing a ringing endorsement of affirmative action': 'we simply have to face up to the fact that affirmative action programs, if they are successful, will result in the displacement of a few individuals.'[44] The final brief was, as Dick Beattie of HEW reported to Califano, 'a win for our side'.[45] It clearly reflected the pressure from black and liberal lobbies, largely directed through the Congressional Black Caucus. It supported the use of racial classifications for affirmative action and called on the Supreme Court to send the case back to California to ascertain whether Bakke's rights had been violated. It did not call on the Court to find for Bakke – which of course, in 1978, it did, though not in a form which disallowed affirmative action; nor did it clearly condemn quotas. The final draft was a victory for HEW and liberal opinion, rather than for the White House. As Eizenstat and Lipshutz reported to Carter in September 1977, the 'final draft' was 'a substantial improvement over previous' efforts, in that it took a 'generally positive thrust' towards affirmative action. However: '*There is simply no direct statement in the brief that we oppose rigid and inflexible quotas based solely on race.*'[46] McCree, himself, in his oral presentation to the Court, adopted a radically supportive posture on affirmative action, setting himself against the evolving Court doctrine that acceptable affirmative action plans should be 'narrowly tailored' to fit particular patterns of past discrimination:

We suggest that it is not enough, really, to look at the visible wounds imposed by unconstitutional discrimination based upon race or ethnic status, because the very identification of race or ethnic status in America today is, itself, a handicap.

The controversy over the Bakke brief contributed to the Administration's reputation for muddle. Califano characteristically blamed Jimmy Carter for not acting like Lyndon Johnson.[48] That the openness of the Administration could, when combined with Carter's leadership style, lead to confusion is not in doubt. However, at least from September 1977, Administration support for the principle of flexible affirmative action was clear. The Solicitor General proffered briefs supporting race-conscious remediation in relation to the Weber decision of 1979 and Fullilove in 1980.[49]

Anti-discrimination, desegregation and voting rights

Carter brought to the cause of civil rights enforcement his customary enthusiasm for governmental reorganisation. One of his very first such plans involved the consolidation of equal employment enforcement in the EEOC. Under Eleanor Norton, the Equal Employment Opportunity Commission enjoyed a bureaucratic resurgence, at last making some headway in the face of its massive case backlog. Norton informed the White House in May 1979:

For the first time in the Commission's history, the backlog diminished rather than grew last year. Using new case processing techniques, we reduced EEOC's total inventory by over 20 per cent, from 100,000 to 79,000 charges.[50]

The OFCC gained new powers and responsibilities. A civil rights unit was set up in the Office of Management and Budget to cost enforcement programmes. Carter's continuing enthusiasm was evidenced in a late Executive Order (2 November 1980) ordering the Justice Department to co-ordinate agency-level civil rights enforcement. (One of the Administration's final acts in 1981 was to scrap entrance requirements for upper-level civil service jobs which many black and Hispanic groups regarded as discriminatory.)[51]

Opportunities to advertise its commitment to desegregation, and to distance itself from racism in other tiers of government, were regularly taken by the Administration. The President's daughter, Amy, attended a desegregated public school in the District of Columbia. Drew Days made clear the Justice Department's concern in the Wilmington Ten case, and filed an *amicus curiae* brief on their behalf in North Carolina. The Department also, in an unprecedented action, filed a civil rights suit against Philadelphia mayor Frank Rizzo and his police department, charging them with 'ethnic brutality'. The Los Angeles police department was sued for allegedly using discriminatory employment procedures. The Justice Department, in an argument eventually upheld by the Supreme Court, opposed tax exemptions for private schools which discriminated along racial lines. It also revived its virtually moribund procedures for challenging housing discrimination under the 1968 Fair Housing Act. (Carter attempted to strengthen the Act in 1980.)[52]

At the heart of school desegregation issues in the late 1970s lay the issue of court-ordered busing of schoolchildren across school district boundaries to achieve integration. Carter did not repeat Gerald Ford's unhappy interventions in this area. As with abortion – and with greater success – the Georgian took shelter behind the Supreme Court. A recent decision (*Milliken* v. *Bradley*, 1974) had significantly narrowed the scope of acceptable busing. Carter and Attorney General Bell were able, within the confines of the Supreme Court ruling, to support busing as a 'last resort'. (Carter frequently invoked the restrictive 'Atlanta plan'). This left them free to oppose legislation (the Biden–Roth bill) which would have restricted busing still further; such restriction was held to be unnecessary in view of the 1974 decision. In 1980, he also vetoed an appropriations bill that would, in effect, have barred the executive from initiating suits to force busing on school districts.[53]

Prolonged deadlock, notably regarding North Carolina, over higher education desegregation illustrated the new complexity of such issues. Joseph Califano, the main opponent of North Carolina's higher education leadership, himself pointed out that all-black colleges in the South had traditionally offered a means of improvement for many Southern blacks. In pursuing desegregation, the Administration exposed itself to the charge that it was undermining valuable institutions. Louis Martin advised Carter that the

White House must present itself as being concerned to strengthen the colleges.[54] Some of the colleges – for example Howard University in the District of Columbia, whence Andrew Young had graduated – enjoyed high reputations. Others, however, were, by the late 1970s, poorly administered and survived primarily as symbols of past struggles. Acting under pressure from the courts and from the National Association for the Advancement of Colored People (NAACP), HEW had come to terms with most Southern states by early 1978. (At least, desegregation plans had been accepted by then. In 1991 the Supreme Court agreed to review a situation where many virtually all-black colleges still existed in the South.)[55] The settlement with Georgia was achieved after Califano invoked the need to save Carter from unnecessary embarrassment over the issue. The situation in North Carolina was more difficult, and deadlock continued until the end of the Carter Administration. North Carolina had more public black colleges – five with more than 95 per cent black students – than the other states. The leaders of these colleges feared that their institutions would be merged out of existence, and pointed out that many of their students had neither the funds nor the Scholastic Aptitude Test scores to move elsewhere. William Friday, president of the North Carolina college system, was adamantly opposed to one of HEW's key criteria for accepting a desegregation plan: the elimination of duplicative non-core-curriculum courses. Key state politicians portrayed the Administration – particularly HEW, with its strong anti-smoking drive – as hostile to tobacco-producing North Carolina. Above and beyond all this, the dispute became enmeshed in the increasing hostility between Califano and the Georgian loyalists in the White House. From Califano's viewpoint, Stuart Eizenstat (a University of North Carolina graduate) was acting as a conduit between Friday (operating under instructions from Governor James Hunt, a Carter supporter) and the President. To Eizenstat, Califano was acting in a confrontational and politically insensitive manner. Eizenstat informed the President on 5 March 1979 (three weeks before HEW was to reject yet another North Carolina desegregation plan) as follows:

I am very concerned that Secretary Califano will not settle this case on a reasonable basis . . .

I think that this would be counter-productive in terms of desegregation and a disaster of the first magnitude politically . . .

At a time when it appeared some progress might be made Secretary Califano sent a team into North Carolina on a highly publicized trip . . .

In that visit several caustic and personal indictments were made against Bill Friday, by HEW officials and the whole visit set back the course of negotiations. Governor Hunt has informed the White House of his extreme displeasure over the trip. He believes it is another instance of the Administration's wounding itself unnecessarily in North Carolina. He has told Tim Kraft's staff that the State can be won in 1980 only if the Administration keeps its people *out* of the State from now on.[56]

Carter did lose North Carolina in 1980, though not by a margin significantly larger than in other Deep or Outer South states.

Black voting was a cause which greatly exercised the Carter Administration. Given the overwhelming support given to Carter in 1976 by black voters, this was hardly surprising. The President frequently argued that poor black turn-out was threatening to undermine the gains of the 1960s. In 1976, about 48 per cent of eligible black voters went to the polls, compared to a figure of 61 per cent for whites. Carter commented:

Both political candidates and incumbents have got to know that you will both vote and act. How are we going to have leadership to fight for equal opportunity and affirmative action in jobs, schools, and housing if even the act of voting is too great an effort?[57]

The Administration's support for enhanced black participation extended to legislative proposals and to more energetic enforcement of existing laws. The White House enthusiastically backed the proposal to amend the Constitution in order to allow the (predominantly black) District of Columbia to be treated as a state for purposes of Congressional and Electoral College representation. (The proposal passed Congress in 1978 but failed to achieve ratification by the states.) Enhancement of black turn-out was also an important goal underlying the wide-ranging electoral reform proposals which Carter submitted to Congress in March 1977. Particularly apposite to the encouragement of black participation was the attempt to redeem the campaign pledge of universal voter registration. The proposals would have followed the practice current in North Dakota, where voters were registered any time up until election day. Opponents of the proposal pointed out the possibilities of fraud, but the more basic reasons for Congressional inaction were summarised in July 1977 by Vice-President Mondale in a memorandum to the President:

There is, unfortunately, no real constituency for this bill. All the members got elected without it and they don't see how it will help them. On the contrary, it inserts a new element of uncertainty into their re-election prospects.

Accepting defeat on the issue, Mondale declared that election day registration 'is clearly an idea whose time is coming, but it's apparently not here yet'.[58] The task of enforcing existing legislation fell chiefly to the Justice Department's Civil Rights Division, under Drew Days. The Division scrutinised over twenty thousand local franchise proposals between 1977 and 1980 (six thousand more than in the previous twelve years), disallowing about 1 per cent of them. At issue were state and local electoral arrangements which potentially diluted the impact of black voting: not only blatant gerrymandering, but also city annexation policies and the imposition of at-large (rather than ward) representation. Many localities undoubtedly observed the law of anticipated reactions, and thought long and hard before submitting controversial proposals to the Division. However, the impact of such policies was to some extent impaired by the Supreme Court, whose decisions in this area tended to uphold contested annexations, at-large systems and reapportionments.[59] In its enforcement of voter registration for (especially) Southern blacks, the Administration tended to favour the sending of federal observers – as in the case of Tallahatchie County, Mississippi, in 1977 – rather than more punitive measures.[60]

Economic policies and the black community

Administration support for affirmative action, desegregation, anti-discrimination measures and black voting rights was relatively inexpensive. Bodies such as the EEOC, the Justice Department Civil Rights Division and the Civil Rights Commission were treated to sharp rises in Carter's budget requests, but much of the increased funding was eaten up by inflation.[61] Such increases as there were hardly constituted a renewed Great Society or a Marshall Plan for blacks. Carter even went so far in 1980 as to veto a civil rights appropriations amendment.[62]

The Administration's disinclination to revive the Great Society, along with the persistence of race-based economic inequality, precipitated – according to Louis Martin's memoranda to Carter – a growing disillusionment of black opinion. In March 1979, for example, Martin reported on the effects of unemployment in Baltimore, Maryland. He urged the President to acknowledge the need to 'defuse the defeatism in the highly charged Black communities':

Many national and local leaders, including some Black elected officials, are placing most of the blame for the current unrest on the widely publicized 'austere' budget . . . They do not buy the linkage between the battle on inflation and the need to cut job programs.[63]

In discussing the impact of federal government policy on black America, it is important to remember that key aspects of anti-poverty and anti-unemployment policy disproportionately affected the African American population. In 1978, 28 per cent of black families had annual incomes (including cash welfare payments, but excluding other benefits such as food stamps) below the official poverty level of $6,662. Black unemployment in 1978 averaged 1.4 million. Over the entire decade of the 1970s, black unemployment rose from slightly less than double that of whites to 2.5 times the white figure at the end of 1979. There were even clear racial dimensions to the women's rights issues discussed in the previous chapter. For example, the abortion rate among African Americans in the mid-1970s was roughly double that among whites.[64]

The Administration regularly claimed credit for its efforts to increase the minimum wage, its youth employment initiatives, and for successful simplification of the food stamp programme (moving in 1977 to a free system).[65] By the end of 1979, black teenage unemployment stood at 36.5 per cent, a slight decrease on the figure of 39.4 which Carter inherited in 1977. In 1979, black families subsisted on incomes averaging 57 per cent of those pertaining to white families.[66] Little wonder that Carter's 'lean and austere' budget for 1980 evoked the kind of response described by Louis Martin!

The evolving edginess in relations between the Administration and black leaders over economic issues was well illustrated in the case of Vernon Jordan, head of the National Urban League and early supporter of Jimmy Carter in Georgia. As early as August 1977, Jordan joined with other black leaders who had campaigned for Carter (Jesse Jackson, Bayard Rustin, Parren Mitchell and Benjamin Hooks) to accuse the Administration of 'callous neglect'.[67] When Carter announced his new urban policy in March, 1978, Jordan commented: 'it's not enough to throw a few billion extra dollars into the pot, add and improve some programs, stir, and present for public consumption.' He reiterated the familiar complaint that the President was more interested in human rights abroad than at home: 'Now was the time to go to the South Bronx, Hough, or Watts, and not to Caracas.' He continued:

As unveiled by the White House, the policy is no new crusade for urban America, no New Frontier of urban revitalization. It is a blend of programs, old and new, large and small, and it represents only the beginning of the long struggle to preserve urban America. It took many billions of dollars of federal aid, federal tax incentives, and federal loans to encourage the movement of jobs and people out of central cities to the suburbs. A similar commitment is required to restore the cities . . . But in this first year, the new urban policy will commit less than a billion dollars in new money for the cities.[68]

Carter's policy did not reverse the 'suburban Marshall plan'[69] of his predecessors; still it was a 'beginning'. Vernon Jordan's reluctance to move to a position of outright opposition was evidenced in correspondence with Hamilton Jordan in April 1978. The Urban League chairman emphasised to his White House namesake that his criticisms were always tempered with 'recognition of good intentions or of positive policies'. Hamilton Jordan was guilty of 'hypersensitivity' in resenting constructive criticism:

To sum up Hamilton, if you think I am against the President, if you think I have been less than constructively critical, if you think I have not given the Administration its due when it deserved it, then you are the victim of staff work that would be rotten anywhere, but is especially disturbing when it takes place in the White House.[70]

Carter's characteristic response to black criticism involved the proclamation of his good intentions; the summoning up of Republican and Congressional demons against whom blacks and the President could unite; references to his prominent black supporters, notably (before his resignation) Andrew Young; invocation of, for example, the food stamp changes and various Comprehensive Employment and Training Act initiatives; and strong support for affirmative action. All this tended to be set against a warning of the dangers of inflated expectations in a post-liberal world of economic constraint. As he complained in an April 1978 interview, 'Black Perspectives on the News', 'people expected so much from a new Democratic President'.[71]

A centrepiece to this interview – it 'will pass this year'[72] – and to the Administration's whole stance towards blacks was the backing given to the Humphrey-Hawkins 'full employment' bill. The measure, which black leaders tended to call the 'Hawkins bill' (after black Congressman Augustus Hawkins of California), was the Congressional Black Caucus's number one priority in the early Carter years.[73] In its original language, the bill called for the establishment of a Job Guarantee Office to be 'responsible for actually enforcing the right of all "able and willing" adults to a job'. Carter's campaign trail conversion to support for the bill had come rather late in the day, and represented part of his attempt to recover lost ground after the 'ethnic purity' gaffe of April 1976.[74]

The Humphrey–Hawkins bill did have some friends in the new Administration, notably Walter Mondale and Labour Secretary Ray Marshall. However, Carter's top budgetary and economic policy advisers – Treasury Secretary W. M. Blumenthal, Budget Director Bert Lance and Council of Economic Advisers chairman Charles Schultze – left him in no doubt as to their view. It was depicted by them as dangerously inflationary, horrendously costly and dangerously provocative of business opinion.[75] Schultze, who saw the bill as economically illiterate, began to draw up an Administration alternative to it. In place of firm commitments, Schultze inserted long range 'goals'. He incorporated a 'commitment' to reduce inflation. As Eizenstat told Carter in May 1977: 'These disagreements go to the heart of the Humphrey-Hawkins bill. They crystallize the distance between the Administration's economic views and those of the Black Caucus and other Congressional liberals.'[76] Mark Siegel, White House staffer and former executive director of the Democratic National Committee, offered his opinion on a letter which Schultze was proposing to send to Congressman Hawkins:

I hope that there is no confusion on anyone's part as to what we are attempting to do here – that is, to change everything about Humphrey-Hawkins except the name of the bill . . .

Politically, we can expect the liberals, black]sic] and labor to be displeased by our position, but Humphrey-Hawkins doesn't have any chance anyway, and no one expects us to come even this close to endorsing its provision. In that context, the Schultz [sic] letter is acceptable, but I would recommend that the coersive [sic] tone of the last sentence be dropped. We do not need to throw down the gauntlet so explicitly.[77]

The President's preference was to endorse Siegel's analysis: to offer symbolic support for the bill, secure in the knowledge that many of its advocates did not seriously expect the Administration to do other than work to emasculate the measure's expensive commitments, especially regarding public works and training. The problem with this strategy was that the White House might eventually displease both black/liberal and business opinion, while also being – not unreasonably – accused of cynicism.[78]

In August 1978, Carter reiterated his support for Humphrey–Hawkins to the Full Employment Action Council, a coalition of elite black, liberal and labour leaders. By this time the bill had passed the House, which had incorporated the goal of 4 per cent unemployment within five years. In the Senate, the Administration had to work not only against efforts to retain the firm commitments of the bill's original language, but also against 'killing' amendments (such as the incorporation of an impossibly rapid zero inflation goal) offered from the right. As Frank Moore informed the President in September 1978, it was somewhat galling to be blamed for lack of enthusiasm for the bill, when 'the conservative Republicans' were its chief opponents.[79] Moore and Louis Martin worked hard to activate Senate support, especially to head off the threatened filibuster. Schultze told Carter on 25 September:

My staff, with DPS, has been working closely with Senate sponsors of the bill to ensure that those provisions we find objectionable in committee versions of the bill can be fixed through floor amendments . . . My staff is monitoring developments closely . . . to ensure that the bill remains acceptable to us should it pass.[80]

The bill's final passage reflected, to some degree, Senate reaction to the death of Hubert Humphrey. Senate Majority Leader Robert Byrd announced that 'he wants to do this for Muriel Humphrey'.[81] It was also, however, the product of Administration mobilisation of the liberal–black–labour coalition which had produced the basis for liberal legislation in the previous decade. The Full Employment and Balanced Growth Act, signed by Carter in October 1978, represented the Administration's most successful accommodation to the 'old' liberal coalition of the Johnson era. At the signing ceremony, Carter declared: 'Human rights also includes economic opportunity'.[82] Coretta King acknowledged that 'we did not get all . . . we would have liked'; nevertheless, the Act was 'an important first step in the struggle for full employment'.[83] In truth, the Act reflected, to a paralysing degree, the three-way fight between its sponsors' original intent, the Administration's demands for greater flexibility, and conservative pressure in the Senate. It represented little beyond good intentions. The Act set a 3 per cent unemployment goal for adults – 4 per cent for all workers – by 1983; an inflation rate of 3 per cent, eventually dropping to zero; and a limit on federal government spending relative to GNP. It embodied a commitment to an improved balance of trade and to a balanced federal budget. All this was to be achieved through economic policy coordination between White House, Congress and the Federal Reserve. The President was given virtually unrestricted discretion to modify the goals and time schedules according to economic circumstances. The *Alice in Wonderland* dimension of the 1978 Act was clearly thrown into relief the following spring, when the White House, in submitting its 'austerity' budget, omitted any reference to full employment targets.

The role of Andrew Young

Young's acceptance of the United Nations ambassadorship was a disappointment to many blacks, who remembered his civil rights activism and wished to see him represent black interests in Washington. (Andrew Young's prominent position in the Southern Christian Leadership Conference, and his famous challenge at Selma in 1965 – 'We come to love the hell out of Alabama'[84] – were potent memories). Young's acceptance appears to have been linked with his personal admiration for Ralph Bunche, the black former UN Undersecretary General, and with his own understanding of the post's potential. He told a public television audience in June 1977:

I really don't think of myself as the UN Ambassador, maybe. I mean I think of myself as an American citizen who's been put in a position to protect American interests and to . . . help the United States of America to resume the rightful leadership role that we ought to have . . . To do that, we've got to relate to the so-called Third World.[85]

Young's major concern as Ambassador was with Africa. He did, however, advise on other issues. His influence, for example, appears to have contributed to Carter's decision to cancel the neutron bomb.[86] Young did not criticise Carter directly, but his outspokenness – his tendency in British Foreign Secretary David Owen's phrase to 'shoot from the "lip" '[87] – severely embarrassed the White House. The accusation of 'racism', levelled by Young at Presidents Nixon and Ford, elicited the following rather unconvincing gloss from Carter: 'an assessment that they were not familiar with the special problems of black people'.[88] At a meeting of the UN Commission on Human Rights, Young gave his opinion that the US record was as 'vulnerable' on this issue as anyone else's. In remarks made regarding the trial of dissidents in the Soviet Union, he referred to 'hundreds, perhaps even thousands' of people 'I would call political prisoners in the US'.[89] At one level, these assertions about the US record on human rights may be interpreted as an attempt to draw attention to the Wilmington Ten case, which much exercised Young at this time.[90] More deeply, however, they reflected a deep unease about his own position within the Administration. A radical commentator put it as follows:

Andrew Young's statement on political prisoners . . . revealed for all to see the insidious nature of President Carter's domestic and foreign policy regarding black people the world over. It revealed Young's neo-colonial position as an international apologist to the Third World and his personal conflicts with such a role.[91]

The President responded to the 'political prisoners' remark by expressing his 'trust' that Young would 'be more careful in future'.[92]

The Reverend Andrew Young was very far from being a revolutionary socialist. In 1980 he outlined those forces which he considered to have been his allies in developing policy on Africa. These included not only various liberal church and intellectual groups (previously engaged in anti-Vietnam war campaigns, now increasingly attuned to South Africa) and Africanists in the State Department, but also big business interests, like Gulf and Mobil oil companies, Boeing and Lockheed – corporations increasingly oriented towards trade with black Africa.[93] From his civil rights movement experience, Young had formed the view that corporate power could be harnessed for progressive purposes. Like many of Carter's foreign policy appointees, Young had been a member of the Rockefeller-backed foreign affairs policy development body, the Trilateral Commission. He believed that, provided they followed fair employment practices (embodied in the Sullivan Code of Corporate Conduct), US corporations could be in the vanguard of change in South Africa.[94]

As guided and interpreted by Andrew Young, the Carter Administration's African policy was intended to generate support (for domestic as well as foreign policy) among blacks at home. In May 1979, Louis Martin gave his opinion to the President that, in the case of Rhodesia, there was significant black opposition to the lifting of sanctions. Organisations like the Congressional Black Caucus were likely to take the Rhodesia–Zimbabwe issue as a measure of the Administration's good faith.[95]

In general terms, Young stood at the head of the 'regionalist' interpretation of African affairs. For him, and his allies in the State Department, Africa was to be considered, as far as possible, in isolation from the Cold War. Apartheid in South Africa should be vigorously opposed, and 'progressive' forces generally supported, without too much concern about Soviet and Cuban influence. As it evolved after 1976, US African policy bore the clear imprint of this 'regionalist' perspective and of the new human rights orientation. (It should be noted, however, that by 1976, even Henry Kissinger had come to the view that, in Rhodesia at least, the US should encourage majority rule.) Against the forces of 'regionalism' stood the 'globalists', concerned above all to combat Soviet influence in Africa. Policy towards the continent essentially represented an uneasy compromise between the two positions, with the 'globalist' perspective gaining ascendancy in the 1979–80 period. (US support for Somalia in the Horn of Africa conflict in 1979 may be taken as an important victory for the 'globalist' camp.)[96]

Young's departure from the Administration, more firing than resignation, was precipitated by the bureaucratic battling within the Administration and also by concern about his 'loose cannon' status. When the possibility of recruiting Richard Hatcher, black mayor of Gary, Indiana, to work for the Administration was being considered in 1978, Hamilton Jordan's advice to Carter clearly reflected the experience of coping with Young: 'Hatcher is tough and strong-willed and we don't want him to feel that to maintain his credibility he can be publicly questioning ... your decisions.'[97] Until mid-1979, Carter was very supportive of his UN Ambassador. However, the July meeting with Palestine Liberation Organisation representatives was in direct contravention of Administration policy, and was reported neither to Carter nor Secretary Vance. Young appears to have been trying to obtain PLO backing for the dropping of an anti-Israeli resolution. However, especially after the Califano and Blumenthal dismissals, Carter felt that Young's errant behaviour could not go unpunished. The White House also was concerned with the impact of all this on domestic Jewish opinion.[98]

In his resignation speech at the State Department, Young accepted that he had been excessively 'impatient', but declared: 'Unfortunately, but by birth, I come from the ranks of those who have known and identified with . . . oppression in the world.'[99] The Black Leadership Forum issued a protest. This group, which included Coretta King, Vernon Jordan and Bayard Rustin, alleged that the US Ambassador to Austria had also met PLO representatives and was still in post. Jesse Jackson's reaction to Young's treatment also finally quashed press speculation that he, Jackson, was about to be recruited into the Administration.[100]

Andrew Young was in many respects a highly effective foreign policy operator. Benjamin Hooks, executive director of the NAACP, declared in 1978: 'No black person has ever had such a forum (especially with the backing of a sympathetic and supportive President) for advocating policies on Africa that challenge white minority rule and oppressive domination.'[101] Young's work on the Rhodesia–Zimbabwe settlement was to bear fruit in 1980. His 'resignation' was perhaps inevitable, but it was unfortunate, both from the Administration's viewpoint, and from that of developing US race relations. It confirmed the growing disaffection of the black political elite who had supported Carter in 1976, as well as raising the level of black–Jewish tension.

Notes

1   *The Presidential Campaign 1976: Vol. I: Part 1* (Washington DC: US Government Printing Office, 1978), p. 136 (5 Apr. 1976).

2   'Remarks and a Q and A Session at a Public Meeting in Yazoo City, Mississippi', 21 July 1977, *Public Papers of the Presidents of the United States: Jimmy Carter, 1977, 2* (Washington DC: US Government Printing Office, 1978), p. 1329.

3   W. L. Miller, *Yankee from Georgia* (New York: Times Books, 1978), p. 47 (Derian), p. 63 (Young).

4   Frank Daniel, ed., *Addresses of Jimmy Carter* (Atlanta: Georgia Dept. of Archives and History, 1975), p. 260 (speech at University of Georgia, 4 May 1974).

5   'Remarks and a Q and A Session . . .', p. 1328. I am indebted here to D. Cunnigen, 'Jimmy Carter as Spokesman for Southern Liberalism', paper presented at the Eighth Presidential Conference, Hofstra University, Nov. 1990.

6   Jimmy Carter, *Why Not the Best?* (Eastbourne: Kingsway, 1977), p. 69.

7   Daniel, ed., *Addresses*, p. 260; *Why Not the Best?*, pp. 66–7. See also James

Wooten, *Dasher* (London: Weidenfeld and Nicolson, 1978), pp. 223–62; B. J. Schulman, *From Cotton Belt to Sunbelt* (New York: Oxford University Press, 1991), p. 166.

8   Rosalynn Carter, *First Lady from Plains* (Boston: Houghton Mifflin, 1984), p. 45.

9   Carter, *Why Not the Best?*, pp. 102–3.

10   Cited in Earl Black, *Southern Governors and Civil Rights* (Cambridge (Massachusetts): Harvard University Press, 1976), p. 70. See also Robert Weisbrot, *Freedom Bound: A History of America's Civil Rights Movement* (New York: Norton, 1990), p. 298; J. Clotfelter and W. R. Hamilton, 'Electing a Governor in the Seventies', in T. L. Beyle and J. Oliver Williams, eds., *The American Governor in Behavioral Perspective* (New York: Harper and Row, 1972), pp. 32–9; Steven F. Lawson, *In Pursuit of Power: Southern Blacks and Electoral Politics, 1965–1982* (New York: Columbia University Press, 1985), pp. 254–5; Wooten, *Dasher*, pp. 292–302.

11   Black, *Southern Governors . . .*, p. 71. See also Gary Fink, *Prelude to the Presidency: The Political Character and Legislative Leadership of Governor Jimmy Carter* (Westport: Greenwood, 1980).

12   See Chuck Stone, 'Black Political Power in the Carter Era', in *The Black Scholar*, 8, 1976–7, pp. 17–21, at 19; Haynes Johnson, *In The Absence of Power* (New York: Viking Press, 1980), p. 177.

13   Cited in Jules Witcover, *Marathon* (New York: Viking Press, 1977), pp. 293–4.

14   Stone, 'Black Political Power . . .', p. 19.

15   Witcover, *Marathon*, pp. 302–8.

16   *The Presidential Campaign 1976: Vol. I: Part 2* (Washington DC: US Government Printing Office, 1978), pp. 1109–10; Witcover, *Marathon*, p. 634.

17   Cited in Lawson, *In Pursuit of Power*, p. 256. See also Stone, 'Black Political Power . . .', p. 19; F. R. Parker, *Black Votes Count: Political Empowerment in Mississippi after 1945* (Chapel Hill: University of North Carolina Press, 1990), p. 150; P. Gunn, S. Hatchett and J. S. Jackson, *Hope and Independence: Blacks' Response to Electoral and Party Politics* (New York: Sage Foundation, 1989), p. 52.

18   *New York Times*, 6 Nov. 1976 (R. Reed).

19   See Dennis F. Thompson, *Political Ethics and Public Office* (Cambridge (Massachusetts): Harvard University Press, 1987), p. 130; Griffin Bell, *Taking Care of the Law* (New York: Morrow, 1982).

20   Cited in B. Adams and K. Kavanagh-Baran, *Promise and Performance* (Lexington (Massachusetts): Heath, 1979), p. 80. See also Joel Dreyfuss and Charles Lawrence, *The Bakke Case* (New York: Harcourt, Brace, Jovanovich, 1979), p. 162.

21   See G. D. Jaynes and R. M. Williams, eds, *A Common Destiny* (Washington DC: National Academy Press, 1989), p. 243; R. C. Smith, 'Black Appointed Officials: A Neglected Area of Research', *Journal of Black Studies*, 14, 1984, pp. 369–88; Michael L. Krenn, ' "Outstanding Negroes" and 'Appropriate Countries': Some Facts and Thoughts on Black U.S. Ambassadors, 1949–1988', *Diplomatic History*, 14, 1990, pp. 131–41; Adams and Kavanagh-Baran, *Promise and Performance*, pp. 84–5; Steven A. Shull, *The President and Civil Rights Policy* (New York: Greenwood, 1989), pp. 95–6; S. Goldman, 'Reorganizing the Judiciary', *Judicature*, 68, 1985, pp. 313–29, at 324.

22 Memo to the President from L. Martin, 4 Sept. 1979, box 39, SO: Chief of Staff Jordan (folder, 'Black Community'). On Martin's appointment, see Hanes Walton, *When the Marching Stopped: The Politics of the Civil Rights Regulatory Agencies* (Albany: State University of New York Press, 1988), p. 131.

23 Memo to the President from F. Moore and Tim Kraft, 22 Sept. 1978, box 103, PHF (folder, '9/25/78 (1)').

24 Memo to the President from P. Cadell, 18 Aug. 1980, box 77, SO: Chief of Staff: Jordan (folder, 'Campaign Strategy').

25 *St Louis Argus*, 9 Aug. 1979. On the award to the Tank battalion, see Bernard C. Nalty, *Strength for the Fight: A History of Black Americans in the Military* (New York: Free Press, 1980), p. 176.

26 See *CQWR*, 21 May 1977, p. 967 (remarks of Rep. Y. Brathwaite Burke: 'The difference in this administration is at least you have a Marshall . . .').

27 V. Jordan, Statement on Urban Policy, 5 Apr. 1978, box 39, SO: Chief of Staff: Jordan (folder, 'Black Community').

28 See Manning Marable, *Black American Politics: From the Washington Marches to Jesse Jackson* (London: Verso, 1985), p. 181. See also Clarence Mitchell, 'Blacks and Carter', *Baltimore Sun*, 10 June 1979.

29 R. L. Stansfield, 'Political Report', *National Journal*, 14 June 1980, p. 966. (According to James Farmer of the Coalition of American Public Employees, 'Carter appeals to the black Baptist . . . He talks their language.')

30 See Herbert B. Asher, *Presidential Elections and American Politics* (Chicago: Dorsey Press, 1988), pp. 180–7; Carter, MC transcript, p. 46.

31 Memo to the President from P. Cadell, 18 Aug. 1980, box 77, SO: Chief of Staff: Jordan (folder, 'Campaign Strategy').

32 Speech by D. S. Days, 11 Nov. 1977, box 22, SO: DPS: Civil Rights and Justice: Gutierrez (folder, 'Human Rights'). On the Haitian refugees, see Alex Stepick, 'Haitian Boat People: A Study in the Conflicting Forces Shaping US Immigration Policy', *Law and Contemporary Problems*, 45, 1982, pp. 163–96.

33 *CQWR*, 21 May 1977, p. 968.

34 Memo to the President from L. Martin, 16 June 1980 (Urban unrest/race relations), box 77, SO: Chief of Staff: Jordan (folder, 'Campaigns and Constituencies').

35 See J. W. Singer, 'Justice Report', *National Journal*, 5 Aug. 1978, p. 1250. For background to affirmative action issues, see J. Dumbrell, 'Affirmative Action during the Reagan Presidency', *Politics*, 8, 1988, pp. 30–4.

36 Office of Louis Martin, 'Fact Sheet 106', Aug. 1979, box 39, SO: Chief of Staff: Jordan (folder, 'Black Community') (also *National Journal*, 5 Aug. 1978, pp. 1248–51). See also Louis Martin, 'Carter Accomplishments in Civil Rights', *Focus*, 8, 1980, pp. 7–8.

37 Office of Louis Martin, 'The First Two Years', 21 Dec. 1978, box 1, SO: Louis Martin (folder, 'Accomplishments (1)').

38 Califano, *Governing America*, p. 233. See also American Jewish Committee, Statement on Affirmative Action, undated (1977), box 148, SO: DPS: Eizenstat (folder, 'Bakke'): 'The use of specific numerical goals and timetables must not be permitted to disguise a de facto quota system.'

39 Letter, Carter to R. Maass, President of the American Jewish Committee, 27 Oct. 1977, box 149, SO: DPS: Eizenstat (folder, 'Bakke').

40 *Regents of the University of California* v. *Bakke*, 438 US 265 (1978). See Dreyfuss and Lawrence, *The Bakke Case*, p. 166; Califano, *Governing America*, p. 236.

41 Memo to the President and Vice-President from S. Eizenstat and B. Lipshutz, 10 Sept. 1977, box 149, SO: DPS: Eizenstat (folder, 'Bakke').

42 Califano, *Governing America*, p. 237.

43 Memo to the President from H. Jordan, undated (1977), box 149, SO: DPS: Eizenstat (folder, 'Bakke').

44 Memo to the Attorney General, Solicitor General and Assistant Attorney General Civil Rights Division from J. Califano, 10 Sept. 1977, box 149, SO: DPS: Eizenstat (folder, 'Bakke').

45 Califano, *Governing America*, p. 242.

46 Memo to the President and Vice-President from B. Lipshutz and S. Eizenstat, 16 Sept. 1977, box 148, SO: DPS: Eizenstat (folder, 'Bakke'). See also Steven F. Lawson, *Running For Freedom: Civil Rights and Black Politics in America since 1941* (Philadelphia: Temple University Press, 1991), pp. 198–200.

47 Dreyfuss and Lawrence, *The Bakke Case*, p. 192.

48 Califano, *Governing America*, p. 230 ('I sensed his (Carter's) desire was to appease constituencies as much as to satisfy a fundamental commitment to civil rights').

49 *US Steelworkers* v. *Weber*, 443 US 193 (1979) (involving a collective bargaining agreement) and *Fullilove* v. *Klutznick*, 448 US 448 (1980) (involving a minority 'set-aside' under the 1977 Public Works Employment Act). See also J. A. Segal, 'Amicus Curiae Briefs by the Solicitor General: The Warren and Burger Courts', *Western Political Quarterly*, 41, 1988, pp. 135–44; Norman C. Amaker, 'The Faithfulness of the Carter Administration in Enforcing Civil Rights', paper presented at the Eighth Presidential Conference, Hofstra University, Nov. 1990.

50 Memo to B. Aronson from E. H. Norton, 1 May 1979, box 3, SO: Speechwriters: SF (folder 'Civil Rights').

51 *Newsweek*, 16 Jan. 1981, p. 52. See also Shull, *The President and Civil Rights Policy*, p. 86.

52 Office of Louis Martin, 'Fact Sheet 106', Aug. 1979, box 39, SO: Chief of Staff: Jordan (folder, 'Black Community'). See also *Public Papers of the Presidents of the United States: Jimmy Carter, 1979, 1* (Washington DC: US Government Printing Office, 1980), p. 911.

53 In *Milliken* v. *Bradley* (418 US 717 (1974)), the Court ruled that federal courts could order busing only if the affected school districts could be proved to have practised discrimination, or if the drawing of district lines had been undertaken to promote segregation. The 'Atlanta plan' involved voluntary busing as a result of policy formulated at the agreement of all relevant racial groups. See Memo to the President from S. Eizenstat, 'Bell Memo on Biden-Roth', 19 July 1977, box 183, SO: DPS: Eizenstat (folder, 'Desegregation').

54 See memo to the President from L. Martin, 7 Aug. 1980, 'Signing Ceremony for the Executive Order on the Black Colleges Initiative', box 198, PHF (folder, '8/8/80'); also, Manning Marable, *Race, Reform and Rebellion* (London: Macmillan, 1984), p. 186.

55 See Lucy Hodges, 'Supreme Court Tackles Racism', *Times Higher Education Supplement*, 10 May 1991.

56   Memo to the President from S. Eizenstat, 5 Mar. 1979, box 246, SO: DPS: Eizenstat (folder, 'North Carolina Desegregation'); Califano, *Governing America*, pp. 244–58.

57   Cited in Lawson, *Pursuit of Power*, p. 257.

58   Memo to the President from W. Mondale, 14 July 1977, box 38, PHF (folder, '7/15/77 (3)'). See also Memo to the President from R. Moe, 19 Feb. 1977, box 9, PHF (folder, '2/19/77'): 'Our registration proposals would produce a system very similar to the North Dakota approach, but with the additions of safeguards against fraud.' The March 1977 proposals also provided for public funding of Congressional campaigns and for direct election of the President. See *CQWR*, 14 May 1977, pp. 909–15.

59   See, e.g., *City of Mobile* v. *Bolden*, 446 US 55 (1980).

60   See Lawson, *In Pursuit of Power*, pp. 259–62: 'The appearance of federal observers . . . generally improved the quality of elections . . .' (p. 261). See also W. E. Leuchtenberg, 'The White House and Black America: From Eisenhower to Carter', in Michael V. Namorato, ed., *Have We Overcome?: Race Relations Since 'Brown'* (Jackson: University Press of Mississippi, 1979), pp. 121–45, at 143.

61   For differing interpretations regarding Carter's budget requests for civil rights enforcement, see Walton, *When the Marching Stopped*, pp. 60–3, 73; and Shull, *The President and Civil Rights Policy*, pp. 88–92.

62   See Shull, *The President and Civil Rights Policy*, p. 89.

63   Memo to the President from L. Martin, 12 Mar. 1979, box 122, PHF (folder, '3/13/79 (1)').

64   See Califano, *Governing America*, p. 73.

65   Office of Louis Martin, 'Fact Sheet 106', Aug. 1979, box 39, SO: Chief of Staff: Jordan (folder, 'Black Community').

66   See Memo to L. Martin from J. Dobbs, 7 Dec. 1979, 'Black Economic Development', box 1, SO: Louis Martin (folder, 'Accomplishments (2)'). Also, Lawson, *In Pursuit of Power*, p. 256; B. E. Anderson, 'Economic Progress', in National Urban League, *The State of Black America, 1980* (New York: National Urban League, 1980), pp. 1–27.

67   Cited in Marable, *Race, Reform and Rebellion*, p. 184.

68   V. E. Jordan, 'Urban Policy: A Missed Opportunity', undated press release, box 39, SO: Chief of Staff: Jordan (folder, 'Black Community').

69   V. E. Jordan, 'Equal Opportunity Day Speech', 17 Nov. 1977, *ibid.*

70   Letter, V. E. Jordan to H. Jordan, 18 Apr. 1978, *ibid.*

71   Interview transcript, 'Black Perspectives on the News', 5 Apr. 1978, box 5, SO: DPS: Neustadt (folder, 'Blacks').

72   *Ibid.*

73   *CQWR*, 21 May 1977, p. 967.

74   Witcover, *Marathon*, p. 306.

75   See Gary M. Fink, 'Fragile Alliance: Jimmy Carter and the American Labor Movement', paper presented at the Eighth Presidential Conference, Hofstra University, Nov. 1990.

76   Memo to the President from S. Eizenstat, 24 May 1977, box 26, PHF (folder, '5/24/77 (1)').

77   M. Siegel, comments on Schultze letter, undated, *ibid.*

78   See R. J. Samuelson, 'Humphrey–Hawkins Hypocrisy', *National Journal*, 7 Jan. 1978, p. 28.

79 Memo to the President from F. Moore, 23 Sept. 1978, box 103, PHF (folder, '9/25/78').

80 Memo to the President from C. Shultze, 25 Sept. 19798, *ibid.*

81 Memo to the President from F. Moore, 23 Sept. 1978, *ibid.*

82 *Public Papers of the Presidents of the United States: Jimmy Carter, 1978, 2* (Washington DC: US Government Printing Office, 1979), p. 1719.

83 Cited in Marable, *Race, Reform and Rebellion*, p. 185.

84 See Roy Wilkins, *Standing Fast* (New York: Viking Press, 1982), p. 309; H.E. Newsum and O. Abegunrin, *United States Foreign Policy Towards Southern Africa: Andrew Young and Beyond* (London: Macmillan, 1987), p. 20.

85 *CQWR*, 18 June 1977, p. 1226; also, Seymour M. Finger, *American Ambassadors at the UN* (New York: Holmes and Meier, 1988), p. 261.

86 See Carl Gershman, 'The World According to Andrew Young', *Commentary*, 66, 1978, pp. 17–23, at 17.

87 David Owen, *Time to Declare* (Penguin: London, 1992), p. 284.

88 *CQWR*, 18 Jan. 1977, p. 1248.

89 Gershman, 'The World According to Andrew Young', p. 20; D. S. Spencer, *The Carter Implosion: Jimmy Carter and the Amateur Style of Diplomacy* (New York: Praeger, 1988), p. 55.

90 Newsom and Abegunrin, *United States Foreign Policy . . .*, p. 16.

91 Richard D. Moore, 'U.S. Black Political Prisoners', *The Black Scholar*, 10, 1979, pp. 17–22, at 22.

92 *Public Papers . . . 1978, 2*, p. 1330.

93 Andrew Young, 'The United States and Africa: Victory for Diplomacy', *Foreign Affairs*, 59, 10980, pp. 648–66, at 652.

94 See Richard W. Hull, *American Enterprise in South Africa* (New York: New York University Press, 1990), p. 305.

95 Memo to the President from L. Martin, 29 May 1979, box 44, SO: Counsel: Lipshutz (folder, 'Rhodesia').

96 See generally, Gaddis Smith, *Morality, Reason and Power* (New York: Hill and Wang, 1986), ch. 6; Robert M. Price, 'U.S. Policy toward Southern Africa', in G. M. Carter and P. O'Meara, eds, *International Politics in Southern Africa* (Bloomington: Indiana University Press, 1982), pp. 45–88, at 50.

97 Memo to the President from H. Jordan, 21 April 1978, box 82, PHF (folder, '4/21/78').

98 See Finger, *American Ambassadors at the UN*, p. 284; D. Bonafede, 'The Undiplomatic Mr. Young', *National Journal*, 25 Aug. 1979, p. 1418.

99 Special briefing: Andrew Young, 15 Aug. 1979, box 79, SO: Powell, (folder, 'Young').

100 Statement of Black Leadership Forum, undated, box 109, SO: Louis Martin (folder, 'Young'); L. Mosher, 'Blacks and Middle East Policy', *National Journal*, 1 Sept. 1979, p. 1455.

101 Cited in Finger, *American Ambassadors at the UN*, p. 285.

5

Compassion and foreign policy: the cases of the Soviet Union and Northern Ireland

Foundations of Carter's foreign policy

Jimmy Carter's two principal foreign policy advisers, Cyrus Vance and Zbigniew Brzezinski, are generally represented as having consistently held opposing views regarding the entire basis of America's position in the world. In fact, at least early on in the Administration, their declared views converged to a considerable degree. Vance, Carter and Brzezinski, for example, all wished to modify what the latter described in his memoirs as America's 'hysterical preoccupations' with Soviet communism.[1]

The views of Vance and Brzezinski were formulated for Carter's benefit in two important position papers. Vance's was presented to candidate Carter in October, 1976. It outlined five foreign policy 'themes': the US must protect its interests *vis-à-vis* the Soviet Union, but the Soviet relationship must not be allowed to distort American relations with other countries; North–South issues must be addressed, along with global questions relating to energy, the environment and nuclear proliferation; the US must take a stand on international human rights; the new Administration should focus on long-term objectives rather than short-term crisis management; the new President must seek to educate both Congress and the public in the complexities of international affairs, and take them into a new, democratic foreign policy consensus.[2] Brzezinski's memorandum, developed from a campaign paper, was presented in April 1977. It posited: 'an unstable world organized almost entirely on the principle of national sovereignty and yet increasingly interdependent socially and economically'. The paper proposed ten objectives: new economic cooperation between Western Europe, Japan and the US; the development of relations with 'regional influentials' – especially oil producers – like Nigeria, Iran, Saudi Arabia and Venezuela; prioritisation of North-South relations, involving a decrease in Third World hostility to the US (ratification of a Panama Canal treaty would be an important step here); pursuit of strategic arms limitation and achievement of an actual strategic arms *reduction* in a US–Soviet treaty by 1980; 'normalization' of relations with mainland China; a comprehensive Middle Eastern settlement; the moving of South Africa towards multi-racial democracy and the achievement of a majority rule settlement in Rhodesia–Zimbabwe by 1978; restriction in international arms transfers; enhancement of 'global sensitivity' over human rights; and development of a defence posture which would deter the USSR, while reflecting 'broad changes in the world'. In his memoir, *Power and Principle*, Brzezinski indicated that these various concerns, at the start of the Carter Administration, coalesced into three main priorities: to 'increase America's ideological impact on the world' by emphasising human rights and, in the process, overcoming the 'spreading pessimism' at home; to 'improve America's strategic position' – an objective which embraced normalisation of relations with China; and 'third . . . to restore America's political appeal to the Third World'.[3]

The Carter foreign policy agenda, as outlined by Brzezinski and Vance, bore the clear imprint of the Trilateral Commission, the Rockefeller-backed study group which represented one elite reaction to international developments since the late 1960s. Brzezinski later recalled meeting Carter at early Trilateral Commission sessions, held shortly after Carter's election to the Georgia state-house:

I remember discussing his membership with my two principal Trilateral Commission colleagues, Gerald Smith and George Franklin. We wanted a forward-looking Democratic governor who would be congenial to the Trilateral perspective.[4]

The 'Trilateral perspective' embraced a programme for inter-capitalist co-operation (notably between the US, Japan and Western Europe), based on a post-Vietnam analysis of America's place in the world. Its key concept was 'complex interdependence'.[5] The days of outright US hegemony, based on the drive towards military and economic superiority were over. Many Trilateralists saw the Soviet Union as a 'status quo' power, no longer engaged in a programme of world domination and constrained by economic problems at home. In such an environment, the US needed to throw itself behind a new collaborative internationalism, with the economic dimension being emphasised above the military. It needed also to focus on the new transnational agenda of environmental, energy, trade and nuclear issues. Above all, the United States must not slide into a pessimistic mood of surly isolationism.

Most of the key foreign policy players in the Carter Administration – Vance and Young, as well as Brzezinski – were Commission members. Carter's foreign policy, especially in its early phase, has been correctly identified with the Commission's general outlook. For Carter himself, the Commission provided a kind of crash course in contemporary international relations theory. What should be avoided, however, is the imputation of conspiracy. Like its parent organisation, the Council on Foreign Relations, the Trilateral Commission has been the subject of conspiracy theories of both left- and right-wing provenance.[6] Such theories overlook important features of the Commission and Carter's relations to it. For one thing, there was never any secret about Carter's membership, although at times it proved a little embarrassing to be associated with a 'too capitalist, too establishment' organisation.[7] Secondly, the views propounded by the Commission were by no means entirely consistent. The Commission's most famous publication was a study of the 'crisis of governability' in Western liberal democracies, involving problems of governmental 'overload' and excessive public and interest group expectations. Such concerns, of course, shaped the outlook of the Carter Administration in domestic affairs. The Commission's report (partly authored by Samuel Huntington, who worked for Carter under Brzezinski) concluded that part of the problem was simply too much democracy.[8] Yet neither authoritarianism nor inveterate hostility to 'big government' formed part of Carter's agenda. When the Commission met in Tokyo and Kyoto in May 1975, the view was forcibly put, notably by Ralf Dahrendorf, that the problem was too *little* democracy, especially in industry. The Commission always contained 'hard' and 'soft' positions. (For example, Stephen Gill has identified two competing factions in the development of Commission attitudes towards the USSR: the 'traders', who sought to draw the Soviet Union into interdependent world economic structures, and the 'Prussians', who looked to Soviet arms concessions being made in the face of NATO military resurgence.)[9] The concerns of the Commission shifted over the years, with security issues predominating after 1978. To an extent, this development was reflected within the Carter Administration, several members of which continued to attend Council on Foreign Relations or Trilateral Commission meetings after 1976.[10] Essentially, however the Trilateral Commission provided a forum for elite debate and accommodation to international change, rather than a focus for conspiracy. Accusations of conspiracy are generally reducible to the charge that Carter was seeking to further the cause of American capitalism in the international arena – scarcely an earth-shattering discovery.

Above and beyond the Trilateral Commission, the outlook of the Carter Administration was shaped by memories of Vietnam and of the Nixon–Kissinger–Ford foreign policy; by the desire to restore consensus; and by the perceived need to adjust to relative US decline in a 'cascadingly' interdependent world.[11] Carter's May 1977 Notre Dame address attacked the entire foundation of US policy in Vietnam:

> For too many years we have been willing to adopt the flawed and erroneous principles of our adversaries, sometimes abandoning our own values for theirs. We have fought fire with fire, never thinking that force is better quenched with water. This approach failed, with Vietnam the best example of its intellectual and moral poverty.[12]

Global containment, the doctrine that had impelled the US into Vietnam, needed to be revised. The communist world was now clearly divided and, as Carter declared in March 1978, old 'ideological labels have lost some of their meaning'. To a large degree, Carter's foreign policy apparatus was staffed by people who felt they had absorbed the 'lessons of Vietnam'.[13] Perhaps most obviously, these lessons included an awareness of the folly of supporting unpopular Third World dictators and elites in the name of freedom. They also involved a perception that an overly secretive, overly exclusive foreign policy-making process could lead to disaster, and that successful policy required democratic consensus. In a book published in 1970, Zbigniew Brzezinski himself argued: 'A profound discrepancy between the external conduct of a democratic society and its internal norms is no longer possible; mass communications quickly expose the gulf and undercut the support needed for its foreign policy.'[14] Vietnam's lessons also embraced a new sensitivity to the limits of American power, especially American military power. Cyrus Vance declared in May 1979:

In seeking to help others meet the legitimate needs of their peoples, what are the best instruments at hand? Let me state first that the use of military force is not, and should not be a desirable American policy response to the internal politics of other nations.

A member of Vance's Policy Planning Staff later recalled that the word 'desirable' was a compromise, between those who worked to rule out military force altogether, and 'those who felt that we could not rule that out in *every* circumstance'. The debate over Vance's speech involved 'a lot of playing out of Vietnam . . .'.[15] By December 1979, Carter felt he had to emphasise that 'not every instance of the firm application of power is a potential Vietnam'.[16]

Criticism of Kissinger's 'Lone Ranger' style as Secretary of State and National Security Adviser under Presidents Nixon and Ford had been a major theme in the 1976 campaign. The new Administration committed itself to an open process. Echoing Brzezinski's 1970 point about the need for democratic consensus, Carter remarked in July 1977:

We've been through some sordid and embarrassing years recently with Vietnam and Cambodia and Watergate and the CIA revelations, and I felt like it was time for our country to hold a beacon light of something pure and decent and right and proper that would rally our citizens to a cause.[17]

The new Administration's doctrine of human rights stood opposed to Kissingerian *realpolitik*. Also at issue, however, were Henry Kissinger's doctrines of detente and linkage. Brzezinski wrote to Carter in December 1975 that detente was 'desirable but it ought to be more reciprocal'.[18] Around the same time, he criticised Kissinger's detente policies as 'highly compartmentalized and essentially static, even conservative'. Nixon and Kissinger had 'elevated amorality to the level of principle'.[19] In effect, Brzezinski was criticising Kissinger for excluding human rights concerns from his linkage doctrine. Linkage in the 'old' Kissingerian sense (of orchestrating arms talks, trade agreements and use of US influence in regional disputes to modify Soviet behaviour) had been severely undermined by the time Carter came into office.[20] The new Administration's 'regionalist' orientation – the view that regional disputes should not always be subjected to Cold War 'East–West analysis'[21] – further undermined it, as did its determination to pursue arms control for its own sake.

Restoration of domestic consensus was a major priority for post-Vietnam policy-makers. The Carter Administration sought to restore consensus not on the basis of anti-communism but upon a restoration of American liberal democratic values in the international context. Alongside the appeal to human rights went a campaign to educate Congress, the bureaucracy and the public in the realities of global interdependence and the politics of global community. In the 1977 Notre Dame address, Carter declared that the bipolar world was giving way to 'a new worldwide mosaic of global, regional, and bilateral relations'.[22] 'Global interdependence', as Vance later remarked, 'had become a reality.'[23] The theory of 'complex interdependence' was expounded by various scholarly authorities in the 1970s, not least by Stanley Hoffman, the major academic influence on the Carter Administration. Developed in opposition to security-oriented 'realism', interdependence theory viewed inter-state relations as disaggregated, and international cooperation as feasible. The line between foreign and domestic concerns was held to have blurred, with 'intermestic' concerns (like the price of oil) being central. (The Carter foreign affairs team had, in its view, learned not only the 'lessons of Vietnam' but also the lessons of OPEC.) Above all, no one nation state could entirely dominate the international system, although stability could be achieved through a co-operative regime of 'world order liberalism'.[24] Carter told the United Nations General Assembly in October 1977 that the 'power to solve the world's problems' no longer lay in 'the hands of a few'. It was 'widely shared among many nations with different cultures and different histories and different aspirations'. American leadership was 'increasingly . . . in need of being shared'.[25]

Retrenchment was inevitably seen as part of the process of adjustment to the new conditions. The US must avoid a dangerous imbalance between commitments and resources. Retrenchment also offered the US the opportunity to rediscover its true moral purpose, which lay not in militarism but in the commitment to human rights. The early Carter Administration's commitment to retrenchment embraced specific proposals – to normalise relations with China, to withdraw from South Korea, to curb the CIA, to control the arms race, to encourage burden-sharing in NATO – with a more general commitment to human rights, the North–South dimension and 'preventive diplomacy' (designed to defuse regional conflicts). Considering the Carter record in this area, Samuel Huntington wrote in an article published in 1979:

consider how different the world would look and what the demands would be on U.S. resources if China were threatening aggression against American interests in Asia, if Egypt were a Soviet ally and military base, and if the Panama Canal were under intermittent attack by guerrilla-terrorists.[26]

By the time Huntington's article appeared in print, the whole 'world order' optimism of the early Carter Presidency was, in fact, crumbling. The shocks of 1979 – Nicaragua, Iran, the 'discovery' of a Soviet 'combat brigade' in Cuba, the Afghanistan invasion, Brzezinski's 'arc of crisis'[27] (stretching from the Horn of Africa to Afghanistan) – caused the Administration to jettison its early world-view. Containment and militarism were rediscovered. In view of this turnabout, it is often presumed that the earlier 'global community' orientation represented only one faction within the Administration, that it was never entirely accepted by leading protagonists, notably Brzezinski. There is some substance to this view. NSC adviser Roger Hansen saw Brzezinski as 'a closet cold warrior from the very outset'. William Odom, Brzezinski's deputy, later recalled how, quite early on, the Administration 'split over whether or not the Soviet Union was a status quo power'. Brzezinski and Odom 'thought it was not', whereas Vance and Leslie Gelb (director of the State Department Bureau of Politico-Military Affairs) saw the USSR – in Odom's words – as 'becoming benign and status quo, and accepting the international order'.[28] Brzezinski made no secret of his worries about the 'post-Vietnam' orientation of the State Department.[29] Even within the State Department, there was considerable opposition to the human rights initiatives. Even in 1977, there were signs of a 'harder' policy existing alongside the 'post-Vietnam' initiatives of retrenchment, human rights and 'preventive diplomacy'. (In 1977, for example, Carter signed Presidential Directive 18, which provided for special military units to be used in Third World conflicts).[30]

The Vance–Brzezinski split will be discussed further in Chapter Seven. That there was such a split is not in question. What is at issue is whether Brzezinski and his associates were ever in sympathy with the early agenda of the Administration at all. Quotations from Brzezinski cited above (and also Jerel Rosati's study, *The Carter Administration's Quest for Global Community*) suggest that he was, although the National Security Adviser was clearly on the 'hard' wing of Trilateralism. The Vance and Brzezinski memoirs gave clear indication of the gulf between the two men, but also (as indicated in Chapter 1) acknowledged a degree of common ground, at least until 1979. Brzezinski was concerned about America 'becoming 'lonely' in the world':

I felt strongly that a major emphasis on human rights . . . would advance America's global interests by demonstrating to the emergent nations of the Third World the reality of our democratic system . . . The best way to answer the Soviet's ideological challenge would be to commit the United States to a concept which most reflected America's very essence.[31]

The emergence of the human rights doctrine

It was the human rights doctrine which provided the glue which, prior to

1979, held together the Administration's foreign policy. The doctrine satisfied a variety of interests and purposes. William Odom, of the National Security Council (NSC) staff, later stated: 'I saw human rights as a brilliant policy. I saw it as the obverse to the Soviet's support of the international class struggle.' For Odom, human rights was 'a very pragmatic tactic', a way 'to really beat up morally on the Soviets'. At the same time it 'offered some basis of a new domestic US foreign policy consensus'.[32]

There was, of course, a significant gulf between the view that here was a good way morally to beat up on the Soviets, and Carter's Inaugural Address promise to make an 'absolute' commitment[33] to human rights. Both Brzezinski and Vance had significant reservations about any such 'absolute' commitment. Yet, although it was undoubtedly interpreted in many different ways, the pursuit of human rights in foreign policy represented the best hope for consensus both in the Administration itself and in domestic opinion generally. As Dan Caldwell notes in his study of the SALT II ratification debate, human rights provided the means whereby Carter was able to 'patch together the fabric of the Democratic party' after it 'had been torn asunder by the Vietnam War'.[34] During the first two years of the Administration at least, otherwise warring factions of the party were able to come together on the basis of the human rights doctrine.

By the time Carter achieved the Democratic nomination in 1976, a well developed lobbying network for the cause of human rights in foreign policy existed, both within and outside Congress. Much of this lobby had a generally left-liberal, 'post-Vietnam' orientation. A shared background in the civil rights and anti-Vietnam war movements gave a strong common feeling to many of the activists, who tended to focus on the activities of the CIA and on US support for rightist dictatorships. A seminal figure in the movement outside Congress was Jacqui Chagnon, a former civil rights and peace activist, who moved in the early 1970s from the organisation Clergy and Laity Concerned to co-ordinate, along with Brewster Rhoads, the Human Rights Working Group of the Coalition for a New Foreign and Military Policy.[35]

Some of these organisations confined their efforts principally to victims of right-wing oppression, notably in South Korea, Latin America, the Philippines and South Africa. In particular, a number of highly effective regional human rights associations sprang up in protest at the burgeoning military authoritarianism in South America. More broad-based organisations, however – notably Amnesty International – did highlight human rights abuses (especially regarding 'political prisoners') in the Soviet Union as well as Latin America, in black as well as in South Africa.

In Congress, the human rights agenda was already well advanced before Carter's name was known outside Georgia. The agenda represented part of the programme of Congressional reassertion which was advanced in the later stages of the Vietnam war. (Indeed, it is possible to argue that part of the

Carter Administration's enthusiasm for human rights derived from a desire to defuse challenges from Congress in this area.) The agenda was promoted particularly in the House of Representatives. It was generally opposed by the Nixon and Ford Administrations, in the name of executive flexibility. It originally drew only limited support in the Senate. Hearings held and reports issued by Donald Fraser's subcommittee of the House International Relations Committee in 1973 and 1974 put the issue of Congressional concern for human rights at the heart of the foreign policy debate. Alongside Fraser, a Democrat from Minnesota, the left-liberal prime mover behind Congressional human rights was Democratic Congressman Tom Harkin of Iowa, who traced his interest in human rights issues to his discovery, in Saigon, of 'tiger cages' for Viet Cong prisoners. Between 1973 and 1976, Congress moved to establish a human rights office in the State Department and to subject various aid programmes to human rights tests.[36]

The Congressional coalition which backed human rights measures was not, however, confined to the left wing of the Democratic party. It regularly included, for example, inveterate opponents of *all* foreign aid. It also included those right-wing Democrats, like Senator Henry Jackson of Washington, who sought to turn the human rights crusade against the Soviet Union. In 1973 and 1974 perhaps the most visible human rights crusade of all on Capitol Hill involved the Jackson–Vanik amendment, which made the granting of 'most-favoured-nation' trading status to the USSR contingent upon Soviet liberalisation of restrictions on Jewish emigration.[37]

Carter in 1975 opposed the Jackson-Vanik amendment, pronouncing it 'ill-advised' and suggesting that the US would react 'adversely' if the Soviets attempted to interfere in American domestic affairs. By late September 1976, however, Carter was praising the amendment as a measure protecting human rights.[38] As the 1976 convention approached, the Carter team began to appreciate the potential which the whole human rights issue presented for party consensus-building. At the platform-drafting meetings, Stuart Eizenstat found that human rights was just about the only issue on which the various party factions could agree. Senator Daniel Patrick Moynihan, widely identified with the Henry Jackson wing, later recalled a remark he made at this time to Sam Brown, former anti-Vietnam War campaigner and representative of the Democratic party left: 'We'll be against the dictators you don't like the most . . . if you'll be against the dictators we don't like the most.' The result, according to Moynihan, was 'the strongest platform commitment to human rights in our history'.[39]

Up to the convention, Carter had not placed emphasis on human rights issues in foreign affairs. After the convention, however, Cadell, Eizenstat and Powell all urged that it should be taken up vigorously. An address to B'Nai B'Rith on 8 September, as well as the October 1976 Notre Dame speech, gave prominence to the new theme. During these months, and notably during the second televised debate with Gerald Ford, it was, in fact, the conservative side of human rights which tended to be prioritised. Ford's extraordinary denial of Soviet influence in Eastern Europe and his apparent rebuff to the Soviet dissident Alexander Solzhenitsyn created opportunities for Carter. Advised by Cadell that human rights was now 'a very strong issue across the board', Carter switched from condemning the 1975 Helsinki agreement as a ratification of 'the Russian takeover of Eastern Europe'.[40] He now assailed the Soviets for not adhering to the 1976 Helsinki ('Basket Three') human rights requirements and President Ford for not pursuing them.

Throughout the Carter Presidency, White House advisers frequently remarked upon the consensual advantages to be gained from emphasising human rights. In December 1977, Hamilton Jordan wrote to Carter:

I agree with Zbig that we need to be more visible and active on the human rights issues. Of our numerous foreign policy initiatives, it is the only one that has a broad base of support among the American people and is not considered 'liberal'. With Panama and SALT II ahead of us, we need the broad-based, non-ideological support for our foreign policy that human rights provides.[41]

A 1978 memorandum from Brzezinski and Anne Wexler similarly invoked SALT. It held that a 'White House event on human rights' would be 'particularly valuable to offset the emphasis that will be placed on SALT'.[42] Late in the Administration, White House personnel Steve Aiello, Al Moses and Bernie Aronson urged that the human rights momentum should be maintained. They pointed to its appeal to ethnic groups and to influential sectors in the Democratic party:

To groups like the Poles, Ukrainians . . . and others human rights is the single most important political issue in the field of foreign policy . . . The issue is of major importance to groups like the Coalition For a Democratic Majority in the Jackson–Moynihan wing of the party.[43]

Human rights also appealed to Carter's desire to restore 'true' American values, and to his most fundamental religious beliefs. Jody Powell declared that the Carter team's attitude was summed up by the reflection: 'If we can't be for that, what the hell can we be for?' An Administration official described Carter's commitment to journalist Elizabeth Drew in 1977 (concentrating, interestingly, on the anti-Soviet side):

The human-rights issue helps him with the Jews if he has to bring pressure on Israel; it helps him with the right; it helps him in the South; it helps him with the Baptists. And he also happens to believe in it. And he won't be deterred.[44]

Having made its commitment to human rights, the Administration then had to decide upon a working definition of the concept. The term, 'political prisoner' had already been abandoned for legislative purposes as too inexact. The most convenient Congressional definition was that contained in the 1974 Foreign Assistance Act. Aid should not be extended, declared the Act, to countries with 'consistent pattern(s) of gross violations' of 'internationally recognised human rights' involving: 'torture or cruel, inhuman, or degrading treatment or punishment; prolonged detention without charges; or other flagrant denials of the right to life, liberty and the security of the person.'[45] The Administration was to find this definition useful in conducting its relations with other countries, judging their records on a 'case-by-case' basis.[46] The 1974 definition raised more questions than it answered, however. As White House staffer Lynn Daft informed Eizenstat in 1977:

The trick, of course, is in defining a . . . 'consistent pattern of gross violations of human rights' and, once defined and the countries identified, figuring out a way to deal with the 'hit list' diplomatically and constructively.[47]

Carter himself found the 1974 definition too narrow. In April 1977, Secretary Vance offered a three-part definition in a speech at the University of Georgia Law School: the right to 'integrity of the person' (especially regarding torture and arbitrary detention); the 'right to fulfilment of such vital needs as food, shelter, health care and education'; and 'civil and political liberties' (especially in relation to voting and free speech and travel). The extent to which 'human rights' should include economic rights – the right, in the words of NSC staffer Jessica Tuchman, to '800 calories a day' – became a matter of public dispute with the Administration.[48] Carter made numerous public statements to the effect that his commitment to human rights included a commitment to economic rights, although his definition conspicuously did not include the 'right to work'. Speaking to the UN General Assembly in December 1978, Andrew Young identified poverty as 'the basic obstacle to the realisation of human rights for most people'.[49] A State Department official interviewed by Elizabeth Drew argued that it would be a 'moral obscenity' to let a 'child starve because its parents' government is abusing human rights'. Another official put it less obliquely: 'Including economic rights allows us to support aid to repressive regimes'.[50] This, of course, was part of the problem with economic rights. 'Social and economic rights' have frequently been championed in international fora precisely by nations with poor records on 'integrity of the person' and 'civil and political liberties'. Further problems were indicated in the following description of NSC deliberations on the issue (described by a participant interviewed by Drew):

We came out that some things are obvious and there is a lot of gray area, that you have to work in the gray area, but you need flexibility. It's pretty easy to say torture, political imprisonment, arbitrary murder violate human rights. Beyond that, you start getting into important political areas. Some say it begins at breakfast, it's having jobs. Then you get into arguments about trade-offs: liberty versus having a job . . . Even if you could establish a natural law of human rights – and there *is* a bit of natural law – thee are other considerations of value to us: a country whose security is at issue.[51]

Besides the three-fold definition given by Vance, the Administration made several stabs at definition. In December 1978, for example, the President told

a meeting of civil and human rights leaders that 'the most basic' right was: 'to
be free of arbitrary violence – whether that violence comes from governments, from terrorists, from criminals, or from self-appointed messiahs
operating under the cover of politics or religion.'[52]

Important definitional appeals were also made to arguments centring on
different levels of economic and political development, and to international
law. The Administration was extremely anxious to avoid the charge that it
was seeking to impose one, 'parochial' form of democracy and liberty. It
declared itself sensitive to the 'stage of a nation's . . . development'. (This
raised the charge that the Administration was attempting to turn 'absolute'
rights into 'relative' ones.)[53] The main defence against parochialism, however, was that Vance's definition of human rights essentially corresponded to
that given in the Universal Declaration of Human Rights, approved by the
UN in 1948. Patricia Derian, State Department spokesperson on human
rights, testified in 1978 that international law was 'our guide to the definition
of human rights'.[54] During his Presidency, Jimmy Carter attempted to gain
Senate ratification of five major human rights treaties: two covenants (on civil
and political, and on economic, social and cultural rights) to the Universal
Declaration; the International Convention on the Elimination of All Forms of
Racial Discrimination; the Convention on the Prevention and Punishment of
the Crime of Genocide; and the American Convention on Human Rights.[55]

The Senate failed to act on the treaties, seeing them as potentially infringing
the authority of Congress. The Administration increasingly, and wisely, saw
the virtue of appealing to international law: to the 1975 Helsinki Final Act,
as well as to the (non-binding) Universal Declaration. However, international law is not only notoriously difficult to enforce but also contains
numerous nods in the direction of 'self-determination'. For example, Article
I of both the covenants declared that 'all peoples have the right to self-
determination'.[56] Invocation under international law, of 'natural' human
rights tends to invite the counter-invocation of 'self-determination'. (For
Woodrow Wilson, often regarded as Carter's principal forebear in foreign
policy, 'self-determination' was the bedrock of world order. The Wilsonian
tradition tended to assume that self-determination would itself ensure the
protection of individual liberties.) Beyond questions of international law and
self-determination, the Carter Administration had also to contend with the
belief, increasingly embraced by Brzezinski, that perhaps anti-communist
policies represented the best way of promoting human rights.[57]

As we have seen, Carter's human rights initiative found significant
difficulty even in leaving the definitional starting-stalls. Effective and even-
handed operationalisation of what was consistently sold as a 'global' policy[58]
proved even trickier. A general assessment of this operationalisation will be
given in Chapter 7. By way of illustration, however, we will now look at,
firstly, the most obvious arena of all: policy towards the Soviet Union.

Human rights and Soviet policy

According to Jessica Tuchman of the NSC staff, the human rights policy's 'bottom line' involved judgements as to its 'seriousness vis-a-vis the Soviet Union'.[59] Intended to underpin a new foreign policy consensus at home, human rights had to be seen to affect the Administration's relations with dictatorships of both left and right. The main problem, from Carter's viewpoint, was the possibility that human rights activism might damage detente in general, and arms control in particular.

Despite having criticised Gerald Ford and Kissinger for having yielded too much to the Soviets in the name of detente, President Carter soon moved to declare his support for the concept. Detente, said Carter, meant 'progress towards peace'.[60] For the new President, it was a dynamic state: not merely an open-ended commitment to superpower co-existence but an emblem of progressive change, including improvements in human rights practices. Carter looked forward to an extension of the 1975 Helsinki Final Act, especially its 'Basket Three' provisions on human rights. As Patricia Derian later remarked, the Helsinki agreement, though it had no legal sanction, had 'assumed a life of its own'.[61] Monitoring groups had been set up in Eastern Europe and the Soviet Union, and human rights activists encouraged. The new Administration looked to future meetings of the Conference on Security and Cooperation in Europe (CSCE) – these eventually took place at Belgrade in 1977–8 and in Madrid in 1980 – to build upon the Helsinki advances.

The human rights orientation of the new Administration made it certain that detente would not proceed in the Nixon–Kissinger–Ford mould. The Carter Administration wished to preserve detente. For some of its members, notably Cyrus Vance, arms control, within the general context of detente, was the major priority. Yet the new regime did not immediately install relations with the Soviet Union, and the preservation of detente, at the centre of its concerns. Its whole Trilateralist, global community outlook militated against any such tendency.[62] Moreover, where President Nixon had asserted in 1970 that the Soviet 'internal order' was 'not an object of our policy',[63] the Carter Administration – if its human rights policy was to gain credibility – had precisely to concern itself with 'internal' Soviet affairs.

A possible solution to this problem, of how to pursue human rights policies without destroying detente and arms control, lay in the rejection of linkage. At an early press conference, in February 1977, Carter reflected:

I think we come out better in dealing with the Soviet Union if I am consistently and completely dedicated to the enhancement of human rights, not only as it deals with the Soviet Union but all other countries. I think this can legitimately be severed from our inclination to work with the Soviet Union, for instance, in reducing dependence upon atomic weapons and also in seeking mutual and balanced force reductions in Europe.

I don't want the two to be tied together. I think the previous administration, under Secretary Kissinger, thought there ought to be this linkage . . .[64]

Carter held that the competitive and cooperative sides of the US-Soviet relationship could be managed simultaneously, but separately. This assertion not only put him in opposition to the Kissinger version of linkage, which stressed the American ability to provide trade and other incentives in order to promote a restraint on Soviet expansionism. It also put him at odds with the so-called 'high pressure' linkage which underpinned the Jackson–Vanik amendment on Soviet Jewish emigration. Though divided on the issue and largely ineffectual in Congress, the Carter Administration, in the name of rejecting linkage and preserving detente, made the difficult decision to push for trade evenhandedness and 'most-favoured-nation' status for the Soviet Union.[65]

For the rejection of linkage to succeed, a degree of Soviet co-operation was essential. In February 1977, Jody Powell gave his opinion to the President as follows:

It seems to me that the Soviets should understand your feeling that it is necessary to build domestic political support for initiatives in arms control and for detente in general. One of the reasons Ford–Kissinger failed in this effort and had to back away from detente was because the American people would not support a policy which seemed to abandon our position in support of human rights.

The Soviets, continued Powell, must understand that the future of detente depended upon the securing of a domestic consensus in the United States. Arms control, and certainly the ratification of any SALT treaty, would depend upon the conciliation of the Henry Jackson–D. P. Moynihan wing of the Democratic party: 'Surely the Soviets are sophisticated enough to understand that the domestic political flexibility we need to make progress in other areas is enhanced by your position on human rights.' Powell suggested that Carter should attempt to convey this message to Soviet Ambassador Dobrynin on a personal basis.[66] The separate pursuit of human rights and of arms control was to prove a difficult course to defend. To many anti-Soviet Democrats it smacked of cynicism. Equally worrying for the Administration were the emerging signs that the Soviets were, in fact, not willing to play along.

The Soviet leadership had initially welcomed the 1975 Helsinki accords, which in effect recognised Eastern Europe as a legitimate Soviet sphere. By 1977, however, Moscow had become alarmed at the growth of dissident opinion in the wake of the Helsinki 'Basket Three' provisions. A new hardness towards dissident intellectuals had, in fact, been evident since the early 1970s. The Sociology Department of Moscow University had been purged in 1972, and a campaign against dissident physicist Andrei Sakharov stepped up in 1973 (two years prior to Sakharov's winning of the Nobel Peace Prize). By the time of Carter's inauguration, a clear decision appears to have been taken to resist any further movement in the CSCE process towards human rights concerns. The policy of allowing oppositional intellectuals to go to the US or Western Europe also was halted, with clear attempts being made to break the lines of communication between domestic dissidents and Western supporters. Above all, a general clampdown on dissident and Helsinki monitoring groups, both in the USSR and Eastern Europe, appeared imminent.[67]

The Carter Administration's position towards human rights issues in the Soviet Union was clearly signalled in the wake of the 1976 election and in the early months of 1977: in, for example, correspondence with the dissident Vladimir Slepak; in the December 1976 reception by Cyrus Vance of the exiled Andrei Amalrik and the early 1977 receiving of Vladimir Bukovsky at the White House; and in State Department protest in February 1977 at the arrests of Aleksandr Ginzburg and of the leader of the Moscow Helsinki Watch Committee, Yuri Orlov. Carter also attempted to revive Radio Free Europe, Radio Liberty and Voice of America as agencies of human rights causes, rather than as CIA-oriented propaganda. Immediately before his arrest, Orlov had praised the White House stance on human rights and declared that the protest at Ginzburg's detention made his own arrest less likely. By May, only four members of the Moscow Helsinki monitoring group remained at liberty. Similar incarcerations occurred in Kiev and Tbilisi. It appeared as if the Soviet leadership was conveying a message to Washington that increased encouragement to dissidence would only stimulate more repression. Yet strong support for the President's stance came from Andrei Sakharov, the best-known Soviet dissident, whose international stature offered at least some protection from the threat of immediate arrest. Interviewed on CBS television on 10 February, Sakharov denied that the new Administration's policy was actually making matters worse:

I have neither the right nor the opportunity to give advice to the new Administration about how it should act . . . I can only permit myself to say that any disagreement, partial uncertainty, or partial retreat will give the Soviet authorities the impression that the new Administration is giving in to blackmail and pressure.

In an ABC television interview on 25 March, Sakharov answered 'Categorically – no!' to the question as to whether Carter's policy had led to greater repression. Repressions, according to Sakharov, were 'our daily life', endemic to the Soviet system.[68]

Sakharov had sent telegrams and letters to Carter both before and after the election. Initially, the response from the White House was slightly equivocal. The State Department delivered a muddled response to Sakharov's temporary detention at the Moscow Procuracy in January. (The physicist, though a consistent admirer of Carter's policy, was later to criticise this lapse and also to describe as 'regrettable' a Presidential tendency to 'back away' in some crucial cases.) However, on 17 February, Sakharov received a strong, written affirmation of support from the President. Meanwhile, the arrests continued. On 5 March, the Soviet press reported charges made by a former dissident,

Sanya Lipavsky, that six prominent Jewish dissidents had worked, or were working, for the CIA. The six included Ginzburg, and also Anatoly Shcharansky, who was arrested two days later. The accelerating repression, along with Soviet rejection of Vance's SALT 'deep cuts' proposal, augured poorly for developing superpower relations.[69]

According to Brzezinski, Carter did take Powell's advice and make 'private efforts to reassure' both Ambassador Dobrynin and Soviet leader Brezhnev that he was not launching an anti-Soviet crusade. Yet Carter's letter to Sakharov had, in Brzezinski's phrase, 'clearly touched a raw nerve'. On 28 February, Carter received a reply to a letter he had written to Brezhnev. Carter's letter had raised human rights issues, but in a context intended to be generally reassuring. Brezhnev now condemned 'interference in our internal affairs', bolstered by 'pseudo-humanitarian slogans'.[70] Implacable Soviet hostility to Carter's human rights interventions continued throughout the Presidency. In mid-June 1978, for example, an article appeared in all Soviet newspapers attacking the President's denunciation of the Russian human rights record in his Annapolis speech of 7 June. Behind 'seemingly nice-sounding' remarks, the Soviets detected a familiar scent: 'We have here the self-same designs to undermine the socialist system that our people have had to encounter in this or that form since 1917.'[71] Cyrus Vance later wrote that the Soviet leadership really did feel that 'our human rights efforts were aimed at overthrowing their system', and that US behaviour was unpredictable.[72]

Encouraged by Sakharov, Carter continued to condemn Soviet human rights violations. He denied that any of the arrested Jewish dissidents had ever worked for the CIA, although it did emerge from a State Department leak that Lipavsky had done so. The President resolved, against the advice of some anti-Soviet critics,[73] to continue with the CSCE process at Belgrade.

Carter's stance was undermined to some extent by his manifest failure to influence events in the Soviet Union. It was also harmed by indications that not all members of the Administration shared the President's commitment. Marshall Shulman, Vance's chief adviser on Soviet affairs, was sceptical about applying the human rights policy to the USSR. The Secretary of State himself was anxious about any threat to arms control. In June 1977, Joyce Starr of the NSC staff complained to Robert Lipshutz and Stuart Eizenstat about an interview given by Andrew Young to *Playboy* magazine. According to Starr, the UN Ambassador had, in effect, said that 'no more . . . can be done for the Soviet dissidents'. They were simply 'a literary elite who have tasted a little freedom . . .'.[74] A year later, various White House foreign policy staff complained about the lukewarm attitude displayed by the US Ambassador in Moscow, Malcolm Toon, and his staff. Starr and Cliff Brody wrote in June 1978:

while the Secretary of State and the President were both confirming publicly and privately our general commitment to human rights and the Helsinki Agreement, our diplomats were not providing official explanations (demarches) of precise expectations. To the extent that individual cases were discussed, prior to Belgrade and thereafter, they have either been left for the President or Secretary to raise or have been taken up on the fringes of non-related discussions.[75]

Joe Aragon in the following month raised the question of whether the human rights policy was 'supported by any tangible evidence of concern at the embassy level'.[76] Toon, who had been retained as Ambassador from the Ford years, made no bones about his scepticism about the human rights policy. His private views encompassed opposition to SALT II. In public, he argued that the Soviet regime simply did not accept 'ideas of free expression and of free individual choice'. The best way to minimise domestic repression was to preserve detente. With detente destroyed, the Soviet authorities would be 'even less concerned about world public opinion'.[77]

Between March 1977 and June 1978 various arguments – from Sakharov's calls for greater human rights activism to the view that detente should be protected above all – vied to influence Presidential policy on the USSR. A major review of the global power structure (Presidential Review Memorandum 10) concluded that the Soviets had fundamental economic vulnerabilities, with the long-term outlook favouring the US.[78] Carter was also advised that arms control was essential. Defence Secretary Harold Brown informed Brzezinski in March 1978 that the Soviets had 'been building up their forces steadily for fifteen to twenty years'. The US needed to pursue both 'equitable and verifiable arms control' *and* strategic and conventional force modernisation.[79]

Carter's Annapolis speech of June 1978 appeared to signal a newly tough line. It was unequivocal on the human rights issue. (The Soviet rejection of US Ambassador Arthur Goldberg's human rights arguments at the recent Belgrade CSCE meeting had made the position clear.) The Annapolis speech also noticeably lacked the conciliatory passages which had been, formulaic in previous statements. The London *Times* interpreted the speech as having moved the US from 'watchful conciliation' to 'wakeful balance'. To some degree, the speech embodied the Administration's response to charges that it had been wrong in continuing with the Belgrade CSCE process after the dissident arrests. *Pravda* blamed Brzezinski's ascendancy for the new toughness.[80] (For his part, Vance, in a 20 June speech in Atlantic City, continued to sound a more conciliatory tone.) The National Security Adviser, opposed by the Secretary of State, now urged Carter to play 'the China card'. Brzezinski saw the normalisation of relations with mainland China as the best way to exploit the Soviet vulnerability outlined in Presidential Review Memorandum 10.[81]

Against this background, in July 1978, the Soviets instituted a series of dissident trials. At first, the US attempted to influence the trials' outcomes by hints that linkage might be revived. Hodding Carter of the State Department declared that the outcomes would 'be an important indication of the Russian attitude on the eve of the SALT talks'.[82] In fact, as an Amnesty International report later documented, there is no case in Soviet history of anyone charged with political or religious offences being acquitted. Between 1975 and 1980, over four hundred people were tried and sentenced in this way.[83] In July 1978, Ginzburg, Victoras Pektus and Shcharansky were all duly found guilty, the latter being sentenced to fourteen years' imprisonment. (He was actually released in 1986.)

Carter condemned the trials as an 'attack on every human being in the world who believes in basic human freedoms'.[84] An offer to exchange Shcharansky for Soviet spies detained in the US was turned down. Ida Milgrom, Shcharansky's mother, wrote the President an open letter, praising his support for her son:

All the difficult days of the trial, I have been standing in front of the iron barriers, in front of a thick wall of KGB men and militiamen . . . All these days I have heard your sincere, authoritative voice in defence of innocent men.[85]

For the first time since the inception of detente under President Nixon, an American Administration now applied economic sanctions to the USSR. Restrictions on the export of gas and oil technology were imposed, scientific exchanges suspended and a computer shipment cancelled. (This action was undermined to some degree by the commencement, by Dresser Industries, of a $141 million drill-bit factory in the USSR.)[86] Once again, the Soviet leaders condemned Carter's interventions as attempts to undermine their system, and simultaneously conveyed their outrage at what they directly referred to as the playing of 'the China card'.

The period between the dissident trials (July 1978) and the end of 1979 was dominated by SALT. The trials stimulated calls, notably on the Henry Jackson wing of the Democratic party, that arms control be abandoned. Representative Samuel S. Stratton (Democrat: New York) insisted that to 'go and sit down and debate SALT' would 'under these conditions of humiliation' make the US look 'weak and grovelling'.[87] It was soon made clear, however, that SALT would continue. Vance met Soviet Foreign Minister Gromyko in Geneva as planned. On 21 July 1978, Carter announced that no further reprisals against the Soviet Union would take place: 'I have not embarked on a vendetta . . . I know that we cannot interfere with the internal affairs of the Soviet Union.'[88] Throughout the SALT negotiations, both sides conscientiously avoided mentioning dissident and human rights affairs. Strobe Talbott relates the story of one American diplomat, newly arrived in Geneva, who raised the Shcharansky case in private conversation with his Soviet counterpart. After reporting this in a 'memcon' to Washington, the diplomat was rebuked and told never again to amalgamate SALT business with human rights.[89]

Between July 1978 and the Soviet invasion of Afghanistan in December 1979, human rights issues impinged on the US–Soviet relationship chiefly in the form of some high-level defections and prisoner exchanges, and in connection with the prospects for SALT ratification.

During the period of the 'high' Cold War, defections from the Soviet Union were occasions of celebration for American leaders. Under the diplomacy of detente, however, they became occasions as much for embarrassment as for propaganda coups. Gerald Ford's coolness towards Alexander Solzhenitsyn, who had been deported to the West in 1974, revealed the new concern for the intricate dynamics of detente. Deputy Secretary of State Warren Christopher declared in 1979:

For us in the United States, these requests for refuge may create temporary abrasions and difficulties. But they are a tribute to our way of life – and to the values we represent in the world. They are also a recurrent challenge to our support for human rights.[90]

During the Carter years, the most important political defection was that of Arkady Shevchenko, who in April 1978 became the highest-ranking Soviet diplomat ever to seek asylum in the US. In June 1978, seven persecuted Pentecostalists – the 'Siberian seven' – forced their way into the US Embassy, remaining there for five years. In March 1979, a Ukrainian seaman, Yuri Vlasenko, entered the Embassy with a US consular officer. Vlasenko was denied asylum. When Vlasenko threatened to ignite an explosive device strapped to his wrist, Soviet police were brought in by Ambassador Toon. The seaman was killed in an explosion and Toon's conduct severely criticised by leading Soviet dissidents. In April 1979, the US arranged a prisoner exchange, with Aleksandr Ginzburg and Georgiy Vins (a leading Baptist dissident) being flown to New York. (Carter described this exchange in his diary as 'one of the most significant things in a human way that we've done . . .'.)[91] A more difficult situation arose in August, shortly before the near-farcical 'discovery' of a Soviet brigade in Cuba. Alexander Godunov, a Bolshoi ballet dancer, defected during an American tour. A plane carrying his wife, ballerina Ludmila Vlasova, was denied permission to leave New York's JFK airport. It was allowed to depart four days late, after State Department officers were convinced that the ballerina actually did wish to return to the Soviet Union.[92]

American protests at Soviet human rights violations did continue during 1979. At the Vienna summit, Carter appealed directly to Brezhnev for the release of Shcharansky. The Soviet leader pointedly noted, on signing the SALT treaty, that arms control touched on 'the most sacred right of any individual – the right to live'.[93] American officials also drew attention to the fact that ratification of the treaty was in the hands of people who certainly would take account of the Soviet human rights record: the US Senate. Immediately prior to the Vienna meeting, Carter warned Brezhnev that human rights violations, along with Soviet involvements in Africa, were bound to harm the prospects for ratification.[94]

Detailed discussion of the deterioration in US–Soviet relations in late 1979 and 1980 is beyond the scope of the current discussion of human rights policies. However, it is reasonable to suggest that Administration perceptions of Soviet behaviour in this period were, at least to some degree, shaped by Carter's failure to make progress on the human rights front. In retrospect, President Carter's reaction to the Soviet brigade in Cuba and (less obviously) to the Afghan invasion appears exaggerated. The Soviet brigade incident was part intelligence failure, part political overreaction.[95] The Afghanistan invasion was a potentially serious departure from the expectations of detente. Carter explained to a group of non-Washington newspaper editors in January 1980 that this was more serious than the 1968 invasion of Czechoslovakia. Afghanistan was 'an independent country'. Pakistan was threatened as was '90 per cent of exportable oil supplies in the world'.[96] Brzezinski was now clearly in the ascendant, SALT ratification was abandoned, the way to a US–Chinese defence relationship was opened and the Carter Doctrine (promising US military protection to the Persian Gulf) promulgated.

Certainly, as Carter later stated, the invasion of Afghanistan was regarded by the White House as a 'launching pad to go directly to the Persian Gulf'.[97] With hindsight, however, the Soviet invasion seems to have been motivated by more local and defensive motives: notably the containment of Islamic fundamentalism, both inside and outside the territorial Soviet Union. It is difficult not to agree with Senator Kennedy's remarks on Carter's response to the invasion:

is this really the gravest threat to peace since World War II? Is it a graver threat than the Berlin blockade, the Korean War, the Soviet march into Hungary and Czechoslovakia, the Berlin Wall, the Cuban Missile Crisis, or Vietnam?

Kennedy pointed out that Moscow had installed a puppet regime in Kabul in 1978 and were intervening openly only when it was threatened.[98] On 2 January, 1980, Hedley Donovan warned Carter that his reaction to the invasion was unwise. The US could not 'do much of anything' there anyway.[99] In April, Donovan reported an assurance from Leonid Zamyatin, a Soviet foreign informant who clearly enjoyed Donovan's confidence, that there was no intention of launching an attack on the Gulf. Donovan's clear implication was that the invasion did not constitute sufficient grounds upon which to base an American termination of detente.[100]

By this time in 1980, Carter's attitude towards the Soviet Union had undergone a paradigm shift from the 'global community' outlook of 1977. The reception of Brezhnev's letter in February 1977 had dented but not destroyed his early optimism. The dissident trials of July 1978 confirmed an already emerging view that, as Sakharov testified, repression was endemic to the Soviet system. This did not mean that Western protest was pointless or counterproductive. Sakharov's own apparent immunity from arrest vindicated the publicity given to human rights by the Carter Administration. But it did mean that the Soviet leadership was almost entirely uncomprehending of the values that underpinned Carter's own political and religious belief system. With the invasion of Afghanistan, Carter came to the view that his early optimism was naive. The Soviet regime was not only morally bankrupt, it was expansionist as well. In late 1979, as NSC staffer Madeleine Albright said, it seemed that the 'real world' had fallen in on the President. For a time, Albright and other NSC staffers 'didn't know how he would come down'.[101] Deeply affected by his experience of the Soviet record on human rights, the President jumped clearly in the direction of Brzezinski.

The Administration did not entirely abandon human rights for *realpolitik* in 1980. Secretary of State Muskie even attempted to revive human rights in preparatory meetings for the CSCE meeting in Madrid, which began in November 1980. In October, he identified the Soviet Union as one of the 'dark corners' of the world 'where Helsinki obligations are ignored'. He promised that the 'United States will make clear in Madrid that we are serious about human rights'.[102] By this time, however, Sakharov had been sent into internal exile. The collapse of detente had indeed, as Ambassador Toon foresaw in July 1979, removed any remaining inhibitions on Soviet behaviour. At Madrid, the Soviet representatives simply countered American accusations by citing human rights abuses in the United States: notably regarding the treatment of blacks (as in the Wilmington Ten case) and native American Indians.[103]

What verdict should be pronounced on what Jessica Tuchman called the 'bottom line' of Carter's human rights policy – policy towards the USSR? General criticisms of the human rights initiative will be considered in Chapter 7. On the narrower issue of Soviet human rights policy, however, it is often argued that (in the words of Strobe Talbott) it was 'little more than a combination of symbolic gestures',[104] which achieved little. Against this view one may cite Carter's view that some improvements – notably over Soviet Jewish emigration – were achieved, and also some evidence in the literature that the Soviet leadership was not entirely impervious to Carter's interventions.[105] It cannot be pretended, however, that such evidence is strong. The dissident movement itself, already buoyed up by the Helsinki agreements, does seem to have gained inspiration from Carter's policy. Most dissidents appeared to favour strong Presidential activism, despite possible dangers. Carter became a hero to some Soviet citizens. In 1979, a Moscow cab driver was reprimanded for displaying a portrait of the President in his taxi. In December 1978, a group of dissidents congratulated Carter for supporting human liberty 'in a world becoming wrapped in lies'.[106]

From a post-Cold War perspective, here is the fundamental justification for Carter's stance. He was at least speaking out clearly for fundamental, human and democratic values. The policy was sometimes confused. Andrew Young's remark about political prisoners in the US, made at the time of the dissident trials, was deeply embarrassing and poorly judged. Carter also never found a truly effective way of communicating with Moscow. The policy was arguably too narrow in focus, concentrating as it did on particular high-profile individuals. Yet it did put the US clearly behind the kinds of values in which the Soviet regime was so manifestly deficient. Moreover, the policy did not – as allied leaders like Helmut Schmidt of West Germany told Carter it would – immediately destroy detente. An arms control agreement, after all, *was* signed and collapsed only in the wake of the Afghanistan invasion. In addition, Carter's policy, at least initially, went a long way towards achieving consensus. It should not be forgotten that Carter's 1977 and early 1978 interventions were supported by a coalition which stretched from Senator Edward Kennedy to Senator Barry Goldwater.

Human rights activists in the Carter Administration repeatedly asserted that every country was unique. Human rights policies had to be global, but they also had to be developed on a pragmatic case-by-case basis. Every instance was unique, but it may also be observed that the Soviet Union, as America's only superpower rival, was exceptionally exceptional. In reviewing the policy, it is now the intention to turn to a far more obscure, and – by comparison with the Soviet example – scarcely noticed area: policy towards the conflict in Northern Ireland. Precisely because of its relative marginality, Northern Ireland constitutes a more 'typical' case and well illustrates the complexities involved in operationalising a global policy of human rights.

Northern Ireland

Conditions in Northern Ireland in the late 1970s appeared to offer the possibility of fashioning a new American policy towards the province, based on human rights considerations. Two aspects of Cyrus Vance's April 1977 Georgia Law School attempt to define the policy appeared particularly apposite. Firstly, there was the question of 'civil and political liberties', notably anti-Catholic employment discrimination. Secondly, and operationally more crucially, the situation raised 'integrity of the person' issues. Improvements had been made by the time Carter entered the White House. Internment – 'prolonged detention without trial', to use the phrase employed in the 1974 Foreign Assistance Act – had been phased out by December 1975. Plastic bullets had replaced rubber. 'Interrogation in depth' (condemned as 'torture' by the European Commission on Human Rights in 1976) had been officially abandoned. Yet the juryless Diplock courts were operating. 'Special category' status, given since 1972 to convicted members of the paramilitaries, was removed in 1976, stimulating the 'blanket' and 'dirty' protests. The 1979 Bennett report into police investigations produced evidence of abuses. Especially influential with American opinion was the report, alleging mistreatment of suspects by the authorities, issued in 1978 by Amnesty International.[107]

Whatever the objective truth concerning British and Royal Ulster Constabulary (RUC) behaviour, there was no easy or obvious course for the Carter Administration to follow. On the one hand, there was the alliance with Britain; on the other, the certainty among sections of Irish-American opinion that British (and especially British army) presence in Northern Ireland itself constituted a violation of human rights. US media reporting of, for example, the Bennett and Amnesty report combined with Carter's high profile on human rights to cause problems for the Administration. Correspondence in the Carter archive illustrates some of these difficulties.

In February 1977, F. B. O'Brien, Washington Director of the Irish National Caucus (INC), wrote to National Security Adviser Zbigniew Brzezinski, advocating that Carter should raise human rights concerns during upcoming talks with Prime Minister James Callaghan: 'British patterns of torture do not seem to change much over the centuries; one need only travel to Charleston, South Carolina and view where the British tortured Americans in their own wine cellars.'[108] The INC was, certainly until 1978, fairly close to the Irish Northern Aid Committee (NORAID), the Provisional IRA's main American fund-raiser. However, protest was not confined to unabashed IRA apologists. The human rights issue was raised, for example, in a 1977 telegram from Paul O'Dwyer, civil rights lawyer and President of New York City council. More extreme was a letter from Thomas Flynn, press officer of the National Council of Irish Americans: 'You support in Ulster the same kind of oppression you fight in South Africa . . .'.[109]

These themes were taken up by Members of Congress sympathetic to Irish-American causes. House Judiciary Committee members Hamilton Fish and Joshua Eilberg visited Belfast in 1978 and addressed Carter on their return:

We admit that it is extremely difficult for the United States to be critical of the British actions in Northern Ireland because of our traditional ally relationships with the United Kingdom. But nonetheless, we submit that the people of Northern Ireland have the same rights as the peoples of the world to call for the protection of . . . human rights . . .[110]

In January 1979, Congressman Mario Biaggi (New York Democrat and organiser of the Congressional Ad Hoc Committee on Irish Affairs) complained to Carter about State Department 'gobbledegook', which boiled 'down to the fact that – when it comes to Northern Ireland – human rights – is an expendable consideration'. Other frequently voiced complaints related to the co-operation extended to British anti-IRA operations within the United States, and the supposed role played by US loans in subsidising British policy in Northern Ireland.[111]

White House and State Department fielding of these criticisms generally involved questioning the propriety of direct American involvement. In May 1977, President Carter himself replied to a request from Congressman Joseph

Addabo to use his forthcoming trip to Britain to promote a 'comprehensive bill of rights for Northern Ireland'. Carter responded:

You may be sure that the British Government is fully aware of my deep, personal commitment to the cause of human rights everywhere – including Northern Ireland . . . I hesitate to become involved in arguing the merits of one proposal over another.[112]

In December 1978, D. J. Bennet, Assistant State Department Secretary for Congressional Relations, told Hamilton Fish that American advice might 'likely be construed as US interference by the principal parties involved . . .'. In June 1979, Bennet refused to support a Congressional resolution criticising Britain's human rights record and calling for a new initiative. He told Clement Zablocki (chairman of the House Committee on International Relations):

The Department believes that H. Con. Res. 122 would be construed as interference by one or more of the parties and governments involved in Northern Ireland . . . the resolution if adopted could be interpreted as taking one side in the communal differences in Northern Ireland and would therefore be contrary to the principle of impartiality which is one of the cornerstones of our policy.[113]

State Department spokesmen also regularly denied that US loans were in any sense subsidising British activities in Northern Ireland, and referred complainees to the brief (and mild) references to the British record contained in the annual Department country reports on human rights. A somewhat different, more pragmatic, note was sounded in State's reply to Thomas Flynn's earlier quoted complaint. Responding to Flynn's suggestion that trade links to Britain should be severed as a human rights protest, the Department's spokesman noted:

When we are dealing with a serious and persistent pattern of violations of human rights, and when other efforts to obtain improvement have been unsuccessful we could consider using trade instruments . . . Even then, we would weigh the benefits which might be achieved against the costs involved in terms of US employment and the balance of payments.[114]

Administration protestations of unwillingness to 'interfere' in Northern Ireland were, at least to some extent, disingenuous. Although its policy disappointed many Irish-Americans, the Carter Administration did, in effect, establish a legitimating precedent for US Presidential involvement in Northern Ireland affairs. This principle was established in direct opposition to the wishes of the British Foreign Office, and was to be further expanded by the Reagan Administration.[115]

Hopes of an end to traditional White House caution on Northern Ireland were raised, to a very limited degree, during the Nixon and Ford years.[116] However, they were ignited during Carter's 1976 Presidential campaign. Candidate Carter cautiously approached the Irish issue in a September address to a Jewish audience: 'Denials of human rights occur in many places and many ways. In Ireland, for example, violence has bred more violence, and caused untold human suffering.'[117] However, it was an apparent promise made in Pittsburgh just a few days before the election which really raised Irish-American expectations. On 26 October, Carter met a delegation from the INC and Ancient Order of Hibernians (the traditional Irish defence group and principal organiser of the New York City St. Patrick's day parade). On the following day, Carter referred to the Democratic Party convention plank on Northern Ireland, with its traditional expression of concern for human rights and support for a united Ireland: 'it is a mistake for our country's government to stand quiet on the struggle of the Irish for peace, for the respect of human rights, and for unifying Ireland.'[118] Six days before the election, Carter issued a statement calling for an 'international commission on human rights in Northern Ireland'. In these last, hectic, pre-election days, he was at one point photographed apparently wearing an 'England Out of Ireland' badge. Such activity provoked rapid condemnation in London and Dublin. In the House of Commons, Northern Ireland Secretary Roy Mason declared that it was 'very dangerous' for 'anyone, irrespective of who he or she is, to make comments that might give aid or succour to the Provisional IRA'. James Molyneaux, Unionist leader at Westminster, spoke of the 'irresponsible opportunism of this peanut politician'. In response to criticism from Dublin, Carter sent a telegram to Irish Foreign Minister Garret Fitzgerald, condemning violence and supporting a 'just solution' which would protect the human rights of both communities.[119]

Carter's clumsy interventions were widely interpreted as designed to attract Catholic votes, especially in New York and Pennsylvania. As an evangelical Protestant Southerner, Carter naturally had anxieties about his ability to mobilise certain traditional sections of the Democratic vote. Some Irish-American leaders, seeking to hold Carter to the Pittsburgh 'commitment', later depicted his attachment to 'the struggle for human rights and self-determination for the people of Ireland'[120] to have been crucial to his 1976 victory. The Pittsburgh remarks may have had some marginal effect. According to the CBS Election Day Survey, Carter took 55 per cent of the potential Irish-American vote (estimated at 12.2 million). However, psephological studies tend to be very sceptical of there being any cohesive 'Irish' vote which takes its cue from US policy affecting Ireland.[121]

Presidential interest in Ireland was sustained during the early part of 1977. Amid considerable publicity, Carter stayed with an Irish family in Massachusetts. The period also witnessed a conscious attempt to put aside the pre-election antics. The White House voiced concern over NORAID and announced an investigation into its activities. On 30 August 1977, Carter issued a statement which was to provide the basis for Administration policy on Northern Ireland for the rest of his Presidency. The statement had been preceded by intense lobbying by the 'Big Four' group of Irish-American politicians: Senators Edward Kennedy of Massachusetts and D. P. Moynihan of New York, House Speaker 'Tip' O'Neill, and Governor Hugh Carey of New York. Intense negotiation had also taken place with Dublin and London. The flurry of leaks and misunderstandings which preceded the statement, although partly attributable to staff blunders, was principally symptomatic of frenetic diplomatic bargaining. In the final version of the statement, Carter pledged the US to 'a just solution that involves both parts of the community' and 'protects human rights'. Any solution required 'widespread acceptance'. Americans were urged not to contribute to unnamed organisations involved in violence. Explaining that there 'are no solutions that outsiders can impose', Carter continued:

a peaceful settlement would contribute immeasurably to stability in Northern Ireland and so enhance the prospects for increased investment. In the event of such a settlement, the United States Government would be prepared to join with others to see how additional job-creating investment could be encouraged.[122]

Despite the conventional coyness about America's role, the statement was a direct expression of a legitimate American interest, and therein lay its chief significance. This point was missed by those who complained about Carter's vagueness; William Craig of the Protestant Vanguard Party, for example, commented: 'One appreciates his interest, but one wonders why he made it.' None the less, the wide support elicited by the statement was undoubtedly indicative of its vague, bromidic qualities. A 'senior Dublin Cabinet source' was quoted as welcoming Carter's 'strongly implied backing for partnership government in Northern Ireland'. (The statement studiously avoided the term 'power-sharing' in deference to loyalist sensibilities.) John Hume of the Northern Irish Social Democratic Party (SDLP) commented that the statement, made as unemployment in the province reached its highest point since 1938, 'shows the people what the real prize of agreement can be'. A lasting settlement might start a dollar bonanza. Harry West, Official Unionist leader, cautiously welcomed the statement, somewhat implausibly interpreting it as a new lease of life for the 1975 Northern Ireland Convention. Another 'leading loyalist' was quoted to the effect that Protestant opinion had been successfully softened up by earlier rumours of a tougher US stand on power-sharing, and by Carter's own religious background.[123]

In the United States, the 'Big Four' rushed to endorse the sentiments which they themselves had done so much to encourage. Edward Kennedy told Carter on 13 September that 'no other President in history has done as well by Ireland'. Only a few voices were raised in criticism. Congressman Eilberg declared that the promises for the future made in the statement could prove empty: 'I think that our Administration should be interested in human rights here and now.' The *Wall Street Journal* offered the thought that once Carter had learned to promote job-creating investment in Northern Ireland, perhaps he might then apply the same policies in the United States. For its part,

Provisional Sinn Fein, having initially given the statement a guarded welcome, moved to condemn American 'counter insurgency' and 'bribes'.[124]

Predictably, the London Foreign Office's response was lukewarm and ambiguous. Indeed, British diplomacy, together with Administration caution about raised expectations, probably lay behind a commentary on the statement issued on 8 September by William Shannon, US ambassador in Dublin. Shannon emphasised that US investment would appear *after* a settlement. Carter was offering his 'good offices', rather than a 'peace plan'. This was in line with a State Department memorandum, prepared for the use of Administration spokespersons in connection with the statement, on 23 August:

we don't normally encourage investment in specific areas abroad, except for an overall policy promoting a sound world economy.
It is difficult to do this in this instance without a peaceful solution of Northern Ireland's problems.[125]

The 'Big Four' at this stage were prepared to support the principle of dollars tomorrow. They were content with establishing a legitimate American interest, and with offering an incentive to revive the peace process from its post-power-sharing torpor. None the less, they continued to seek specific commitments. The Administration seems at one point to have been committed to a figure of $100 million, significantly below Kennedy's pre-statement 'bid' of $500 million. Kennedy continued to pressure Carter to commit himself to 'a Marshall-type program':

American assistance could take a variety of forms, including not only direct appropriations by Congress under the foreign aid program, but also loans, loan guarantees, and other incentives and subsidies for US firms to invest in Northern Ireland.[126]

Kennedy's hopes were not fulfilled. Between 1977 and 1979 neither the Administration nor Congress showed any eagerness to move further without any initiative being taken across the Atlantic. Carter contented himself with meeting Mairead Corrigan in March 1978 and expressing support for the 'peace people', while the FBI continued to investigate the INC, NORAID and the republican newspaper, *The Irish People*.[127]

Blame for the lack of movement was widely laid at the door of Prime Minister Callaghan and his reliance upon unionist votes to sustain his House of Commons majority. Following a December 1978 meeting with Roy Mason and Foreign Secretary David Owen, Moynihan declared that the British government had 'no intention of doing anything about Northern Ireland except keeping the British there'. The 'Big Four's' 1979 St Patrick's Day statement was far more critical of British policy than its two predecessors. In April 1979, 'Tip' O'Neill accused Callaghan of treating Ulster like a 'political football'. Hugh Carey and Mario Biaggi both embarked upon (separate) schemes for 'peace fora' and 'summits' to resolve the Irish conflict. Carey's was rebuffed by the new Conservative government in London in

August 1979, the same month in which Biaggi was personally persuaded by Carter to abandon his scheme.[128]

The defeat of Callaghan's government in May, and the consequent lessening of unionist influence at Westminster, appeared to open new opportunities. By the summer of 1979, Carter was under intense Congressional pressure to replicate his Camp David success and urge on Mrs Thatcher what became known as the 'American solution'. In June 1979, Kennedy exhorted the President to act at the forthcoming Tokyo summit. He should tell the new British PM:

a British policy that emphasized 'security' concerns while ignoring a political initiative could inflame Irish-American opinion, undercut the responsible leadership that Speaker O'Neill and the rest of us are trying to provide; upset other important aspects of the US and British relationship; fuel anti-British sentiment in America; and even become a hair-curling issue in the 1980 election.

An undated, handwritten reply from Carter indicates that he did, indeed, converse with Mrs. Thatcher in Tokyo along these lines.[129]

As outlined in Kennedy's letter, the 'American solution' consisted essentially of a return to Sunningdale power-sharing in all but name. Kennedy suggested that the term 'participatory democracy', within the framework of a 'revived regional' government led by a 'moderate Unionist' Prime Minister, should be preferred to 'power-sharing'. Protestant support could be won through the promise of American investment, strong condemnation of the IRA, acceptance that Irish 'reunification' was 'not likely to occur in the foreseeable future', and through exploitation of intra-Protestant divisions. Kennedy told Carter that a 'monolithic Unionist party' was unlikely to be reconstituted. Consequently, 'the Official Unionists may be inclined to develop an independent policy' which would leave stranded 'the pure negativism of Paisley and his faction'. Kennedy contented himself with recommending that 'the British Government should do nothing to widen the breach between Ireland and Northern Ireland'; however, it was widely accepted that the 'American solution' would involve an 'Irish dimension', possibly on Sunningdale Council of Ireland lines. As Eilberg and Fish found in their trip to the province in 1978, there was also some support for importation into Northern Ireland of American constitutional practices, notably checks and balances and a bill of rights.[130]

US arms sales to the RUC had long been the subject of protest by the INC and its allies in Congress. By early 1979, the 'Big Four's' growing impatience with Britain was evidenced by O'Neill joining the protest. On 3 August, the State Department announced that any new applications to export arms to the RUC would be frozen, pending a policy review. The announcement derived from action in Congress by Mario Biaggi to effect a complete ban. State's slightly ambiguous language, which reflected a compromise engineered by Clement Zablocki, enabled London to characterise as 'simply . . . a review' what was, in fact, an arms ban which continued into the Reagan years.[131]

London sources were further quoted as implying that, if no fuss were made, the Administration would soon overcome its temporary discomfiture at the hands of Congressional extremists, and 'quietly . . . resume' sales.[132] Such a view misrepresented the White House position. For one thing, Administration acceptance of the arms ban may have been the price demanded by Biaggi for abandoning his Irish 'summit'. Clearly also, Carter's ability quietly to resume sales – or, indeed, to reverse the State Department's increasingly liberal attitude towards visa applications by Irish republicans – was likely to be limited by the exigencies of fighting Kennedy for the 1980 Presidential nomination. In fact, Administration complicity in the arms ban, together with the new visa policy, amounted to a concerted effort to elicit a new political initiative from London.

The initiative came in October. Its American provenance was widely discussed, and was evident in its premature announcement in Washington by British Ambassador Sir Nicholas Henderson. (In 1983, Ulster Unionist leader James Molyneaux alleged that British subservience to American pressure derived from a 'high powered conference . . . in London' between Foreign Secretary Lord Carrington and Secretary of State Vance in June 1979). The plan amounted to an attempted revival, in line with the 'American solution' outlined in Kennedy's June letter to Carter, of devolved regional government while avoiding the term 'power-sharing'. The declaration by Northern Ireland Secretary Humphrey Atkins that the initiative could proceed on the basis of 'the highest level of agreement' (rather than complete acceptance) echoed the 'widespread acceptance' mentioned in Carter's 1977 statement. It also pointed to an abandonment of the Paisleyites, as indicated in Kennedy's letter.[133]

By the later part of 1979 and during 1980 important factors were beginning to push the Administration away from the apparently developing high profile on Northern Ireland. Firstly, the fizzling out of the 'Atkins initiative' indicated the difficulties in achieving 'widespread acceptance' of the 'American solution'. Secondly, a relatively discrete regional conflict (especially one occurring within the territory of an ally and unrelated to problems of energy resource access) was unlikely to command priority in Carter's frenetic last year in office. Even Kennedy, in the face of the new Cold War and Iranian hostage crises, neglected to focus on Irish issues in the nomination race. His prediction that Ireland would become a major issue in the election was not fulfilled.

The policy was shaped by powerful forces both within and outside the Administration. Within the foreign policy bureaucracy, the State Department stood for caution on Irish issues. On 6 September 1979, Cyrus Vance indicated, after the assassination of Lord Mountbatten and less than a month after the arms ban: 'For us to intrude ourselves into the Irish question would not be wise.' It would 'be resented by the parties concerned'.[134] Among republican sympathisers in the US, the State Department had a reputation for extreme Anglophilia. Democratic Congressman Lester Wolff complained to Carter in December 1977 that 'our State Department is still very much receptive to the biased influence of England'.[135] Certainly, as late as June 1979, State was describing arms sales to the RUC as 'fully consistent with our human rights and arms control policies'.[136]

Beyond the State Department, interest in Northern Ireland was maintained by White House aide Bob Hunter, who kept Carter informed on the issue and had an important role in drafting the 1977 statement. The elements in the Administration most critical of British policy were Vice-President Mondale (who quickly moved to support O'Neill's 'political football' remark in April 1979) and UN Ambassador Young. In December 1977, Andrew Young spoke publicly against British use of torture at Riverside church in New York City, with pickets from NORAID circling the building.[137]

Outside the Administration, the 'Big Four' represented the weightiest influence on the development of White House policy. Working closely with the government of the Irish Republic (notably diplomats Sean Donlon and Michael Lillis), the four politicians had, by early 1977, arrived at the position which underpinned Carter's August statement: strong condemnation of the IRA's American supporters, combined with encouragement for a British initiative along 'American solution' lines. This position surfaced in their 1977 St Patrick's Day statement, whose tone was at variance with, for example, Kennedy's evidence before the 1972 Congressional hearings on Northern Ireland. The 'Big Four's' 1977–80 position also embodied a recognition of the legitimacy of Protestant aspirations. In 1979, Kennedy actually met Andy Tyrie, Ulster Defence Association chairman.[138]

The four's position was not without political costs. They ran the risk of becoming outflanked by less cautious Congressional forces, especially members of Biaggi's Ad Hoc Committee. The four's post-1978 impatience with Britain, their renewed enthusiasm for Irish reunification after the demise of the 'Atkins initiative', and the 1981 launching of Friends of Ireland, were all, at one level, efforts to shore up their position as pre-eminent Irish-American spokesmen.[139]

Figures like Biaggi – and even Senator George McGovern, who visited Belfast in 1977 – could not compete with the 'Big Four' in terms of influence with the Carter Administration. It was not simply that the four represented a powerful force within the Democratic party. In Speaker O'Neill, the group contained someone with immense influence over the fate of legislation. In Kennedy, despite the open animosity between him and Carter's staff, it contained someone with whom some accommodation would have to be made if Carter were to be re-elected. In addition, Kennedy's implied threat, that 'responsible' Irish-American leadership required some recognition and response if it were to be maintained, had force not only for London but also for the Administration itself.[140]

The 'Big Four' were way ahead of their rivals in their ability to keep pace with and mould Irish-American opinion. Of course, the IRA has long acquired money, guns and support from the United States. However, while exact figures are difficult to come by, it is likely that, by the late 1970s, NORAID was sending about $150,000 annually to Ireland; this compared with about $600,000 in the early 1970s. (Contributions surged once again during the 1981 hunger strikes.) The fall in support for the IRA in the late 1970s was partly due to the 'Big Four' but also reflected an ebbing away of earlier emotionalism. As William Shannon wrote in 1976, for many suburban Irish-Americans any extended commitment on Northern Ireland 'would require a journey into the past they are reluctant to make'. American Catholics were arguably more exercised over Carter's blocking of tuition tax credits for parochial schools than by policy on Ireland. For its part, the Roman Catholic hierarchy in the US has been anxious to disassociate itself from republican events; it was also notable that the US Catholic Conference public stance on human rights in the 1970s embraced the Third World and Poland rather than Northern Ireland.[141]

As noted previously, American media coverage of perceived human rights abuses (and certainly of the 1981 hunger strikes) had an impact on public opinion. Generally, however, American journalists, usually situated in London rather than Belfast, have tended to reflect the official British view and to portray the conflict principally in sectarian terms.[142] In formulating its policy, the Carter Administration had to take account neither of a unified, highly mobilised Irish America, nor of a consistently sensitised wider public opinion. This left it freer to adapt its position to take account of developing political configurations in Dublin and London. The 1977 statement was timed so as to influence the forthcoming meeting between Callaghan and Jack Lynch, the new Irish Prime Minister. The 'Big Four' seem to have pointed out to Carter that Fianna Fail was likely (precisely because of its anti-partitionist traditions) to prove a credible counter to the IRA. Lynch consistently attacked American friends of violent republicanism, a group to which he consigned Biaggi. At one level, the 1977 statement and the putative 'American solution' were functions of the Republic's successful diplomacy. It was even suggested in Washington that the first draft of the statement had been made by Irish diplomat Michael Lillis. This strategy had been prepared during visits to Washington in 1975 and 1976 by Garret Fitzgerald (Foreign Minister in the Cosgrave government). In stressing the continuity between Irish diplomacy and US policy, it is interesting that the official briefing book for Carter's November 1979 meeting with Lynch indicated that Foreign Minister Michael O'Kennedy was a Trilateral Commission member: 'On his trips to the United States, he has particularly welcomed US efforts to boost industrial developments in Ireland and Northern Ireland and to stem the flow of arms supplies to terrorists in Northern Ireland.'[143] At his 1979 meeting with Carter, Lynch in effect urged the President to mediate openly on the

Camp David model and unambiguously to promote the 'American solution'. The fact that Carter stood by his more restrained policy of pressuring London (notably through tacit support for the arms ban) indicates the Administration's sensitivity to British views.

The late 1970s did witness some significant Anglo-American tensions; though it is interesting that, listing them in his memoirs, Brzezinski did not mention Northern Ireland.[144] (It is also poignant to note that in one of the areas of tension – Concorde landing rights at Washington DC and New York airports – the British sought the support of Speaker O'Neill and Governor Carey.) Callaghan, however, was regarded, in the words of the briefing book for his March 1977 visit, as 'well disposed towards the United States', with his 'commitment to Europe' being 'totally pragmatic'.[145] Conservative shadow minister Geoffrey Howe was rebuffed in a July 1977 effort to meet Carter.[146] Approval of Callaghan was reflected in the Administration's sensitivity to his reliance on unionist votes at Westminster. Mrs Thatcher's election victory caused some initial tensions. Staffer Jim Rentscher suggested to Brzezinski that Carter should personally congratulate the new Prime Minister: 'the call will . . . help counter some of the distorted speculation we saw during the campaign (to the effect that we were hoping for a Labor win and 'troubled' by the idea of the Tories taking over).'[147] Relations with the Thatcher government rapidly improved, however; this was due partly, no doubt, to the response to US pressure embodied in the 'Atkins initiative', but more importantly to British support during the Iranian hostage crisis.[148]

In considering extra-American influence on Carter's policy, mention should also be made of the SDLP's John Hume. During his period as a Harvard fellow in 1976, Hume developed a close relationship with Edward Kennedy and his adviser Carey Parker. Hume is thought to have drafted the 'Big Four's' 1977 St Patrick's Day statement. He outlined his version of the 'American solution' in a 1979 article. American investment had already helped the Republic; although it had stagnated in the North since 1969, it was the hope for the future there as well. Hume also drew attention to American security interests. Northern Ireland was: 'a strategically placed area in the Atlantic approaches to Northwest Europe, potentially ripe for subversion if political neglect continues'.[149] (The view that US policy towards Ireland has consistently been driven by security considerations is commonly heard and has been advanced from varying viewpoints by, for example, Sean Cronin and Enoch Powell.[150] Security considerations undoubtedly have affected US policy toward Northern Ireland. However, Carter's policy was more a product of complex domestic pressures than an expression of American security interests).

The case of policy in Northern Ireland clearly demonstrates the complex problems associated with the wider human rights stance: notably, raised ethnic group expectations and inevitable charges of inconsistency. The Administration's definition of 'human rights' proved difficult to maintain, with policy increasingly being justified in terms of the simple 'human right' to live in peace.[151] (In September 1991, Amnesty International announced that human rights abuses by the paramilitaries, as well as by the authorities, would henceforth come under its scrutiny.[152] It is also often pointed out that Belfast's homicide rate is typically less than one-third that of Washington DC.)

From all this it may nevertheless be argued that the Carter Administration fashioned a coherent policy: the successful assertion of a legitimate American interest, combined with carrot (investment promises) and stick (tacit endorsement of the arms ban, the threat of Irish-American leadership falling into 'irresponsible' hands) pressure on Britain to adopt the 'American solution'. This policy led, indirectly, to the December 1980 agreements between Mrs Thatcher and the Irish Taoiseach Charles Haughey, and eventually to the 1985 Anglo-Irish Agreement.

Notes

1 Zbigniew Brzezinski, *Power and Principle* (London: Weidenfeld and Nicolson, 1983), p. 149. See also Jerel A. Rosati, *The Carter Administration's Quest for Global Community* (Columbia: University of South Carolina Press, 1981), p. 151.

2 Cyrus Vance, *Hard Choices* (New York: Simon and Schuster, 1983), pp. 441–2.

3 *Power and Principle*, pp. 52–4, 3.

4 *Ibid.*, p. 5. See also Brzezinski, MC transcript, p. 58 and Lloyd Cutler, MC transcript, p. 35.

5 See Stephen Gill, *American Hegemony and the Trilateral Commission* (Cambridge: Cambridge University Press, 1990), p. 222. See also Holly Sklar, 'Trilateralism: Managing Dependence and Democracy', in H. Sklar, ed., *Trilateralism* (Boston: South End Press, 1980), pp. 1–58; Jenny Pearce, *Under The Eagle* (London: Latin America Bureau, 1982), pp. 103–21.

6 See L. H. Shoup and W. Minter, *Imperial Brain Trust* (New York: Monthly Review Press, 1977) and P. Thompson, 'Bilderberg and the West' in Sklar, ed., *Trilateralism*, pp. 157–89, 188 (note 57, on right-wing conspiracy theory).

7 Gill, *American Hegemony and the Trilateral Commission*, p. 171 (remark of Jimmy Carter).

8 See M. Crozier, S. P. Huntington and S. Watanuki, *The Crisis of Democracy: Report to the Trilateral Commission on the Governability of Liberal Democracies* (New York: New York University Press, 1975).

9 See Gill, *American Hegemony . . .*, p. 223.

10 Hedley Donovan informed Carter in March 1980 that he intended to attend the Bilderberg conference in Aachen the following month. The 'more or less familiar Trilateral types' would be there. He added that the underlying reason for his European trip was to see his grandchildren in Rome (Memo to the President from H. Donovan, 18 Mar. 1980, box 2, SO: Donovan (folder, 'Memos').

11 See James N. Rosenau, 'A Pre-Theory Revisited: World Politics in an Era of Cascading Interdependence', *International Studies Quarterly*, 24, 1984, pp. 245–305.

12 *Public Papers of the Presidents of the United States: Jimmy Carter, 1977, 2*

(Washington DC: US Government Printing Office, 1978), p. 956.

13   See Richard A. Melanson, *Writing History and Making Policy: The Cold War, Vietnam, and Revisionism* (Lanham: University Press of America, 1983), p. 178. Carter's March 1978 remark is cited in R. A. Melanson, *Reconstructing Consensus: American Foreign Policy since the Vietnam War* (New York: St Martin's Press, 1991), p. 101.

14   Z. Brzezinski, *Two Ages: America's Role in the Technocratic Era* (New York: Viking, 1970), p. 255.

15   Vance and Policy Planning staffer cited in Melanson, *Writing History and Making Policy*, pp. 181–2.

16   *Washington Post*, 13 Dec. 1979 (cited in T. P. Lomperis, *The War Everyone Lost – and Won* (Baton Rouge: Louisiana University Press, 1984), p. 2).

17   *Public Papers of the Presidents . . . 1977*, 2, p. 1274.

18   Brzezinski, *Power and Principle*, pp. 5–6.

19   Z. Brzezinski, 'From Cold War to Cold Peace', in G. R. Urban, ed., *Detente* (London: Temple Smith, 1976), p. 252–73, 269. See also Z. Brzezinski, 'America in a Hostile World', *Foreign Policy*, 28, 1976, pp. 65–96; G. Schweigler, 'Carter's Detente Policy: Change or Continuity?', *The World Today*, 34, 1978, pp. 81–9; and Raymond L. Garthoff, *Detente and Confrontation: American-Soviet Relations from Nixon to Reagan* (Washington DC: Brookings, 1985), p. 564.

20   See S. R. Ashton, *In Search of Detente* (London: Macmillan, 1989), pp. 132–7. See also Henry Kissinger, *The White House Years* (London: Weidenfeld and Nicolson, 1979), pp. 128–130.

21   See Andrew Young, 'The United States and Africa: Victory for Diplomacy', *Foreign Affairs*, 59, 1980, pp. 648–66, 666.

22   *Public Papers of the Presidents . . . 1977*, 2 at 956.

23   Vance, *Hard Choices*, p. 87.

24   See Stanley Hoffman, *Primacy or World Order* (New York: McGraw Hill, 1978); Robert O. Keohane and Joseph S. Nye, *Power and Interdependence* (Boston: Little, Brown, 1977).

25   Cited in Rosati, *The Carter Administration's Quest for Global Community*, pp. 42–3.

26   S. P. Huntington, 'Coping with the Lippmann Gap', *Foreign Affairs*, 58, 1979, pp. 448–61, 457. See also Michael Genovese, 'Jimmy Carter and the Age of Limits: Presidential Power in a Time of Decline and Diffusion', paper presented at the Eighth Presidential Conference, Hofstra University, Nov. 1990.

27   Brzezinski, *Power and Principle*, pp. 3, 53–6.

28   Brzezinski (with Madeleine Albright, Leslie Denend and William Odom), MC transcript, p. 56 (Odom); D. Moreno, *US Policy in Central America* (Miami: Florida International University Press, 1990), p. 182 (Hansen remark).

29   Brzezinski, MC transcript, p. 69.

30   See Fred Halliday, *The Making of the Second Cold War* (London: Verso, 1983), p. 218; Michael Klare, *Beyond the 'Vietnam Syndrome'* (Washington DC: Institute for Policy Studies, 1981), p. 69.

31   *Power and Principle*, p. 124. For the view that Brzezinski was never 'on board', see Alexander Moens, review of Rosati's *The Carter Administration's Quest for Global Community*, *International Journal*, 46, 1991, pp. 353–5. See also, Thomas J. McCormick, *America's Half-Century: United States Foreign Policy in the Cold War*

(Baltimore: Johns Hopkins University Press, 1989), pp. 199–200; Joanna Spear and Phil Williams, 'Belief Systems and Foreign Policy: The Cases of Carter and Reagan', in Richard Little and Steve Smith, eds., *Belief Systems and International Relations* (Oxford: Blackwell, 1988), pp. 190–208, at 196; and Henry Brandon, *Special Relationships: A Foreign Correspondent's Memoirs from Roosevelt to Reagan* (London: Macmillan, 1988), p. 336 (on Brzezinski and human rights).

32   Brzezinski *et al.*, MC transcript, p. 49 (Odom).

33   *CQWR*, 22 Jan. 1977, p. 106.

34   Dan Caldwell, *The Dynamics of Domestic Politics and Arms Control: The SALT II Treaty Ratification Debate* (Columbia: University of South Carolina Press, 1991), p. 12.

35   See Sandy Vogelgesang, *American Dream; Global Nightmare* (New York: Norton, 1980), pp. 122–3; Lars Shoultz, *Human Rights and United States Policy toward Latin America* (Princeton: Princeton University Press, 1981), pp. 74–108.

36   See T. M. Franck and E. Weisband, *Foreign Policy by Congress* (New York: Oxford University Press, 1979), at p. 84; C. W. Whalen, *The House and Foreign Policy* (Chapel Hill: University of North Carolina Press, 1982), pp. 122–6; J. P. Salzberg, 'A View from the Hill', in David D. Newsom, ed., *The Diplomacy of Human Rights* (Lanham: University Press of America, 1986), pp. 13–20; D. Carleton and M. Stohl, 'The Foreign Policy of Human Rights', *Human Rights Quarterly*, 7, 1985, pp. 205–29; A. G. Mower, *Human Rights and American Foreign Policy: The Carter and Reagan Experiences* (Westport: Greenwood, 1987), pp. 60–6; D. M. Fraser, 'Congress's Role in the Making of International Human Rights Policy', in D. P. Kommers and G. D. Loescher, eds., *Human Rights and American Foreign Policy* (Notre Dame: University of Notre Dame Press, 1979), pp. 247–54.

37   See Dan Caldwell, 'The Jackson–Vanik Amendment', in John Spanier and Joseph Nogee, eds, *Congress, the Presidency and American Foreign Policy* (New York: Pergamon Press, 1981), pp. 1–21.

38   *The Presidential Campaign, 1976, Vol. I: Part 1* (Washington DC: US Government Printing Office, 1978), pp. 83–4; Garthoff, *Detente and Confrontation*, p. 569.

39   D. P. Moynihan, 'The Politics of Human Rights', *Commentary*, Aug. 1977, p. 22.

40   Cited in Elizabeth Drew, 'A Reporter at Large: Human Rights', *The New Yorker*, 18 July 1977, pp. 36–62, 36. See also J. Muravchik, *The Uncertain Crusade* (Lanham: Hamilton Press, 1986), pp. 2–8.

41   Memo to the President from H. Jordan, 3 Dec. 1977, box 34, SO: Chief of Staff: Jordan.

42   Memo to the President ('through Phil Wise'), 24 Oct. 1978, box HU-3, WHCF: SF: Human Rights.

43   Memo to J. Watson from S. Aiello, A. Moses and B. Aronson, undated, box HU-4, WHCF: SF: Human Rights (folder, '8/1/80 – 1/20/81').

44   Drew, 'A Reporter at Large', p. 41.

45   See Carleton and Stohl, 'The Foreign Policy of Human Rights', p. 207: 1974 Foreign Assistance Act (section 502B).

46   See *American Foreign Policy: Basic Documents, 1977–1980* (Washington DC: US Government Printing Office, 1983), p. 425 (remarks of Patricia Derian).

47   Memo to S. Eizenstat from L. Daft, 22 Nov. 1977, box 208, SO: DPS:

Eizenstat.

48 Jimmy Carter, *Keeping Faith* (London: Collins, 1982), p. 144; *American Foreign Policy: Basic Documents*, p. 433 (Vance); Muravchik, *The Uncertain Crusade*, p. 96 (Tuchman).

49 *Basic Documents*, p. 409.

50 Drew, 'A Reporter at Large', p. 42.

51 *Ibid.*, p. 54.

52 *Basic Documents*, p. 427.

53 See Address by Deputy Secretary of State Warren Christopher to the American Bar Association, 9 Aug. 1977, *Basic Documents*, pp. 412–17; Charles Frankel, *Human Rights and Foreign Policy* (New York: Foreign Policy Association, 1978); David P. Forsythe, 'American Foreign Policy and Human Rights: Rhetoric and Reality', *Universal Human Rights*, 2, 1980, pp. 35–53.

54 Derian, cited in Muravchik, *The Uncertain Crusade*, p. 75. See also D.P. Forsythe, 'Human Rights in U.S. Foreign Policy: Retrospect and Prospect', *Political Science Quarterly*, 105, 1990, pp. 435–54. A good summary of the status of international law and institutions in this area in the late 1970s may be found in R. J. Vincent, *Human Rights and International Relations* (Cambridge: Cambridge University Press, 1986), pp. 61–108. See also A. Glenn Mower, *The United States, the United Nations, and Human Rights* (Westport: Greenwood, 1979), pp. 91–2.

55 See Natalie Hevener Kaufman, *Human Rights Treaties and the Senate: A History of Opposition* (Chapel Hill: University of North Carolina Press, 1990); David P. Forsythe, 'The United States, the United Nations and Human Rights', in M. P. Karns and K. A. Mingst, eds, *The United States and Multilateral Institutions* (London: Routledge, 1992), pp. 261–88.

56 Muravchik, *The Uncertain Crusade*, p. 79.

57 See M. Glen Johnson, 'Historical Perspectives on Human Rights and U.S. Foreign Policy', *Universal Human Rights*, 2, 1980, pp. 1–18, at 11.

58 *Basic Documents*, p. 425 (Derian).

59 Memo to Z. Brzezinski from J. Tuchman Mathews, 7 July 1978, box HU-2, WHCF: SF: Human Rights.

60 Cited in Garthoff, *Detente and Confrontation*, p. 564.

61 *Department of State Bulletin*, Jan. 1979, p. 7.

62 See Robert W. Tucker, 'America in Decline: The Foreign Policy of Maturity', *Foreign Affairs*, 58, 1979, pp. 449–84.

63 Cited in Strobe Talbott, 'Social Issues', in Joseph S. Nye, ed., *The Making of America's Soviet Policy* (New Haven: Yale University Press, 1984), pp. 183–208, at 199.

64 *Basic Documents*, pp. 558–9.

65 See Garthoff, *Detente and Confrontation*, p. 730; Brzezinski, *Power and Principle*, p. 151; P. Stern, *Water's Edge: Domestic Politics and the Making of American Foreign Policy* (Westport: Greenwood, 1979).

66 Memo to the President from J. Powell, 21 Feb. 1977, box 46, SO: Counsel: Lipshutz (folder, 'Soviet Dissidents').

67 See generally, Donald R. Kelly, ed., *Soviet Politics in the Brezhnev Era* (New York: Praeger, 1980); Ronald J. Hill, *The Soviet Union: Politics, Economics and Society* (London: Pinter, 1985), ch. 3; *Prisoners of Conscience in the USSR: Their Treatment and Conditions* (London: Amnesty International Report, 1980).

68 Andrei D. Sakharov, *Alarm and Hope* (London: Collins and Harvill, 1979), pp. 49, 53. See also Garthoff, *Detente and Confrontation*, pp. 568–74; Donald S. Spencer, *The Carter Implosion* (New York: Praeger, 1988), ch. 3; A. D. Sakharov, *Memoirs* (London: Hutchinson, 1990), pp. 462–70.

69 See Sakharov, *Alarm and Hope*, ch. 4; Martin Gilbert, *Shcharansky: Hero of Our Time* (London: Macmillan, 1980), pp. 133, 145, 188–90; Avital Shcharansky, *Next Year in Jerusalem* (London: The 355, 1980), pp. 88–90; Sakharov, *Memoirs*, p. 464.

70 Brzezinski, *Power and Principle*, pp. 155–6.

71 *The Times*, 19 June 1978.

72 Vance, *Hard Choices*, p. 101.

73 See Walter Lacqueur, 'The World and President Carter', *Commentary*, 65, 1978, pp. 56–63.

74 Memo to R. Lipshutz and S. Eizenstat from J. Starr, 6 June 1977, box 208, SO: DPS: Eizenstat (folder, 'Foreign Affairs and Human Rights').

75 Memo to R. Lipshutz, S. Eizenstat and J. Aragon, 19 June 1978, box 46, SO: Counsel: Lipshutz (folder, 'Soviet Jewry').

76 Memo to H. Jordan from J. Aragon, 7 July 1978, *ibid.*

77 *Department of State Bulletin*, Sept. 1979, p. 46.

78 See Banning Garrett, 'China Policy and the Constraints of Triangular Logic', in K.A. Oye, R.J. Lieber and Donald Rothchild, eds., *Eagle Defiant: United States Foreign* (Boston: Little, Brown, 1983), pp. 237–71, at 246.

79 Memo to Z. Brzezinski from H. Brown, 8 Mar. 1978, box 77, PHF (folder, '3/17/78 (1)').

80 *The Times*, 8 and 9 June 1978.

81 See Garrett, 'China Policy', p. 246; Brzezinski, *Power and Principle*, pp. 177, 403–25.

82 *The Times*, 9 July 1978.

83 See *Prisoners of Conscience in the USSR* pp. 1–3.

84 Cited in Spencer, *The Carter Implosion*, p. 45.

85 Cited in Gilbert, *Shcharansky*, p. 275.

86 See Samuel P. Huntington, 'Renewed Hostility', in Nye, ed., *The Making of America's Soviet Policy*, pp. 265–91, at 280.

87 CQWR, 15 July 1978, p. 1835.

88 *The Times*, 22 July 1978.

89 See Strobe Talbott, *Endgame: The Inside Story of SALT II* (London: Harper and Row, 1979), pp. 92–3.

90 *Department of State Bulletin*, Jan. 1980, p. 37.

91 Jimmy Carter, *Keeping Faith* (London: Collins, 1982), p. 147.

92 See Vladislov Krasnov, *Soviet Defectors* (Stanford: Hoover Institution, 1986); Charles Fenyvesi, 'The Unwelcome Defector: An Embarrassment to Both Sides', *New Republic*, 22 Apr. 1978, p. 9; Spencer, *The Carter Implosion*, p. 105.

93 See Garthoff, *Detente and Confrontation*, p. 739; also, Elmer Plischke, *Diplomat in Chief* (New York: Praeger, 1986), p. 408.

94 Vance, *Hard Choices*, p. 100.

95 See Richard E. Neustadt and Ernest L. May, *Thinking in Time* (New York: Free Press, 1986), pp. 92–6; David D. Newsom, *The Soviet Brigade in Cuba* (Bloomington: Indiana University Press, 1987); Brzezinski, *Power and Principle*, pp.

346–52; Vance, *Hard Choices*, pp. 358–64.

96   Briefing in Cabinet room, 15 Jan. 1980, box 79, SO: Powell (folder, 'Soviets in Afghanistan (2)').

97   Carter, MC transcript, p. 61.

98   Kennedy, Georgetown University, 28 Jan. 1980, box 13, SO: Speechwriters: SF (folder, 'Kennedy').

99   Memo to the President from H. Donovan, 2 Jan. 1980, box 2, SO: Donovan (folder, 'Memos to the President').

100   Memo to the President from H. Donovan, 10 April 1980, *ibid.*

101   Brzezinski (with Albright *et al.*), MC transcript, p. 52 (Albright).

102   *Basic Documents*, p. 445.

103   See Ashton, *In Search of Detente*, p. 145.

104   Talbott, 'Social Issues', p. 199.

105   See, e.g., R. J. Hill, *Soviet Union: Politics, Economics and Society* (London: Pinter, 1985), p. 143.

106   *A Chronicle of Current Events*, nos. 55–6 (London: Amnesty International, 1981), p. 59; Vogelgesang, *American Dream*, p. 104.

107   See Charles Townshend, 'Northern Ireland', in R. J. Vincent, ed., *Foreign Policy and Human Rights* (Cambridge: Cambridge University Press, 1986), pp. 119–40; *Report of the Committee of Inquiry into Police Interrogation Procedures in Northern Ireland*, Cmnd. 7497 (Mar. 1978) (Bennett report); *Report of an Amnesty International Mission to Northern Ireland* (London: Amnesty International, 1978).

108   Letter, F. B. O'Brien to Z. Brzezinski, 7 Feb. 1977, box CO-65, WHCF: SF: Countries CO 167 (executive).

109   Telegram, Longshoremen's Association and P. O'Dwyer to the President, 17 June 1977, box HU-17, WHCF: SF: Human Rights HU 2–1 (executive). Letter, W. Kelly to the President, 18 Jan. 1978, box CO-33, WHCF: SF: Countries CO 73 (general).

110   Letter, H. Fish and J. Eilberg to the President, 17 Oct. 1978, box CO-33, WHCF: SF: Countries CO 73 (general); *Northern Ireland: A Role for the United States?*, Committee print, report by two members of the Committee on the Judiciary, House of Representatives, 95th Congress, 2d session (Dec. 1978), p. 203.

111   Letter, M. Biaggi to F. Moore, 19 June 1979, box CO-64, WHCF: SF: Countries CO 167 (executive); letter, J. Heaney to Z. Brzezinski, 11 Feb. 1978, box CO-65, WHCF: SF: Countries CO 167 (executive).

112   Letter, President Carter to J. Addabo, 21 May 1977, box CO-64, WHCF: SF: Countries CO 167 (executive).

113   *Northern Ireland: A Role for the United States?*, pp. 216–17; letter, D. J. Bennet to C. Zablocki, undated (certainly June 1979), box CO-64, WHCF: SF: Countries CO 167 (executive).

114   Letter, R. Thompson (State Department Officer-in-Charge, Irish Affairs) to T. Flynn, 26 Jan. 1979, box CO-65, WHCF: SF: Countries CO 167 (executive).

115   See Mary Holland, 'Kennedy's New Irish policy', *New Statesman*, 11 May 1979, pp. 678–9; Bernard Crick, 'The Pale Green Internationalists', *New Statesman*, 7 Dec., 1979, pp. 888–91; Adrian Guelke, 'The American Connection to the Northern Ireland Conflict', *Irish Studies in International Affairs*, 1, 1984, pp. 27–39; Sean Cronin, *Washington's Irish Policy: 1916–1986* (Dublin: Anvil Books, 1987), p. 313; Jack Holland, *The American Connection: US Guns, Money and Influence in*

Northern Ireland (Dublin: Poolbeg Press, 1989), pp. 114–15, 128; Adrian Guelke, *Northern Ireland: The International Perspective* (Dublin: Gill and Macmillan, 1988), ch. 7.

116 See Barry White, *John Hume: Statesman of the Troubles* (Belfast: Blackstaff Press, 1984), pp. 190–1 (joint 1976 communique issued by President Ford and Irish Prime Minister Liam Cosgrave).

117 *The Presidential Campaign 1976, Vol. I: Part 2* (Washington DC: US Government Printing Office, 1978), p. 715.

118 Cited in Cronin, *Washington's Irish Policy*, p. 312. See also George C. Osborn, *The Role of the British Press in the 1976 American Presidential Election* (Smithtown (New York): Exposition Press, 1981), pp. 106–7.

119 Holland, *The American Connection*, p. 121; Kevin Kelley, *The Longest War: Northern Ireland and the IRA* (Dingle, Co. Kerry: Brandon, 1982), p. 227; *The Times*, 29 Oct. 1976; *Parliamentary Debates*, 5th series, vol. 918, 28 Oct. 1976, p. 687 (remarks of Roy Mason).

120 Letter, F. B. O'Brien and Fr S. McManus (of the INC) to Margaret Costanza, 18 Feb. 1977, box CO-65, WHCF: SF: Countries CO 167 (executive).

121 Mark A. Siegel, 'Ethnics: A Democratic Stronghold?', *Public Opinion*, 1, 1978, pp. 47–8.

122 The statement is printed in Holland, *The American Connection*, pp. 127–8. See also *The Times*, 16 Feb. 1977, 17 Mar. 1977, 25 Aug. 1977 and 31 Aug. 1977.

123 *The Times*, 31 Aug. 1977 and 1 Sept. 1977.

124 Letter, E. Kennedy to the President, 13 Sept. 1977, box CO-64, WHCF: SF: Countries CO 167 (executive); *Northern Ireland: A Role for the United States?*, p. 202; *Wall Street Journal*, editorial 'Aside', 6 Sept. 1977; *The Times*, 1 Sept. 1977.

125 *The Times*, 9 Sept. 1977; 'Northern Ireland Statement: Press Questions and Answers', 23 Aug. 1977, box CO-64, WHCF: SF: Countries CO 167 (executive).

126 Holland, 'Kennedy's new Irish policy'; letter, E. Kennedy to the President (see note 124).

127 *The Times*, 3 Apr. 1978. See also *CQWR*, 6 Apr. 1977, pp. 702–3; *Daily Telegraph*, 14 Sept. 1979.

128 See Crick, 'The Pale Green Internationalists'; *The Times*, 16 Nov. 1978; *Daily Telegraph*, 21 Apr. 1979 and 8, 9 and 24 Aug. 1979; *Congressional Record*, 19 Mar. 1979, Senate 5482 ('Big Four' 1979 St Patrick's Day statement).

129 *Daily Telegraph*, 14 Aug. 1979 (Carter urged to mediate in Northern Ireland 'Camp David style' by 130 Congressmen); letter, E. Kennedy to the President, 21 June 1979, box CO-64, WHCF: SF: Countries CO 167 (executive); handwritten note to 'Sen (Ted) Kennedy' from the President, 25 June 1979, *ibid.*: 'I discussed Northern Ireland with P.M. Thatcher and will report results of our conversation the next time I see you – Jimmy.'

130 Letter, E. Kennedy to the President, 21 June 1979 (see note 129); *Northern Ireland: A Role for the United States?*, p. 136.

131 See *New York Times*, 8 Apr. 1979 and 3 Aug. 1979; Desmond Hamill, *Pig in the Middle: The Army in Northern Ireland 1969–1985* (London: Methuen, 1985), pp. 236–7; *Parliamentary Debates*, 5th series, vol. 974, 22 Nov. 1979, p. 547 (remarks of Humphrey Atkins).

132 *Daily Telegraph*, 4 Aug. 1979.

133 See *ibid.*, 17 Sept. 1979 (Henderson); Paul Arthur and Keith Jeffrey,

Northern Ireland since 1968 (Oxford: Blackwell, 1988), pp. 86–7 (Molyneaux); *New York Times*, 12 Nov. 1979 (interview with Mrs Thatcher); Sean Cronin, *Irish Nationalism* (Dublin: Academy Press, 1980), p. 225. See also Adrian Guelke, 'British Policy and International Dimensions of the Northern Ireland Conflict', *Regional Politics and Policy*, 1, 1991, pp. 140–60, at 146.

134   *Daily Telegraph*, 6 Sept. 1979.

135   Letter, L. Wolff to the President, 29 Dec. 1977, box CO-64, WHCF: SF: Countries CO 167 (executive).

136   Letter, R. Thompson (State Department) to E. M. McCarthy (Irish Foundation of Arizona), 27 June 1979, box CO-33, WHCF: SF: Countries CO 73 (general).

137   *New York Times*, 12 Dec. 1977. See also White, *John Hume*, p. 192; *Daily Telegraph*, 23 Apr. 1979; *Northern Ireland: A Role for the United States?*, p. 204.

138   See Holland, *The American Connection*, p. 249; Hearings before the Subcommittee on Europe of the Committee on Foreign Affairs, *Northern Ireland*, House of Representatives, 92nd Congress 2nd session (Feb./Mar., 1972), pp. 2–16 (testimony of Senator Kennedy).

139   See *The Times*, 24 Oct. 1977.

140   *Ireland in 1977*, Committee print for the Committee on Foreign Relations, US Senate, 95th Congress 1st session (1977) (report of Senator McGovern); Kennedy letter of 21 June 1979 (see note 129). In this section I have drawn on an interview given to me by Robert Blancato (aide to Mario Biaggi), Washington DC, 14 July 1988.

141   William Shannon, 'The lasting Hurrah', *New York Times* magazine, 14 Mar. 1976; Lowell W. Livezey, 'US Religious Organizations and the International Human Rights Movement', *Human Rights Quarterly*, 11, 1989, pp. 14–81.

142   See Jo Thomas, 'Bloody Ireland', *Columbia Journalism Review*, 27, 1988, pp. 31–7.

143   'Biographies of Prime Minister Lynch's party', 2 Nov. 1979, box CO-33, WHCF: SF: Countries CO 73 (general). See also *Daily Telegraph*, 25 Sept. 1979 (Lynch reprimand of Biaggi); Raymond Smith, *Garret: The Enigma* (Dublin: Atherlow, 1985), p. 236; Garret Fitzgerald, *All in a Life* (London: Macmillan, 1991).

144   Brzezinski, *Power and Principle*, pp. 140–3, 517; *Observer* editorial, 'The Greening of America', 11 Nov. 1979; *Public Papers of the Presidents . . . 1979* (Washington DC: US Governing Printing Office, 1980), pp. 2093–7 (Lynch visit).

145   'Briefing Book for 10 Mar. 1977 visit of Callaghan, box CO-64, WHCF: SF: Countries CO 167 (executive). See also James Callaghan, *Time and Chance* (London: Collins, 1987), pp. 482–3.

146   Memo to Z. Brzezinski from P. Tarnoff (State Dept.), 16 July 1977, box CO-64, WHCF: SF: Countries CO 167 (executive).

147   Memo to Z. Brzezinski from J. Rentscher, 4 May 1979, *ibid.*

148   See Carter, *Keeping Faith*, p. 486.

149   John Hume, 'The Irish Question: A British Problem', *Foreign Affairs*, 58, 1979–80, pp. 300–13, 311. See also John Wallace, 'America – and the Hume Connection', *Belfast Telegraph*, 2 Sept. 1977. On US investments in Northern Ireland, see Kelley, *The Longest War*, pp. 278–9 and 1972 Hearings, *Northern Ireland*, pp. 116–22.

150   See Cronin, *Washington's Irish Policy*; *Parliamentary Debates*, 6th Series, vol. 87, 27 Nov. 1985, pp. 954–5 (Powell contribution to the debate on the Anglo-Irish agreement). Powell depicted British policy as dancing to America's tune, with the

Irish Republic exacting its price for collaborating with NATO.

151   See 'Northern Ireland Statement: Press Questions and Answers' (see note 125).

152   See *Fortnight*, Oct. 1991, p. 31.

6

Human rights and revolution: the cases of Nicaragua and Iran

The Carter Administration's attempt to create a new foreign policy consensus based on ideas of 'global community' and international interdependence, and centred on human rights, came under pressure in 1978, especially in relation to the conflicts in Angola, Zaire and the Horn of Africa. In 1979, however, it disintegrated. Perceived changes in public opinion, shifts in intra-Administration power relations and the emergence of a well organised New Right critique of Carter's foreign policy all contributed to this disintegration, and to the substitution of a more orthodox, security-oriented Cold War approach. Central to these changes were the Administration's increasingly unhappy and compromised efforts to accommodate its 'global community' approach to the crises of 1979. The next chapter will discuss the implications of and background to the 1979 shift in policy. The present chapter will examine the attempts to adapt US policy towards revolution in the developing world, focusing on two major 1979 'shocks': the upheavals in Nicaragua and in Iran.

Nicaragua

Applying human rights policies to Nicaragua
In the words of Robert Pastor, the Latin American specialist in Carter's National Security Council staff, there 'was no specific policy toward Nicaragua early in the Carter Presidency'; rather, 'there were only human rights policies that applied to Nicaragua'.[1] The President had a personal commitment to Latin America, and undertook an extensive tour there in May–June 1977. However, apart from the issue of the Panama Canal, policy towards Central America was subsumed under a general commitment to human rights and to rejecting the legacy of Kissinger and Nixon. The President's preferred policy combined non-intervention with multilateralism. If at all possible, Central Americans should forge their own political decisions; if US action were needed, it should be taken in concert with America's allies in

the Organisation of American States (OAS).[2]

During 1977, with detailed policy development being carried out in a decentralised fashion at intermediate levels of the bureaucracy, there occurred a kind of judicious distancing from the regime of Anastasio Somoza. As Mauricio Solaun, a Cuban-American appointed as Ambassador to Managua, the Nicaraguan capital, in mid-1977, recalled:

This policy became known among some of its supporters in the State Department and the National Security Council as a policy of 'neutrality'. It was 'neutral' in that, following the described interventionist constraints [*sic*] of our human rights policy, we were not to place ourselves entirely within either the camp of the government of Nicaragua or the opposition. In effect, Washington was periodically critical in public of the Somoza regime but the embassy was not to side with opposition to the extent of organizing the overthrow of the government, nor was it to help organize the opposition or finance any of its factions.[3]

The whole corrupt *Somocismo* system – a mixture of brutal dictatorship and dynastic opportunism – derived from past American patronage. Somoza himself was firmly of the view that his future depended upon adapting to the winds blowing from Washington. He was profoundly worried that his anti-communism might no longer guarantee US support, as it had done under previous Administrations. Former Congressman John Murphy, a close Somoza ally, told Robert Pastor in 1984 that the dictator 'knew that he was in deep trouble' when the Carter Administration, five days after taking office, cancelled export licences for ammunition. (Pastor's interview with Murphy was conducted in Danbury Federal Penitentiary, where the former Representative had been committed on corruption charges.) Somoza was not prepared, however, to countenance meaningful reform. Rather, he emulated the examples of his father and brother who had reacted to unfavourable signals from Washington by crawling into their shells 'like an armadillo' and waiting 'for the wind to pass'.[4]

American human rights policy towards Nicaragua in the first year of Carter's Presidency was developed in the Interagency Group on Human Rights and Foreign Assistance, chaired by Deputy Secretary of State Warren Christopher, and in the US Congress. The Christopher Group, set up in April 1977, provided a forum for a case-by-case consideration of the link between human rights and foreign assistance. During 1977, it attempted to assess Somoza's record, to calculate the effects of aid cut-offs on the stability of his regime, to argue whether a distinction could be made between military and economic aid, and to assess the prospects for meaningful reform. The main bureaucratic contenders were the State Department's Bureau of Inter-American Affairs, which tended to argue that Somoza should be patronised and that he would reform if the carrot of aid were dangled in front of him, and the Bureau of Human Rights, which favoured a tougher line. Patricia Derian and her deputy Mark Schneider saw Somoza as exactly the kind of dictator the US had so often supported in the past and as a symbol of the kind of legacy which Carter had been elected to relinquish. A battle between the two bureaux broke out in 1977 over the provision of sling swivels (to attach a rifle to a carrying sling) for Somoza's National Guard. Wade Matthews, Central American chief on the Inter-American Affairs Bureau, felt the Derian-Schneider line to be redolent of empty, 'feel good' symbolism. (He was defeated over the swing swivels in the Christopher Group.) The Group was influenced during 1977 by apparent evidence that Somoza's repression was both brutal and effective. The brutality was exposed in a series of articles in the *New York Times*, written by Alan Riding. The Christopher Group was also influenced by State Department perceptions that Somoza was winning the war, and that there was little danger of apparently pro-communist forces taking over. The oppositional Sandinistas (the FSLN) were described in June 1977 as a 'small, pro-Castro, Marxist terrorist group' in terminal retreat from the National Guard.[5]

The battle on Capitol Hill centred on an attempt by Congressional liberals (notably Edward Kennedy in the Senate and Ed Koch of New York in the House) to eliminate all military aid for Somoza. Against these liberals stood a Somoza-funded lobby whose Congressional champions included Murphy and the conservative Democrat Charles Wilson of Texas, a strong opponent of Soviet activism in Central America who occupied a pivotal position on the House Appropriations Foreign Operations Subcommittee. Over the next two years, Murphy, Wilson and other members of the Congressional 'Somoza lobby' constantly threatened to force Administration compromises on Nicaragua as a price for soft-pedalling their hostility to the Panama Canal treaties.[6]

The Administration nevertheless sent encouraging signs to the anti-Somoza lobby on Capitol Hill. Lucy Benson, Assistant Secretary of State for Security Assistance, testified that military aid to Nicaragua was not vital to US security interests. Charles Bray, Latin American specialist at the State Department, promised in April 1977 that Administration support for aid depended on human rights improvements.[7] In July, Ed Koch protested to the State Department about 'a lobby organized and paid for by the Nicaraguan government', which had succeeded in having military aid approved on the House floor. Koch alleged that sections of the State Department were sympathetic to the 'Somoza lobby' and hostile to the Department's own Bureau of Human Rights.[8] By this time, however, the Administration had made it clear that no military aid agreement would receive the Presidential signature without significant human rights changes. John Murphy protested that this would leave Nicaragua without the means to defend itself against 'the enemies of the United States'.[9]

In July and August 1977 Somoza received treatment in Miami for his heart condition. In September he responded to Carter's policy by lifting the 'state of siege' which had been in force in Nicaragua since December 1974. In a survey of Administration policy the following February, Warren Christopher listed the September relaxation in Nicaragua as a victory for Washington's human rights initiative.[10] In fact, the lifting of the 'state of siege' had thrust the Christopher Group into a quandary. Few regarded the move as anything other than cosmetic and cynical. Yet Somoza had responded to US pressure, albeit in a situation where opposition appeared in any case to have been crushed, and perhaps he should be rewarded. The result was a rather botched Christopher Group compromise, whereby a $2.5 million arms agreement was signed but future economic aid frozen.[11]

The state of US-Nicaraguan relations in September 1977 was summarised in a State Department briefing for Vice-President Mondale, to be used in connection with his 9 September meeting with the President of the Nicaraguan Congress, Cornelio Hueck. The briefing asserted that 'our traditionally close bilateral relations' had recently 'stiffened due to U.S. concern over violations of human rights in Nicaragua'. These violations stemmed mainly 'from interaction between the National Guard and the FSLN, a leftist guerrilla movement'. At present, the Guard 'seems to be heeding President Somoza's recent instructions to avoid human rights violations'. Future aid must depend on 'improvement' in human rights having taken place to the satisfaction of both State Department and Congress. Among 'talking points', Mondale was asked to emphasise: 'The maintenance of stability in the . . . region is of mutual concern . . . and we view our security assistance as a means toward maintaining that stability.' He was also requested to tell Hueck that the US was looking 'for the Government of Nicaragua to increase its commitment to assisting Nicaragua's rural poor'.[12]

Somoza's father had once responded to a Costa Rican rural education scheme by declaring that he did not want educated people: 'I want oxen.'[13] Few people in the State Department in late 1977 felt that Anastasio Somoza's attitudes differed greatly from those of his parent. Some, notably Assistant Secretary of State for Inter-American Affairs Terence Todman, however, continued to argue against policies which might destabilise the dictator and usher in confusion and Soviet influence. Todman appealed to signs that the Sandinistas were regrouping and forging links with the moderate opposition. Todman's position, however, was under attack both from the Derian–Schneider faction in the Department and from the Managua embassy. In February 1978, Todman (who was, incidentally, one of the leading black diplomats at the State Department) publicly broke with the human rights policy. He characterised it as selective morality, 'punishing the poor' by denying them assistance in order to show US dissatisfaction with their governments, and as assuming that issues may be dealt with in isolation 'without considering the consequences for other aspects of our relationships'.[14] He was soon replaced by Viron Vaky, who accepted the view that US 'neutrality' should be abandoned in favour of a policy of easing Somoza out. In December 1977, the White House appeared to side with the

emerging anti-Somoza mood at State by deciding to oppose important
Nicaraguan development loans at the Inter-American Development and
World banks.[15]

January 1978 to February 1979

The assassination of Pedro Joaquin Chamorro, newspaper editor and leading
constitutionalist opponent of the regime, seemed to indicate that the dictator
was not prepared to tolerate meaningful opposition. The domestic political
violence which greeted the assassination also raised sensitive regional security
questions. By January 1978, Nicaragua had moved, in Viron Vaky's phrase,
'a little closer to the front burner'.[16]

On 10 February, the Administration suspended military aid. Between
February and July 1978, various signals were sent to Managua. Shifting
Administration policies reflected intense bureaucratic battles. Vaky was
clearly coming to the view that the US should begin to organise a moderate
coalition to oust Somoza. (He put this view to an interagency conference on
the Nicaraguan crisis held on 29 August 1978.) Robert Pastor of the NSC
staff and Anthony Lake (now State's Director of Policy Planning) disagreed.
In Pastor's words, he and Lake 'believed that the United States should not
pursue a policy of overthrowing governments'.[17]

President Carter was urged by regional leaders, notably President Carlos
Andreas Perez of Venezuela, to avoid another Cuba by acting quickly to
remove Somoza and replace him by a moderate coalition. Meanwhile, in
Congress, Murphy and Wilson threatened to torpedo the entire 1978 Foreign
Assistance bill unless aid to Somoza were released. The dictator himself
persisted with his policy of using cosmetic changes as a painless means of
extracting concessions. In February 1978, he announced that he would step
down in 1981.

The result of these countervailing pressures, still exerted on a decentralised
policy process, was a hesitant restoration of aid. A loan package was allowed
to proceed in May. The State Department quickly facilitated some military
training funds. Israeli arms sales to Somoza were allowed to proceed without
any American protest.[18] On 30 June, Carter completed his letter to Somoza,
welcoming the dictator's promises to restore human rights and to allow the
moderate oppositional 'Group of Twelve' to return from exile.[19]

The Carter letter was subsequently attacked from virtually all sides.
According to Viron Vaky, it showed that the President simply 'did not
understand dictators'.[20] (Even Somoza later condemned the letter as a trick
'designed to give us a false sense of security'.)[21] As Anthony Lake noted, the
letter was generally in accord with Carter's February 1978 human rights
directive, which held that a full range of diplomatic tools should be employed.
Somoza *had* recently indicated his willingness to co-operate with the Inter-
American Human Rights Commission. The original idea for the letter came
from Carter, who instructed Brzezinski to prepare it. The human rights

personnel in the State Department were deeply dismayed. Mark Schneider, according to Anthony Lake, 'went through the roof'. He thought it 'a stupid idea, since Somoza was sure to publicize the letter' for his own purposes.[22] Derian was 'horrified' at the prospect, seeing the letter as an effort by the NSC staff to 'give Somoza praise, encouraging him to do better'.[23] Even Robert Pastor had severe doubts. Delegated by Brzezinski to do the drafting, he told his boss on 28 June:

our historical relationship with Somoza makes it very difficult for us to take any step which could be interpreted as supportive of Somoza without it antagonizing the democratic opposition in Nicaragua and our human rights supporters in Nicaragua.[24]

The State Department–NSC staff conflict was reflected in various word changes and in a delay in the letter being delivered. Yet essentially the letter had exactly the consequences feared by Pastor. In his own memoir, Pastor focuses on the leaking of the letter by an unnamed human rights officer at the State Department. But the problem was not the leak but the letter itself. Regional and human rights experts at State opposed the letter, as did Ambassador Solaun and the Latin American specialist on the NSC staff. Carter seems to have been unaware of all this, and neither Vance nor Brzezinski appears to have done anything to make him so aware. As Frank McNeil, former Ambassador to Costa Rica, later wrote, the President's letter – which, as Schneider foresaw, Somoza immediately turned to his own purposes – convinced regional leaders that Carter wanted Somoza to stay in power. Their distrust of Washington mounted, and Venezuela, Costa Rica and Panama significantly stepped up their clandestine arms shipments to the Sandinistas.[25]

In August 1978 Pastor attempted successfully to head off any further friendly White House communications with the Nicaraguan regime. He advised Brzezinski that the President should not respond to overtures from the Nicaraguan Ambassador, Sevilla Sacasa. According to Pastor, the Ambassador 'papers his walls with letters from his 'good friends' in the White House, over five administrations'.[26] By this time, various events – the Carter letter and its leaking, the emergence of the 'broad opposition' (the FAO) in Managua, and the Sandinista capture of the National Palace on 22 August – were propelling Nicaraguan policy from the human rights to the national security arena. Control over decision-making passed from the Christopher Group to an interagency group in which Pastor and Vaky took the lead. By September the Somoza regime appeared to be falling. As the dictator unleashed the National Guard, any pretence at human rights improvements was dropped. Vaky argued that the US must take the initiative in securing power for a moderate opposition. Pastor favoured a regional mediation effort which would enable the US to keep its distance. All agreed with Douglas Bennet of the State Department, who informed Congressman Lee Hamilton in October that some kind of initiative was needed to 'help steer developments towards a moderate, independent course which will avoid Marxist or revolutionary excess'.[27]

William Jordan, former Ambassador to Panama, was dispatched to organise an OAS mediation, and also gently to persuade Somoza that the longer he remained, the more likely it was that Nicaragua would go communist. The mediation began in October 1978 and involved a US delegation headed by William Bowdler, together with delegations from the Dominican Republic, Guatemala and the moderate Nicaraguan 'broad opposition'. Regional leaders saw the main task as the removal of Somoza, and were sceptical about the apparent US preference for retaining the National Guard and even Somoza's political party in a new interim coalition regime (the so-called '*Somocismo* without Somoza' policy). The dictator himself was recalcitrant and Bowdler did not have instructions to issue an ultimatum. Even when the US did, in January 1979, begin to issue threats, Somoza was unmoved. For a time it appeared as if some kind of plebiscite might form the basis of a compromise. Essentially, however, Nicaragua was now in revolution. The centre would not hold. The Sandinistas were now more united than ever, and gaining in popularity and credibility. In Sergio Ramirez Mercado they even had an unofficial representative in the FAO mediation team. US perceptions were still, however, dominated by the assumption that a strong moderate centre could be found. As Pastor put it, the Administration 'drew unconsciously from . . . a political culture that reflected a wariness of sharp breaks and a preference for gradual change'.[28]

The degree to which the human rights perspective had now receded was evidenced in a memo from Pastor to Brzezinski on the Nicaraguan 'broad opposition', written on 10 January 1979. The memo referred to a letter written to President Carter by the 'broad opposition' (the FAO), referring to the recent Inter-American Human Rights Commission report on Nicaragua. Pastor advised his chief:

In view of the current status of the mediation effort, State recommends that the President not make a written response to the FAO letter. I concur in this. We should instruct Ambassador Solaun to respond orally to the FAO: (a) acknowledging the receipt of the letter, (b) expressing appreciation for the FAO's views, and (c) reiterating U.S. support for the IAHRC. We will tell the Ambassador to refrain from commenting on the genocide charge.[29]

Revolution

The failure of the mediation effort stimulated political polarisation in Nicaragua. According to Pastor, it was the very nearness which the mediation had come to a solution which 'motivated the FSLN to bury their differences and develop a winning strategy'.[30] With the OAS mediation abandoned, the Administration imposed diplomatic and economic sanctions on Somoza. (Vaky and Bowdler had wanted them applied during the mediation.) Meanwhile, elements within the CIA, without the knowledge of CIA Director

Stansfield Turner, began to investigate covert means of helping Somoza.[31]

Between January and June 1979, the US looked to the prevention of a Sandinista victory. Confirmed in May as the new Ambassador to Nicaragua, after Solaun's resignation, Lawrence Pezzullo later recalled that the White House 'was obsessed with the 'vacuum' that Somoza would leave behind him'.[32] By this time Vaky and William Bowdler were arguing that direct contact should be established with the Sandinistas, with a view to obtaining a moderation and broadening of their provisional government. This was successfully resisted by the White House, and especially by Zbigniew Brzezinski, who was now increasingly concerning himself with the Central American crisis. Even Warren Christopher, who tended to straddle the Vaky–Bowdler and Brzezinski positions, appeared to believe that Somoza could still be prevailed upon to release power to the FAO. Protesting the arrest of 'moderate' leaders like Alfonso Robelo on 30 April, Christopher again dangled before the dictator the prospect of 'extremist elements seeking a violent solution to the problems of Nicaragua'.[33]

As the FSLN launched its final offensive in late May, any notion that Somoza might weather the storm had to be abandoned. With excruciatingly unfortunate timing, the US, in mid-May, supported Nicaragua's request for a $66 million loan from the IMF. According to Pastor, the decision reflected the Administration's opposition to the introduction of 'political criteria . . . into the Fund's decision making'. Nicaragua had adopted an acceptable economic plan. Therefore, the issue:

> represented a classic tradeoff between a global interest in maintaining 'the rules of the game' for the international monetary system and a specific interest in avoiding any indication of support for a regime like Somoza's. The latter interest will prevail only when there is a compelling security crisis. In mid-May, there was a continuing security problem in Nicaragua, but it was difficult to argue that it was either compelling or a crisis at that time.[34]

Pastor's equivocations notwithstanding, the decision to support the IMF loan application represented the survival of the '*Somocismo* without (or maybe even with) Somoza' policy. The White House was especially eager to ensure the survival of the US-trained National Guard who, at the very worst, could provide a counterweight to the Cuban-trained Sandinista army in a post-Somoza Nicaragua. At this time, as Dario Moreno has pointed out, the differences between Vance and Brzezinski 'on SALT, China, and Iran were beginning to spill over into the Nicaraguan conflict'. The National Security Adviser took issue with what he saw as the naive Vance–Vaky–Pezzullo assumption that 'some middle-of-the-road regime would somehow miraculously emerge in the wake of Somoza'.[35] In early June, the President approved Brzezinski's plan to create an OAS military force to move in to fill the vacuum on Somoza's departure. Despite his personal belief that the suggestion would not gain regional support, Vance proposed to OAS foreign

ministers on 21 June that only an OAS 'peacekeeping presence' could 'facili-
tate the formation by the Nicaraguans of a transitional government of
national reconciliation'.[36]

The OAS rejected the idea. Events in Nicaragua were now reaching
denouement. The murder of ABC newsman Bill Stewart on 20 June
illustrated how far the National Guard had veered out of any control. (To
some extent, Stewart's murder undermined the position of the Somoza lobby
in Congress. Yet the Congressional thunder from the right remained intense.
On 19 June a group of Senators, led by Jesse Helms of North Carolina,
accused Carter of 'cold hostility toward our friends', and warned of a
'Cuban-style regime' emerging. Murphy reminded the President that the
Nicaraguan situation could be even more serious: 'Cuba was surrounded by
water; Nicaragua is not . . .').[37] Brzezinski was now lobbying the President,
Defence Secretary Brown, Vice-President Mondale and Hamilton Jordan to
back a plan for unilateral American military intervention. Carter was
unmoved by his suggestion. At a crisis meeting held on 25 June, the Administration's Special Coordination Committee considered whether it would be
possible to establish a 'second pillar of power', independent of Somoza and
capable of negotiating with the Sandinistas. Vaky supported his policy of
attempting, through negotiation, to prevail upon the Sandinistas to widen
and broaden their junta. The meeting opted, in effect, to pursue both strategies.[38]

American efforts to include former stalwarts of Somoza's political party in
the post-revolutionary government were rejected by the Sandinistas. On 11
July, Congressman Ted Weiss of New York wrote to the President:

It is most disturbing to note that the conditions which the United States seeks to
impose in return for Somoza's resignation are akin to those stipulated by the dictator
himself. These prerequisites – the preservation of the National Guard and the
inclusion of United States selected individuals in the junta – have likewise been
repeatedly rejected by all groups in the Nicaraguan opposition.

According to Weiss, US 'insistence on attempting to alter the character of the
Provisional Government' was serving only 'to prolong the civil war'.[39]

Plans to retain the National Guard fell away as the force disintegrated.
Through Bowdler, the Administration, in effect, accepted the Sandinista
decision to appoint a 'moderate' government, but without former pro-
Somoza people. (John Murphy characterised the 'national reconstruction
government' as consisting of 'communists and frightened "liberals" '.)[40]
Somoza finally resigned on 17 July. The State Department issued a statement
which attempted to re-focus attention on human rights issues. It proclaimed
the 'end of the most prolonged remaining system of personal rule in the
modern world'. Signalling its acceptance of the junta, it continued:

A caretaker regime is in place to begin the process of national reconciliation. A
government of national reconstruction, formed initially in exile, will assume power

from the caretaker regime. It has pledged to avoid reprisals, to provide sanctuary to those in fear, to begin immediately the immense tasks of national reconstruction, and to respect human rights and hold free elections.[41]

But conflicting signals continued. On 19 July an American DC-8 with false Red Cross markings landed at Managua airport to take away defeated National Guard officers. On 27 July a special flight brought emergency food and medical supplies to the new regime.[42]

After the revolution

In his memoir of policy in Nicaragua, Robert Pastor emphasises that there was no entirely neat contrast between the attitudes of the Carter and Reagan Administrations towards the Sandinista regime. Both 'sought to moderate and contain the revolution'. The Carter Administration 'was on the verge of terminating its aid program to Nicaragua when it left office'. The Reagan team 'entered with a mandate to end aid but did not do so for nearly ten weeks'.[43] Nevertheless, the Carter Administration, quite unlike its successor, did display some degree of understanding regarding the roots and rationale of the Sandinista revolution. Pezzullo told Congress soon after the revolution:

Sandinismo . . . is a Nicaraguan, home-grown movement. Sandino predates Castro. He was a man; he lived . . . The nature of this thing is such that you have to see it take its own form, rather than make prejudgements about it.[44]

Attempting to gain substantial aid for the new regime through Congress in September 1979, Administration spokesmen emphasised that here was an opportunity for the United States to demonstrate that it could respond positively to revolutionary change in the developing world. The mistakes of Cuba and Vietnam did not have to be endlessly recycled. As Vaky pointed out, the 'course of the Nicaraguan revolution' would be profoundly affected 'by how the United States perceives it and relates to it'.[45]

Robert Pastor's analysis of the post-revolutionary situation emphasised opportunities rather than dangers. On 20 September 1979, Pastor described the 'political situation' to Brzezinski as 'still quite fluid'. The Sandinistas had 'established their propaganda instruments' but also allowed 'other newspapers and radio stations' to criticise their regime. On 25 October, Pastor reported on an address given by Rafael Solis, the new Nicaraguan Ambassador to the United States. Solis had made 'a genuine effort to demonstrate a reasonable approach . . .'. He had 'pointedly' indicated that US aid 'would be channelled through the private sector'. Solis had, however, responded sharply to a journalist's question about Cuban–Nicaraguan relations and Cuba's status as 'a puppet of the USSR'. Solis replied that, given the history of US support for Somoza, America 'was not in a very credible position to complain about puppetry anywhere'. Four days later Pastor again reported favourably on the continuing pluralism in the Nicaraguan media. As late as

August 1980, Pastor was assuring Brzezinski that 'the Sandinistas not only listen to press criticism, but they are responsive to it'.[46]

By August 1980, hopes for avoiding a breakdown in US-Sandinista relations had receded. Even when Pastor was praising the relative freedom of the Nicaraguan media, he wrote that the country was 'largely directed by pro-Cuban, anti-American Marxists'.[47] By mid-1980, a number of developments – the postponement of free elections until 1985, the opening up of trade agreements between Managua and Moscow, the resignation of 'moderate' junta members like Violeta Chamorro and Alfonso Robelo – had convinced many in Washington that Nicaragua was indeed going the way of Cuba. Yet throughout this period, many officials concerned with the detailed management of policy – people like Pezzullo and Agency for International Development mission director Lawrence Harrison – remained convinced that a strategy of patient accommodation could prevent another Cuba. Central to this strategy, which was accepted at the highest levels of the Administration, was the re-incorporation of Nicaragua into the US-dominated international system of lending. During the latter part of 1979, the Administration encouraged World Bank and Inter-American Development Bank loans of $262 million. A deal to re-structure debt to North American, Japanese and European banks, inherited from the Somoza years, was made in September 1980. The domestic American political debate centred on Administration efforts to secure Congressional passage of a substantial aid programme. President Carter himself implored the chairman of the Senate Appropriations subcommittee on Foreign Operations in February 1980:

Unless we provide assistance to Nicaragua before the growing season begins, there will be shortages of food, further economic deterioration, and demoralization of private business. If assistance from the United States is not forthcoming soon, we can expect an exodus of middle class Nicaraguans as they conclude that the United States has turned its back on Nicaragua.[48]

A 75 million dollar aid package was stalled in Congress between September 1979 and June 1980, when it finally passed. Somoza had always boasted that he had more friends on Capitol Hill than Carter had. The dictator's old friends joined with Members who were concerned about helping pro-Soviet forces and inveterate opponents of all foreign aid to strengthen the hand of those in Managua who argued that nothing worthwhile could be extracted from Washington. The accelerating Cold War crisis atmosphere further exacerbated relations. Candidate Ronald Reagan effectively argued that Carter was financing America's enemies, not only in Nicaragua but also in neighbouring countries (notably El Salvador) whose left-wing guerrillas were being supported by Managua. In such a climate, the Sandinistas' requests for *military* aid against former Somoza supporters were bound to go unanswered. Viron Vaky later commended that 'what the U.S. did from July 1979 onward to gain influence in Nicaragua was ineffective' compared to the efforts of Cuba and the Soviets. In January 1981, the Administration declared that it had 'compelling evidence' that arms were being supplied to the El Salvador guerrillas. By the time Reagan took office, the Carter Administration had spent possibly as much as $1 million in covert funds to bolster the anti-Sandinista forces in Nicaragua. The final days of the Presidency saw the restoration of 'non-lethal' aid to the government of El Salvador.[49]

Iran

Applying human rights policies to Iran

A strategically important, oil-rich country, Iran had long formed a key part of the American dominated anti-communist security structure. Restored to power in a CIA-inspired coup in 1953, Muhammad Reza Shah Pahlavi represented to the diplomacy of Nixon and Kissinger a vital bulwark against the Soviet Union, a guaranteed source of oil and a massive consumer of American arms. By the mid-1970s, the Shah was directing Iran's huge post-1973 oil profits towards the absorption of over half of all US arms sales. Anxious to reject Kissinger's legacy in other areas, Carter appeared broadly to accept the inherited positive views of America's Persian ally. In *Keeping Faith*, Carter recorded his early appreciation of the Shah's 'ability to maintain good relations with Egypt and Saudi Arabia', while also providing 'Israel with oil in spite of the Arab boycott'. In November 1977, when the Shah visited Washington, President Carter was also 'especially eager to secure his influence in support of Sadat's dramatic visit to Jerusalem'. But, as Gary Sick, NSC staff specialist on Iran, put it, the 'security relationship was paramount'. This meant inevitably that 'some accommodation' would be required in human rights and arms sales policies. As Congressional human rights activist Donald Fraser acknowledged in the early 1970s, US human rights policies were bound to be influenced by economic, strategic and other 'interests' – 'in Iran we have them all in one place'.[50]

There was awareness in Washington of the Shah's poor record on human rights and, in particular, of the abuses perpetrated by SAVAK, the Iranian secret police. The CIA had long-standing links with SAVAK. When he was confirmed as Ambassador to Tehran in May 1977, William Sullivan was informed that the CIA–SAVAK links would continue.[51] Since 1973, Tehran had, in fact, been the headquarters of the CIA in the Middle East. Carter was aware throughout 1977 of the existence of some two and a half thousand political prisoners in Iranian goals. For a time, Tehran and Washington eyed each other with some suspicion. In May 1977, Michael Hornblow of the NSC staff reported as follows on Sullivan's confirmation. The new Ambassador would:

be arriving in Iran at a particularly critical time since a number of policies adopted by the Carter Administration in the fields of human rights, nuclear proliferation, and the

Indian Ocean are viewed by the Shah as directly affecting the entire range of US-Iranian relations.[52]

For his part, Carter recorded in his diary on 31 July 1977 that he did not care whether the Shah purchased his arms from the US or not.[53]

By the later months of 1977, the US–Iranian relationship had become warmer. Carter appears to have formed the view that, despite some continuing human rights problems, the Shah was making genuine attempts to liberalise his regime. On 25 October, the President recorded his opinion that the Shah had 'moved very rapidly' in a liberal direction. A 1977 visit to Iran by the International Committee of the Red Cross concluded that 'a substantial and significant improvement' had occurred in the treatment of prisoners.[54]

Positive perceptions of the Shah were strengthened by a series of bureaucratic victories in the State Department for pro-Tehran forces. Patricia Derian and her allies continually argued against indulging the Shah. William Sullivan saw the Derian group within the State Department as aligning 'themselves with the opponents of his regime, regardless of what cause those opponents might serve'.[55] (Brzezinski later wrote in similar terms that Henry Precht, head of the Iran Desk, was 'motivated by doctrinal dislike of the Shah and simply wanted him out of power altogether'.)[56] The State Department leadership, however, felt that the Shah should be supported. Cyrus Vance intervened to ensure that tear gas would be sold to Tehran. Peter Tarnoff reported to Brzezinski from the State Department on 23 September 1977:

It is true that Iran has not abided by some international standards related to due process. That has been particularly true in the relatively small number of criminal cases having to do with state security crimes.

I am encouraged by changes in the relevant practices during recent months. One involves a more open approach to the entire subject of human rights. Another relates to an important law, recently passed by the Iranian parliament, which introduces . . . new and potentially important guarantees of due process for defendants.[57]

Even allowing for the fact that some liberalisation was occurring, Tarnoff's report seems to hover between naivety and cynicism. Critics of the Tehran regime sought to puncture such attitudes in the 1977 debate over major arms sales to Iran, and in the extended Washington debate on Iranian human rights which attended the Shah's November 1977 visit.

Cyrus Vance promised the Shah during a visit to Tehran in May 1977 that the US would honour all arms contracts and was prepared to offer also the AWACs airborne early warning system. These promises were given in spite of a 1976 campaign commitment and a directive (issued in May 1977) that arms sales would be restrained and modulated to correspond to their recipients' record on human rights. The AWACs and other high technology military sales provoked a major reaction on Capitol Hill. Senator Thomas Eagleton declared that the sales violated 'the tenets of restraints in the arms sales policies which are being developed by the new Carter Administration'. Others in Congress pointed to the fragility of the Pahlavi regime and to the danger of sophisticated technology falling into hostile hands. Senator John Culver opined that 'the sales of AWACs to Iran goes counter to the President's own expressed principles'. The White House embarked on a sustained lobbying programme. In July, the President himself wrote personally to House Speaker O'Neill. He described his decision to make the AWACs sales in the following terms:

I took particular account of the excellent security record of Iran during our long military relationship, and the totally successful security measures Iran has used in maintaining the high technology system we have already transferred.

By October a 'compromise' had been worked out. This ensured, in effect, that the flow of arms to Iran would maintain the momentum built up during the Nixon–Ford era.[58]

The Shah's November visit was regarded by both sides as a success. Hamilton Jordan thought the Shah 'easily the most impressive' of the many heads of state the President had hitherto encountered.[59] However, significant embarrassment was caused when the police resorted to tear gas in an attempt to control anti-Pahlavi Iranian student demonstrators. Rosalynn Carter later commented that 'Jimmy knew from intelligence briefings' that there was much 'more to these demonstrations' than the Shah was prepared to admit. Pahlavi characterised the Iranian opposition as 'just a few communists'.[60]

Critics of the Shah were naturally anxious that the President should – if he insisted on meeting Pahlavi at all – at least raise human rights issues with him. Prince M. Firouz, a former Iranian minister and Ambassador to the USSR, argued this point,[61] as did Amnesty International. Within the Administration, Margaret Costanza offered the following analysis of Amnesty's reports on the 'liberalisation':

Fewer political prisoners have been officially executed in Iran in the past year than previously, but Amnesty International notes with regret that the number of political activists (who may be terrorists as stated by the government) who have been shot in the street or 'while resisting arrest' has grown.[62]

During the actual visit, Heidi Hanson of the State Department Bureau of Human Rights wrote a note to Jody Powell to the effect that the President must resist all pressure to skirt around the human rights issue: 'The bureaucrats here have to know we're here to stay – that human rights is still a part of our Foreign Policy – no matter who we are talking with.'[63] Carter did raise the issue. It may indeed, as Rosalynn Carter remembered, have been the first time an American official had ever addressed it with him. However, the President was simply told that harsh measures were needed to combat communism.[64] The competing priorities underpinning the Carter-Pahlavi dialogue were neatly encapsulated in a note of congratulation sent to President Carter after the Shah's visit by Arthur Burns, chairman of the Federal Reserve Board: 'I and my colleagues at the Federal Reserve were ever so pleased that you succeeded in persuading the Shah of Iran to forgo an increase in the price of oil next year.'[65] These competing priorities, along with a degree of Presidential self-delusion, were clearly on display when Carter visited Tehran for the 1977–8 New Year's holiday. Two days prior to the President's arrival, Iranian police occupied all dwellings along the route between the airport and the Shah's palace. Carter's toast to the Shah and remarks to journalists about Iran's 'enlightened monarch' were to become notorious. A letter written by Carter to the Shah on New Year's Day 1978 made no mention of human rights, pressed the claims of the Ford Motor Company to Iranian markets and exalted the shared US–Iranian 'objective in controlling the proliferation of nuclear weapons'.[66]

Carter's sentiments appeared to signal to the Shah that it was business as usual between Tehran and Washington. To the Iranian opposition – especially the Islamic fundamentalist opposition – they seemed to demonstrate that the American President was a dangerous hypocrite. A month after Carter's disastrous trip, Ayatollah Khomeini wrote that the President 'uses the logic of bandits':

The head of a government that has signed the Declaration of Human Rights says, 'We have military bases in Iran; we can't talk about human rights there. Respect for human rights is feasible only in countries where we have no military bases'.[67]

Revolution
Carter's election had initially encouraged all elements among the Iranian opposition. Ibrahim Yazdi, a naturalised American and a close adviser to Khomeini, gave his opinion to the Ayatollah in November 1976 that the 'liberals' were back in power in Washington. The 'Shah's friends are out', he advised, it 'is time to act'. Among the more prosperous opponents of the regime it even became fashionable to give and receive copies of *Why Not the Best?*. Some oppositionists continued to hope, even after the New Year visit, that Carter would extend his human rights policies to Iran. (Most such opponents appear to have believed that even the Shah's detailed behaviour could be controlled from Washington.) From February 1978 onwards, however, Khomeini in particular seems to have developed a strong personal hatred and distrust of the American President.[68]

On 9 January 1978, only eight days after Carter's departure from Iran, police fired on a group of students, in the holy city of Qom. They were demonstrating against government attacks on the exiled Ayatollah Khomeini. Within the American foreign policy bureaucracy, most top Middle East personnel were preoccupied with the Egypt–Israel negotiations. Iranian affairs were handled primarily by Henry Precht, regional desk head at the

State Department, Gary Sick at the NSC and Robert Murray at the Pentagon. Beset by poor intelligence from Tehran and a general lack of comprehension regarding the potency of the Islamic fundamentalist movement, the American response to the events of 1978 was cumbersome and dilatory. The first White House meeting on Iran did not take place until 2 November. By this time violent rioting, strikes and massacres – for example the Black Friday killings in Tehran on 8 September – had pitched the entire country into revolutionary confrontation.[69]

While Washington was dithering on the Iranian disturbances, it was at least not sending contradictory signals. The Administration simply pressed for better intelligence and offered the Shah generalised support. On 10 September, Carter telephoned Tehran to wish Pahlavi 'the best in resolving these problems and . . . in his efforts to implement reforms'.[70] The Shah's announcement that free elections would be held in 1979 confirmed many State Department officers in their view that the regime could survive through liberalisation. State produced its first comprehensive plan for the crisis on 24 October. It recommended that reform should continue, that the US should oppose any military takeover and that contacts should be established with Khomeini. The plan was opposed within the Administration at one level by Ambassador Sullivan, who wrote that America's destiny was to work with the Shah. At a higher level still, it was opposed by Brzezinski, who, in effect, suppressed State's analysis so that Carter would not see it. By the end of October 1978, Brzezinski had, to some extent because of the influence of Iranian Ambassador Ardashir Zahedi, become converted to the view that only a military crackdown – the 'iron fist' – could save the Shah. As Brzezinski averred in 1982: 'I favoured a military coup before things fell apart.'[71]

Against this background of high-level disagreement arrived Ambassador Sullivan's admonition of 9 November that perhaps Washington should 'think the unthinkable' and contemplate an Iran with no Shah. At the 2 November meeting of the Special Coordination Committee in the White House, Brzezinski attempted, with only a limited degree of success, to sell his 'iron fist' solution to his fellow participants. A telephone call from Brzezinski to the Shah, however, appeared to suggest that there was widespread support for military crackdown. Cyrus Vance meanwhile made his position clear: the restoration of order was vital, but this could not be achieved by force alone. Explaining State Department policy to a Congressional critic in December, Douglas Bennet emphasised that Iran's upheavals were 'primarily an internal matter . . . which the Iranians themselves have to resolve'. The Shah, Bennet pointed out, 'has committed his government to a program of political liberalisation'.[72] The huge rift between the NSC and the State Department was reflected in a letter sent in December 1978 by Henry Precht to Ambassador Sullivan. Precht referred to a top secret list of questions that had been sent to the Shah – a list which he, Precht, had not been shown, 'such is the level of distrust that exists in the White House towards the State Department . . .'.[73]

The Shah's response to the messages coming from Washington was a disjointed amalgam of reform and 'iron fist'.

In November 1978, Secretary of the Treasury Michael Blumenthal, a recent visitor to Tehran, managed to persuade Brzezinski that an independent study should be commissioned on the Iranian crisis. George Ball, a senior foreign policy adviser from the Kennedy and Johnson years, was called upon. Ball concluded that the Shah was 'on the verge of collapse', that military repression would not work and that power should be transferred to a Council of Notables recruited by the US. Discreet contacts should be made with Khomeini. Ball's recommendations were rejected, on 12 December, by Carter and Brzezinski. Ball did manage to persuade the President not to send his National Security Adviser to Tehran, but emerged with the view that Brzezinski was 'trying to emulate Kissinger's rise to prominence by inflating and manipulating the NSC'.[74]

Ball's perception that the State Department was being excluded from the process in Washington was essentially accurate. In Tehran, however, Sullivan was still precariously in post, and was able to implement a strategy of maintaining contact with the oppositional groups, and of refusing to confirm to the Shah that the US wanted a military crackdown. During the Shah's final days, however – he left Iran for good on 16 January 1979 – US policy was in chaos. Brzezinski was still advocating a military 'solution', but was held back by Carter and Mondale. The President, in Brzezinski's phrase, found the idea of a coup 'morally troublesome'.[75] A mission led by General Robert Huyser attempted to pull together the disintegrating Iranian military behind Shapur Bakhtiar, the new civilian leader designated by the Shah. Huyser sought also to protect US electronic spy surveillance posts. The General's reports, both to Carter and along an independent channel established with the Pentagon, indicated the rift with Sullivan. Defence Secretary Harold Brown later recalled: 'I was on the phone every day with Huyser. Vance was with Sullivan. They gave conflicting advice.' Commenting on Sullivan's attempts to establish contact with the fundamentalist Islamic opposition, Huyser subsequently complained that Washington 'not only conceived but actually implemented conflicting policies simultaneously'.[76]

In reality, despite Huyser's hopes, the condition and morale of the Iranian military had collapsed to such an extent that doubt must be cast on the assumption that an effective 'iron fist' solution was ever feasible. It was precisely the condition of the military which caused Harold Brown to steer away from Brzezinski's hard line.[77] The 'soft' option of attempting to conciliate the fundamentalists was not being advanced only by Sullivan. Carter seriously considered sending a mission under former State Department official Ted Eliot to meet the Ayatollah in Paris. Cyrus Vance wanted the Eliot mission to proceed if for no other reason than to attempt to delay Khomeini's return. The Secretary of State pointed out that the Ayatollah was 'strongly anti-Communist' and might be amenable to the view that 'unless he allowed

Bakhtiar time to form a viable government, the Communists might seize the leadership of the radical Left'. The Eliot mission was opposed by Brzezinski and rejected by Carter, who, according to Vance, felt that 'such a step would be taken to mean we had abandoned the Shah'. Informal contacts were made with Khomeini. According to Vance, the 'case for actively urging the parties to negotiate an understanding was impeded by Brzezinski's determined opposition to direct contacts' with Khomeini.[78] On 1 February 1979, the Ayatollah returned to Iran and, within days, in Richard Cottam's phrase, 'the revolution had become an accomplished fact'. The US, as Sullivan reported, had become 'identified with evaporating institutions'. On 11 February, General Huyser was asked by (then) Deputy Defence Secretary Charles Duncan if he 'would be willing to go back to Tehran and conduct a military takeover'. Huyser felt that, for a variety of reasons – from the objective difficulties facing US intervention to the state of Presidential and public opinion – this was impossible.[79]

After the revolution – the hostage crisis

In the immediate post-revolutionary period, the Department of State took the lead in attempting to retrieve a viable policy. State's position embodied the assumption that a working relationship could be fashioned with a post-revolutionary 'moderate' regime. Those Pahlavi supporters in the US who pointed to the danger of Soviet influence in Iran were ignored. As Vance put it, it was believed that 'over time U.S. and Iranian interests in a strong, stable, non-Communist Iran' would allow a new relationship to develop.[80] The success of Deputy Prime Minister Ibrahim Yazdi in terminating the first, mid-February, assault on the US Embassy (which involved the temporary seizure of Sullivan and his staff) seemed to attest to the feasibility of Vance's approach. The Secretary of State's immediate concerns were for the integrity of sensitive electronic surveillance equipment and intelligence, and for the safety of US citizens. On 16 February, it was announced that the US would maintain normal diplomatic relations with the provisional government of Mehdi Bazargan.

The provisional government, in fact, was but one of many factions contending for power. The State Department strategy was based on the assumption that some kind of 'moderate' force could emerge from the chaos, and that the US should identify itself with that force. This policy stance was, to a large extent, the product of ignorance. As Henry Precht wrote in July: 'We simply do not have the bios, inventory of political groups or current picture of daily life as it evolves at various levels in Iran.'[81] In this frenetic and confusing atmosphere, the policy of seeking out the 'moderates' was to some extent neutralised by a kind of fatalism about the eventual success of the religious fundamentalists.[82] However, no contact was made with Khomeini. As Assistant Secretary Harold Saunders informed Vance in September: 'We have had no direct contact with the man who remains the strongest political leader in

Iran.'[83]

Iranian political opinion, so long attuned to the watching of events in Washington, began to see American interference everywhere: in Senator Javits' May resolution in Congress, condemning the revolutionary executions; in Senator Henry Jackson's condemnations of the revolution; and, above all, in the heavy-handed attempts by the CIA to insinuate itself into the 'moderate' wing of the revolutionary leadership. All Iranian factions half expected a replay of 1953. The CIA's attempted wooing of Abolhassan Bani-Sadr and of the 'moderate' Liberation Movement was exposed in November when student revolutionaries stormed the US Embassy and seized, along with the hostages, intelligence documents.[84]

The taking of the hostages was precipitated by Carter's decision to admit the Shah to the US to receive medical treatment. Initially, the President had felt that Pahlavi was 'just as well off playing tennis in Acapulco as . . . in California'.[85] However, the diagnosis of the Shah's cancer (from which he was to die in July 1980) changed the President's mind. There was also, of course, the familiar question of US 'credibility' and promises to its allies. Henry Kissinger and Nelson Rockefeller, strong supporters of the Shah in the US, urged threse arguments vigorously. Veteran diplomat John McCloy, whose law firm now represented the Shah, had written to Warren Christopher in April 1979 that a refusal to admit Pahlavi 'or any equivocation on our part, I fear, would be taken as persuasive evidence of our unreliability as a protector of our former friends when the consequences of such assistance appeared inauspicious'.[86] Both humanitarian arguments and McCloy's point about 'credibility' also ruled out any later accession to Tehran's demand that the Shah be handed over to atone for his sins. (A parallel demand, that all the Shah's financial assets be transferred to Tehran, was not feasible for Washington to comply with, and illustrated the extraordinary omnipotence which the Islamic fundamentalists assumed that the US government enjoyed over international affairs.) In December, the Shah was, in Hedley Donovan's phrase, 'shunted along' to Panama.[87]

Between November 1979 and January 1981, US policy towards Iran was centred on the hostages. Indeed, to a large degree, the entire focus of the Administration, and indeed the country (especially until summer 1980), became fixed on events in Tehran. Agriculture Secretary Robert Bergland recollected: 'The Iranian hostage crisis brought everything to a screeching halt.' CIA Director Stansfield Turner remembered everything being 'totally consumed by Iran'.[88] Walter Cronkite took to ending the CBS *News* every evening by enumerating how many days the hostages had been held. As George Ball complained, the crisis rapidly acquired an element of national soap opera. More profoundly, the crisis resonated with myth, cultural memory and racially-charged emotion. It recalled the frontier tradition of narrative dealing with hostage-taking by Indians. It fed on suspicions and cultural stereotypes of the Near East which had already been released during the oil price hikes of the early 1970s. Above all, it touched on deep collective fears of national decline and vulnerability. State Department spokesman Hodding Carter recalled America's self-image in this period: that of a muscle-bound superpower, a tethered giant, eternally exposed to humiliation at the hands of lesser powers: 'a little country of Muslims and people who ran around in robes and looked funny could do all this to us and we couldn't do anything about it.'[89] The note of national alarm was set by the White House, rather than by press and television. On 2 December 1979, Carter declared his re-election campaigning 'postponed'. He compared his stance to that of President Lincoln who, at 'the height of the Civil War' decided that his only task was to save the Union, not to worry about his own political future: 'Now I must devote my concerted efforts to resolving the Iranian crisis.' For Carter, hostage release became, in his own words, 'almost . . . an obsession'.[90]

Carter's reactions were intensely personal. As Harold Saunders, Assistant Secretary of State for Near Eastern Affairs, later wrote, the President was 'simply acting as Jimmy Carter – an outraged and concerned American who happened to be President'. Carter regarded anything less than an all-out, unrelenting public commitment to the hostages as morally unacceptable. He also felt that the best way of meeting Senator Kennedy's challenge was to do – and be seen to do – what was right.[91]

The extreme prioritisation of the hostage issue, embedded in the wider post-Afghanistan invasion crisis atmosphere, yielded initial benefits to the Carter cause in the nomination race. However, as the President's team acknowledged in its 1980 electoral post-mortem, the 'rose garden' strategy was a long-term disaster.[92] Failure to secure hostage release humiliated the American leadership. As Brzezinski later remembered, the crisis significantly (and in Zbig's view, unfairly) increased Carter's reputation for 'waffling', ineffective symbolism and indecision.[93] By November 1980, the American people had simply endured too many Presidentially-defined crises from which the President seemed unable to rescue them. For all its inclination towards the proclamation of 'crisis', the Carter Administration never developed a convincing rhetoric of public crisis.[94]

The promise not to campaign – to abjure 'political' activity – was naive and misconceived. Virtually any activity in election year can plausibly be regarded as a species of 'campaigning'. Thus, Carter's promise not to engage in 'politics' simply led to a situation where *any* activity on the part of the White House could be attacked as hypocritical. When Carter attempted, as he did, to use the advantages of incumbency and patronage to further his electoral cause, he was berated and abused all the more fiercely.[95]

According to Gary Sick, the bureaucratic processes developed to handle the crisis operated in 'almost textbook fashion'. They appeared (except in the rescue mission) to illustrate that crisis management can, by decreasing bureaucratic obstruction and facilitating information flows, maximise decisional rationality. For one thing, Carter was clearly in charge. Brzezinski chaired the Special Coordination Committee meetings which met virtually every morning to consider the crisis; but the President annotated Sick's summary of proceedings, with these Presidential annotations forming the basis of the following morning's business. The Committee included the regular foreign policy and defence leaders but also Treasury Secretary William Miller, Energy Secretary Charles Duncan and Attorney General Benjamin Civiletti. The articulation of perspectives from outside the national security establishment was regarded as valuable, and the Committee developed a strong sense of purpose and directed flexibility.[96]

What it could not do was produce results. Above all, the Administration was faced with the fearsome difficulty of trying to read, and second-guess, the situation in Iran. The precise motives of the hostage-takers – intimately bound up with their desire to force Khomeini's hand – were not clearly understood. The US had no 'stay-behind assets' in Tehran, picking up information for Washington.[97] The Administration did not know who was in control in Iran. Enormous efforts were expended in, as Deputy US Representative to the United Nations W.J. Vanden Heuvel described his conversations with Iran's UN delegation, 'talking to the wind'.[98]

Despite the relatively smooth functioning of the Special Coordination Committee, the Vance–Brzezinski rift continued. The Secretary of State felt that 'the hostages were pawns in a power struggle and valuable only as long as they were unharmed'. The US would not hand over the Shah, allow the hostages to be tried or offer any demeaning apology for past American actions. All 'possible channels of communication' would be opened to Tehran – secret back-channels were even established to the Palestinian Liberation Organisation – and international opinion mobilised to isolate Iran.[99] Essentially this strategy was followed. Brzezinski, however, favoured a much tougher line. According to Stansfield Turner, the National Security Adviser repeatedly canvassed the CIA in pursuit of 'unrealistic' covert operations in Iran.[100] Zbig later gave his opinion that Carter could have won the 1980 election had he been willing 'to take a position that at stake' in the crisis was 'national honor, national security and not lives'. At some point Carter should, declared Brzezinski in 1982, have taken the decision that 'we will preserve national security and national honor, but not lives' and 'bomb the hell out of Tehran and have the hostages killed'.[101]

The Vance–Carter 'softly softly' approach became actually even more conciliatory after the Soviet invasion of Afghanistan. In the early part of 1980, it was feared that the crumbling of any Iranian leadership might tempt a Soviet intervention. Amir Taheri, editor of *Kayhan* (a leading Iranian newspaper before the revolution), has argued that Carter's attention was actually insufficiently attuned to the preservation of the hostages' lives. According to Taheri, the President was pursuing 'multiple objectives': attempting to turn the crisis to his own electoral advantage, helping Tehran 'moderates' and preventing a Soviet advance. This policy resulted in the mullahs seeing him as weak, and in the USSR obstructing moves to release the hostages.[102] Republicans regularly criticised Carter for trying to 'hype' the crisis and feared a neatly engineered 'October surprise' – a pre-election release. To much domestic opinion, Carter was simply not acting forcefully enough. Indeed, in view of the Iranians' blatant violations of international law, it can be argued that the US reaction was very restrained. George Kennan told the Senate Foreign Relations Committee in February 1980 that the US should have declared the hostage seizure a hostile act, which inaugurated a state of war.[103]

Despite all the misery and frustration, some successes were achieved. The hostages *were* eventually released. (However, subsequent assertions that the Carter Administration did not offer an 'arms for hostages' deal need to be treated with caution. Following the outbreak of the Iran–Iraq war, the US became further concerned about the possibility of a complete Iranian collapse. The Administration did offer – without success – to release arms negotiated by the Shah if the hostages were released.)[104] It is nevertheless arguable that the hostages' release was delayed as much in response to machinations involving the Reagan team as to the policies of the Carter Administration.[105] On two occasions before the end of 1979, the UN Security Council was successfully persuaded to call upon Iran to give up the hostages. Even James Fallows congratulated the Administration in May 1980 for having beaten 'the Iranians to the punch' by cutting off oil imports and freezing assets, and for 'managing the transition from tough guy to soft guy' after the Afghanistan invasion.[106]

The major debacle, of course, was the rescue mission. At the heart of the problem, predictably, was the Vance-Brzezinski split. Military options had been considered ever since the hostages had been taken, but had been ruled out as impractical or counterproductive. Vance had consistently opposed them. By April 1980, all other major participants, as is clear from their memoirs, felt considerable pressure to take decisive action. The frustrations were becoming intolerable. On 25 March, Edward Kennedy had beaten Carter, 59–41 per cent, in the New York primary. The 'rose garden' strategy was in tatters. Hamilton Jordan told Defence Secretary Brown: 'We're in a box.' Sanctions had been imposed, but still the US had no leverage on Khomeini.[107] The crucial, deciding meeting took place on 11 April. Present were Carter, Mondale, Brown, Christopher, Brzezinski, David Jones (Chairman of the Joint Chiefs of Staff), Stansfield Turner, Jody Powell and Jordan. Not only was this group significantly smaller than the regular crisis management team, it excluded Vance, who was on vacation in Florida. Warren Christopher was alarmed to find that the plan was so far advanced and was, in effect, being approved; but he assumed Vance had been informed about it. When the Secretary of State returned, he was 'dismayed and mortified'.[108] Vance reiterated his objections:

even if the rescue mission did free some of our embassy staff, the Iranians could simply take more hostages from among the American journalists still in Tehran. We would then be worse off than before, and the whole region would be inflamed by our action. Our national interests in the whole region would be severely injured and we might face an Islamic–Western war. Finally, . . . there was a real chance that we would force the Iranians into the arms of the Soviets.[109]

Vance was overruled. The mission went ahead with no proper rehearsal, no overall plan and a naive faith in technology. At the implementation level, inter-service rivalry compounded the political errors. Major General John Singlaub later commented: 'We tried to bring disparate units from all over the Armed Forces, from all over the world – and then put them into an ad hoc arrangement to do a very complicated plan.'[110] It is tempting to agree with the President that the mission's failure was due to 'a strange series of mishaps'[111] – Carter's notorious bad luck. Yet it is clear that the whole episode was redolent with poor planning, unreflective 'groupthink' among key advisers and the damaging spin-off from the Vance–Brzezinski rivalry. On 27 April, Vance became the first Secretary of State to resign over matters of substantive policy since William Jennings Bryan in 1915.

Reflections on Nicaragua and Iran

There are striking parallels between the Nicaraguan and Iranian experiences: the bureaucratic battling, the centrality of the Vance–Brzezinski split, the poor intelligence, the assumption at certain points by factions in Nicaragua and Iran of virtual American omnipotence, the debates about whether to open contacts with 'extremists' – even the admittance of the two dictators to the US for medical treatment. Both cases illustrated the limits of human rights policies and the strong hold of past commitments.

There was, however, at least one crucial difference. In Nicaragua, the human rights policy was a reality, albeit compromised and orchestrated by Somoza for his own purposes. Containment of Soviet power was always potentially an important consideration, even in the Administration's early days.[112] However, the Administration did attempt to disassociate itself from the dictator, in the assumption that American interests were best served by encouraging reform and wooing 'progressive' forces in Nicaragua. In Iran, the policy was little more than a gesture. The Administration was prepared simply to take the Shah's word that liberalisation was proceeding. Thus were hopes raised and eventually disappointed among 'moderate' Iran opinion.

The two cases demonstrate the extreme difficulty in exorcising the legacy of the past. 'Global community' activists within the Carter Administration did not fully appreciate or anticipate these problems. Institutionalised resistance at home always threatened to cause the 'new agenda' to degenerate into symbolism, or to be applied only to countries (like pre-1979 Nicaragua) with little apparent security or economic significance. Abroad, the Administration's insistence that now was the 'age of limits', that the days of indiscriminate and adventuristic globalism were over, was – with some reason – not widely accepted.

With hindsight, it can be argued that the US should have disengaged from Somoza much earlier. 'Moderates' *within* the ranks of the Sandinistas were ignored. There was an unwillingness, both in Iran and Nicaragua, to re-think policy. In Iran, for example, a full-scale review following the January 1978 killings in Qom might have given American policy a sense of informed purpose. Serious pursuit of human rights initiatives in 1977 and 1978 might have encouraged a serious reform process in Iran and headed-off extreme anti-Americanism. As it was, with decisional circuits severely overloaded, policy in both cases limped along behind events. In Iran and Nicaragua, Carter himself made some important blunders – notably the letter to Somoza and the 1977–8 New Year visit to Tehran. Above all, American policy-makers showed little understanding of the dynamics of revolution, especially regarding social and economic forces. The Administration tended to assume either that all change was dangerous or that extremism could be assuaged by human rights liberalisation rather than by fundamental social and economic upheavals.

In both revolutions the US policy process evolved from a relatively open, decentralised system to a more secretive, centralised one in which the National Security Adviser contended with the Secretary of State. Brzezinski's conduct regarding Iranian policy in 1978 amounted to a conscious attempt to undermine collectively agreed policy. Also, in the case of the hostage crisis, it should be noted that, in the words of Harold Hongju Koh, the Administration undertook 'one of the most dramatic exercises of presidential powers in foreign affairs in peacetime United States history'.[113] The freezing of Iranian assets and suspension of Iranian claims pending in US courts enjoyed little, if any, statutory or constitutional authority. (This was made evident in a 1981 Supreme Court decision.) Moreover, the Administration made no effort clearly to bring itself into line with the 1973 War Powers Resolution by informing Congress prior to the hostage rescue mission.[114]

James Theberge, President Ford's Ambassador to Managua, concluded that the lesson of Carter's experience in Nicaragua was that security must come before human rights.[115] The following chapter, a general account of Carter's foreign and human rights policies, will, *inter alia*, examine that conclusion.

Notes

1 Robert A. Pastor, *Condemned to Repetition: The United States and Nicaragua* (Princeton: Princeton University Press, 1988), p. 52. See also R. D. Schulzinger, 'Patterns in the Mess: The United States and Nicaragua', *Diplomatic History*, 13, 1989, pp. 255–63.

2 Pastor, *Condemned to Repetition*, pp. 50, 77–8.

3 Cited in Bernard Diederich, *Somoza and the Legacy of US Involvement in*

Central America (London: Junction Books, 1982), p. 144.

4   Pastor, *Condemned to Repetition*, pp. 53, 55. See also J. A. Booth, *The End and the Beginning: The Nicaraguan Revolution* (Boulder: Westview, 1982), p. 129.

5   *Ibid.*, pp. 51–2; Dario Moreno, *US Policy in Central America: The Endless Debate* (Miami: Florida International University Press, 1990), p. 48; Anthony Lake, *Somoza Falling* (Boston: Houghton Mifflin, 1989), pp. 71–2. See also James Theberge, 'The Collapse of the Somoza Regime', in Daniel Pipes and Adam Garfinkle, *Friendly Tyrants: An American Dilemma* (London: Macmillan, 1991), pp. 109–29.

6   See Lars Schoultz, *Human Rights and United States Policy Toward Latin America* (Princeton: Princeton University Press, 1981), pp. 60, 103; Holly Sklar, *Washington's War on Nicaragua* (Boston: South End Press, 1988), p. 24; Jimmy Carter, *Keeping Faith* (London: Collins, 1982), p. 181.

7   See Alex R. Hybel, *How Leaders Reason: US Intervention in the Caribbean Basin and Latin America* (Oxford: Blackwell, 1990), p. 237.

8   Letter, E. Koch to the President, 1 July 1977, WHCF: SF: Foreign Affairs, box FO-31 (folder, 'FO 3–2/CO 114').

9   Letter, J. Murphy to the President, 1 July 1977, *ibid.*

10   *American Foreign Policy: Basic Documents, 1977–1980* (Washington DC: Department of State, 1983), p. 423. See also R. A. Pastor, 'The Carter Administration and Latin America: A Test of Principle', in J. D. Martz, ed., *United States Policy in Latin America* (Lincoln: University of Nebraska Press, 1988), pp. 61–97, at 82.

11   See Walter LaFeber, *Inevitable Revolutions: The United States in Central America* (New York: Norton, 1983), pp. 230–1.

12   Memo to Z. Brzezinski from P. Tarnoff, 6 Sept. 1977, box CO-46, WHCF: SF: Countries (folder, 'CO 114').

13   Cited in Sklar, *Washington's War Against Nicaragua*, p. 10.

14   See Joshua Muravchik, *The Uncertain Crusade* (Lanham: Hamilton Press, 1986), pp. 37–8.

15   See Moreno, *US Policy in Central America*, p. 51.

16   Hybel, *How Leaders Reason*, p. 239.

17   *Condemned to Repetition*, p. 79.

18   On US aid to Somoza, see Jenny Pearce, *Under The Eagle* (London: Latin America Bureau, 1982), pp. 117–21.

19   Letter printed in Sklar, *Washington's War on Nicaragua*, p. 15.

20   Hybel, *How Leaders Reason*, p. 241.

21   A. Somoza (as told to Jack Cox), *Nicaragua Betrayed* (Boston: Western Islands, 1980), p. 147.

22   Lake, *Somoza Falling*, p. 85.

23   Moreno, *US Policy in Central America*, p. 53.

24   Lake, *Somoza Falling*, p. 86.

25   Pastor, *Condemned to Repetition*, pp. 66–71; Lake, *Somoza Falling*, p. 86; Frank McNeil, *War and Peace in Central America: Reality and Illusion* (New York: Scribner's Sons, 1988), pp. 111–12; Booth, *The End and the Beginning*, p. 161; Thomas M. Franck and Edward Weisband, *Foreign Policy by Congress* (New York: Oxford University Press, 1979), p. 96.

26   Memo to Z. Brzezinski from R. Pastor, 1 Aug. 1978, box CO-46, WHCF: SF: Countries (folder, 'CO 114').

27   Letter, D. J. Bennet to L. Hamilton, 24 Oct. 1978, *ibid.* See also Pastor,

Condemned to Repetition, p. 70; Richard R. Fagen, 'The Carter Administration and Latin America: Business as Usual?', *Foreign Affairs*, 57, 1978, pp. 652–69, at 662.

28 *Condemned to Repetition*, p. 74. See also McNeil, *War and Peace in Central America*, p. 112.

29 Memo to Z. Brzezinski from R. Pastor, 10 Jan. 1979, box CO-46, WHCF: SF: Countries (folder, 'CO 114').

30 *Condemned to Repetition*, p. 120.

31 See Sklar, *Washington's War Against Nicaragua*, p. 22.

32 Lake, *Somoza Falling*, p. 230.

33 Diederich, *Somoza*, p. 244.

34 Pastor, *Condemned to Repetition*, p. 129.

35 Moreno, *US Policy in Central America*, p. 59.

36 *American Foreign Policy: Basic Documents*, p. 1319.

37 Letter, Senators Helms, Hatch, McClure, Jepsen, Thurmond, Gordon Humphrey to the President, 19 June 1979, box CO-47, WHCF: SF: Countries (folder, 'CO 114'); letter, J. Murphy to the President, 28 June 1979, box CO-46, WHCF: SF: Countries (folder, 'CO 114').

38 See Moreno, *US Policy in Central America*, pp. 59–60; Pastor, *Condemned to Repetition*, pp. 147–49.

39 Letter, T. Weiss to the President, 11 July 1979, box CO-47, WHCF: SF: Countries (folder, 'CO 114').

40 Letter, J. Murphy and L. McDonald to the President, 28 June 1979, box CO-46, WHCF: SF: Countries (folder, 'CO 114').

41 *American Foreign Policy: Basic Documents*, p. 1320.

42 *Ibid.*, p. 1321; Moreno, *US Policy in Central America*, p. 62.

43 *Condemned to Repetition*, p. 191.

44 Cited in LaFeber, *Inevitable Revolutions*, p. 239.

45 Pastor, *Condemned to Repetition*, p. 208.

46 Memo to Z. Brzezinski and D. Aaron from R. Pastor, 20 Sept. 1979, box CO-47, WHCF: SF: Countries (folder, 'CO 114'); memo to Z. Brzezinski from R. Pastor, 25 Oct. 1979, ibid.; memo to Z. Brzezinski, D. Aaron and H. Owen from R. Pastor, 29 Oct, 1979, *ibid.*; memo to Z. Brzezinski and D. Aaron from R. Pastor, 15 Aug. 1980, *ibid.*

47 15 Aug. 1980 memo, *ibid.*

48 Letter, President Carter to D. Inouye, 25 Feb. 1980, *ibid.*

49 See Peter Kornbluh, 'The Covert War', in T. W. Walker, ed., *Reagan Versus the Sandinistas: The Undeclared War* (Boulder: Westview, 1987), pp. 21–38, at 21.

50 Subcommittee on International Organizations, House Committee on International Relations, Committee print: *Human Rights Conditions in Selected Countries and the U.S. Response*, July 1978, p. 143 (Fraser, 1971); Carter, *Keeping Faith*, p. 435; Gary Sick, *All Fall Down: America's Tragic Encounter with Iran* (New York: Random House, 1985), p. 25. See also Cyrus Vance, *Hard Choices* (New York: Simon and Schuster, 1983), p. 317; D. S. McLellan, *Cyrus Vance* (New Jersey: Bowman and Allanheld, 1985), p. 127; Muravchik, *The Uncertain Crusade*, p. 141 (interview with Stephen Cohen).

51 W. H. Sullivan, *Mission to Iran* (New York: Norton, 1981), p. 21. On the Shah's human rights record, see House Committee on International Relations, *Human Rights Conditions in Selected Countries*, pp. 123–144; Muhammad Reza

Pahlavi, *The Shah's Story* (London: Michael Joseph, 1980), pp. 169–73.

52   Memo to T. Smith from M. Hornblow, 19 May 1977, box CO-31, WHCF: SF: Countries (folder, 'CO 71'); *Keeping Faith*, p. 435. See also E. J. Epstein, 'Secrets from the CIA Archive in Tehran', *Orbis*, 51, 1987, pp. 33–42.

53   *Keeping Faith*, p. 434.

54   William Shawcross, *The Shah's Last Ride: The Fate of an Ally* (New York: Simon and Schuster, 1988), p. 201; *Keeping Faith*, p. 438. See also D. C. McGaffey, 'Policy and Practice: Human Rights in the Shah's Iran', in D. D. Newsom, ed., *The Diplomacy of Human Rights* (Lanham: University Press of America, 1986), pp. 69–79.

55   Sullivan, *Mission to Iran*, pp. 147–8.

56   Z. Brzezinski, *Power and Principle* (London: Weidenfeld and Nicolson, 1983), p. 355.

57   Memo to Z. Brzezinski from P. Tarnoff, 23 Sept. 1977, box CO-31 (folder, 'CO 71'); Sullivan, *Mission to Iran*, p. 148.

58   James A. Bill, *The Eagle and the Lion: The Tragedy of American–Iranian Relations* (New Haven: Yale University Press, 1988), pp. 229–30 (Eagleton and Culver); letter, President Carter to T. O'Neill, 28 July 1977, box CO-31, WHCF: SF: Countries (folder, 'CO 71'). See also Michael A. Ledeen and William Lewis, *Debacle* (New York: Knopf, 1981), p. 80; Sam C. Sarkesian, ed., *Defense Policy and the Presidency: Carter's First Years* (Boulder: Westview, 1979).

59   H. Jordan, *Crisis* (New York: Putnam's Sons, 1982), p. 89.

60   R. Carter, *First Lady from Plains* (Boston: Houghton Mifflin, 1984), p. 306.

61   Letter, M. Firouz to the President, 18 Oct. 1977, box CO-31, WHCF: SF: Countries (folder, 'CO 71').

62   Memo from M. Costanza to Z. Brzezinski, 11 Nov. 1977, *ibid.*

63   Memo (handwritten) from H. Hanson to J. Powell, 16 Nov. 1977, *ibid.*

64   *Keeping Faith*, p. 436; R. Carter, *First Lady from Plains*, p. 306.

65   Letter, A. Burns to the President, 28 Nov. 1977, box CO-31, WHCF: SF: Countries (folder, 'CO 71'). See also Vance, *Hard Choices*, p. 321.

66   Letter, President Carter to the Shah, 1 Jan. 1978, box CO-31, WHCF: SF: Countries (folder, 'CO 71').

67   Cited in Bill, *The Eagle and the Lion*, p. 234.

68   See Amir Taheri, *The Spirit of Allah: Khomeini and the Islamic Revolution* (London: Hutchinson, 1985), pp. 211–14; Gary Sick, *October Surprise* (London: I. B. Tauris, 1991), pp. 85, 157; John Simpson, *Behind Iranian Lines* (London: Robson Books, 1988), p. 154; Richard W. Cottam, *Iran and the United States* (Pittsburgh: University of Pittsburgh Press, 1988), p. 157; Dilip Hiro, *Iran under the Ayatollahs* (London: Routledge and Kegan Paul, 1985), p. 170.

69   See Barry Rubin, *Paved With Good Intentions: The American Experience in Iran* (London: Penguin, 1981), pp. 206–8.

70   See *Keeping Faith*, p. 438; Alexander Moens, 'President Carter's Advisers and the Fall of the Shah', *Political Science Quarterly*, 106, 1991, pp. 211–37, at 218; Said Amir Arjomand, *The Turban and the Crown: The Islamic Revolution in Iran* (New York: Oxford University Press, 1988), p. 128.

71   Brzezinski, MC transcript, p. 69. See also Alexander Moens, *Foreign Policy Under Carter: Testing Multiple Advocacy Decision-Making* (Boulder: Westview, 1990), pp. 142–4; Brzezinski, *Power and Principle*, p. 394; Sick, *All Fall Down*, p. 60;

John D. Stempel, *Inside the Iranian Revolution* (Bloomington: Indiana University Press, 1980), p. 290.

72 Letter, D. Bennet to R. Dellums, 22 Dec. 1978, box CO-31, WHCF: SF: Countries (folder, 'CO 71'). See also Moens, 'President Carter's Advisers . . .', p. 219; Anthony Parsons, *The Pride and the Fall* (London: Butler and Turner, 1984), p. 91.

73 Cited in Bill, *The Eagle and the Lion*, p. 252.

74 George Ball, *The Past Has Another Pattern* (New York: Norton, 1982), pp. 457–9.

75 *Power and Principle*, p. 382. See also Sullivan, *Mission to Iran*, pp. 222–4; Sick, *All Fall Down*, pp. 128–36.

76 Robert E. Huyser, *Mission to Iran* (London: Andre Deutsch, 1980), pp. 292–3; Moens, 'President Carter's Advisers . . .', p. 230 (Brown).

77 *Ibid.*, p. 233.

78 Vance, *Hard Choices*, pp. 336–40.

79 Huyser, *Mission to Iran*, pp. 283–4; Vance, *Hard Choices*, p. 341; Cottam, *Iran and the United States*, p. 185.

80 Vance, *Hard Choices*, p. 343; *Time*, 22 Sept. 1980, pp. 16–21 (Brzezinski blamed for loss of Iran).

81 Cited in Bill, *The Eagle and the Lion*, p. 276.

82 See Cottam, *Iran and the United States*, p. 207.

83 Cited in Bill, *The Eagle and the Lion*, p. 281. See also Sick, *All Fall Down*, p. 172.

84 See Bill, *The Eagle and the Lion*, pp. 278–93; also, John Ranelagh, *The Agency: The Rise and Decline of the CIA* (London: Weidenfeld and Nicolson, 1986), pp. 651–3.

85 Carter, MC transcript, p. 37.

86 Letter, J. McCloy to W. Christopher, 16 Apr. 1979, box CO-31, WHCF: SF: Countries (folder, 'CO 71'). See also Jordan, *Crisis*, pp. 28–32.

87 H. Donovan, *Roosevelt to Reagan* (New York: Harper and Row, 1985), p. 173. Warren Christopher gives a good account of the legal and practical limits on US policy in W. Christopher, 'Introduction' to W. Christopher *et al.*, *American Hostages in Iran: The Conduct of a Crisis* (New Haven: Yale University Press, 1985), pp. 1–34, at 2.

88 Cited in Ranelagh, *The Agency*, p. 653; K. Thompson, ed., *The Carter Presidency* (Lanham: University Press of America, 1990), p. 125 (Bergland).

89 Cited in J. P. Wallach, 'Leakers, Terrorists, Policy makers and the Press', in Simon Serfaty, ed., *The Media and Foreign Policy* (London: Macmillan, 1990), pp. 81–94, at 84. See also *Time*, 17 Nov. 1980 (Ball); Edward W. Said, *Orientalism* (London: Penguin, 1985), pp. 285–8; K.C. McAdams, 'Power Prose: The Syntax of Presidential News', *Journalism Quarterly*, 67, 1990, pp. 313–22.

90 *Keeping Faith*, p. 594; Mary E. Stuckey, *The President as Interpreter-in-Chief* (Chatham: Chatham House, 1991), p. 110.

91 H. H. Saunders, 'Diplomacy and Pressure', in Christopher *et al.*, *America's Hostages in Iran*, pp. 72–143, at 49.

92 *New York Times*, 9 Nov. 1980. See also Carter, MC transcript, p. 63.

93 Brzezinski, MC transcript, pp. 84–5.

94 See Carol Winkler, 'Presidents Held Hostage: The Rhetoric of Jimmy Carter and Ronald Reagan', *Terrorism*, 12, 1989, pp. 21–30; K. V. Erickson, 'Jimmy Carter:

The Rhetoric of Private and Civic Piety', *Western Journal of Speech Communication*, 44, 1980, pp. 221–35.

95   See Stuckey, *The President as Interpreter-in-Chief*, p. 110; *New Republic*, 10 Nov. 1979, p. 5.

96   Sick, *All Fall Down*, p. 212; Hargrove, *Jimmy Carter as President*, p. 141; James Fallows, 'Washington: The Joy of Crisis', *The Atlantic Monthly*, May 1980, pp. 8–24. See also J. R. O'Neal, 'The Rationality of Decision Making during International Crises', *Polity*, 20, 1988, pp. 598–627.

97   C. A. Beckwith and Donald Knox, *Delta Force* (London: Arms and Armour Press, 1984), p. 22. See also Robin Wright, *In The Name of God: The Khomeini Decade* (London: Bloomsbury, 1990), p. 79; R. D. McFadden *et al.*, *No Hiding Place* (New York: New York Times Books, 1981).

98   Cited in L. M. Fasulo, *Representing America: Experiences of US Diplomats at the UN* (New York: Facts on File, 1984), p. 273.

99   Vance, *Hard Choices*, pp. 377–8.

100   Stansfield Turner, *Secrecy and Democracy: The CIA in Transition* (Boston: Houghton Mifflin, 1985), pp. 87–9.

101   Brzezinski, MC transcript, p. 90.

102   Amior Taheri, *Nest of Spies: America's Journey to Disaster in Iran* (London: Hutchinson, 1988), pp. 126–30.

103   See Fallows, 'Washington: The Joy of Crisis'.

104   See Sick, *All Fall Down*, p. 314; also, Amitav Acharya, *U.S. Military Strategy in the Gulf* (London: Routledge, 1989), pp. 126–8.

105   Sick, *October Surprise*; Abolhassan Bani-Sadr, *My Turn to Speak: Iran, the Revolution and Secret Deals with the US* (New York: Brassey's, 1991).

106   Fallows, 'Washington: The Joy of Crisis'.

107   Jordan, *Crisis*, p. 249; also, Brzezinski, *Power and Principle*, p. 490; Carter, *Keeping Faith*, p. 512. See also J. der Derian, *Antidiplomacy* (Oxford: Blackwell, 1992), p. 33.

108   Brzezinski, *Power and Principle*, pp. 493–4. See also Steve Smith, 'Groupthink and the Hostage Rescue Mission', *British Journal of Political Science*, 15, 1984, pp. 117–23, at 120; Jordan, *Crisis*, p. 251.

109   Vance, *Hard Choices*, p. 410.

110   Cited in Paul B. Ryan, *The Iranian Rescue Mission: Why It Failed* (Annapolis: Naval Institute Press, 1985), p. 132. See also Steve Smith, 'The Hostage Rescue Mission', in S. Smith and Michael Clarke, eds, *Foreign Policy Implementation* (London: Allen and Unwin, 1985), pp. 11–33; Beckwith and Knox, *Delta Force*; Richard A. Gabriel, *Military Incompetence* (New York: Hill and Wang, 1985), pp. 85–116.

111   *Keeping Faith*, p. 518.

112   See Martha L. Cottam, 'The Carter Administration's Policy toward Nicaragua: Images, Goals and Tactics', *Political Science Quarterly*, 107, 1992, pp. 123–46.

113   H. Hongju Koh *The National Security Constitution* (New Haven: Yale University Press, 1990), p. 122.

114   See *Dames and Moore* v. *Regan*, 453 US 654 (1981); Michael J. Glennon, *Constitutional Diplomacy* (Princeton: Princeton University Press, 1990), p. 96.

115   Theberge, 'The Collapse of the Somoza Regime', p. 127.

7

From human rights to the Carter Doctrine

Human rights

Implementation and the bureaucracy

In Chapter 5, we examined the problems faced by the Carter Administration in achieving a working definition of 'human rights' in the foreign policy context. The studies of the Soviet Union, Northern Ireland, Nicaragua and Iran illustrated the complex difficulties faced in implementing the policy. Successful, even-handed operationalisation proved exceedingly problematic, and the Administration failed to develop a bureaucratic process adequate to the task. It was not merely a case of lack of will, nor of bureaucratic obstruction. The path to successful implementation was overshadowed by all kinds of practical difficulties, so much so that it may well be judged that the Administration's performance was not all that discreditable.

These difficulties were well summarised in a 1978 report prepared by the Congressional Research Service for the House Committee on International Relations (as the House Foreign Affairs Committee was then called). The CRS isolated three main areas of difficulty in attempting fairly to implement human rights policies. Firstly, there was the problem of obtaining high quality data. Information held in the US was frequently impressionistic and reflective of particular ethnic group or press interests, as well as of the penetrability of the country being studied. Amnesty International information was felt to be reliable but was generally built around individual cases and responsive to the needs of the adoption groups. The US government, of course, had its own information-gathering processes, but these were rarely geared to human rights monitoring. Moreover, as the report noted, data collection 'must cover a given period of time', whereas 'levels of human rights violation often fluctuate dramatically within countries over time'. Secondly, there was the problem of ranking countries according to their human rights record, and adjusting US policy accordingly. As the CRS report noted:

When one is dealing with such emotion-laden matters as electric shock torture, years in prison without trial, and summary execution or mysterious disappearance without trial, it is difficult indeed to achieve even impressionistic consensus on relative weightings.

Thirdly, and related to the ranking problem, the report raised the question of realistic expectations. Were human rights absolute or relative? According to the CRS study, the:

problem of expectation relates to the fact that countries vary in their levels of political and economic modernization, their social heterogeneity, their cultural patterns and values, their prevailing ideologies and the extent to which they are under threat from external forces. These characteristics, in turn, relate to the extent to which human rights are likely to be respected[1]

The problems raised in the CRS study were, unsurprisingly, never solved by the Carter Administration.

In judging the policy further it is important to draw attention to its 'bureaucratic politics' dimension. One of the principal goals of the Congressional human rights lobby in the early 1970s was to institutionalise the cause of human rights within the executive decision-making process. To some extent this had been achieved before Carter came to the White House, with the 1976 establishment of the Bureau for Human Rights and Humanitarian Affairs in the State Department. The first human rights 'co-ordinator', James Wilson, however, had little impact on policy and his marginalisation reflected the lack of commitment exhibited by the Nixon–Kissinger–Ford regime in this area. Patricia Derian enjoyed a far higher profile, and was soon upgraded to Assistant Secretary. Speaking in 1978, Mark Schneider gave an upbeat account of the institutionalisation of human rights. According to Schneider, Derian, as head of the Human Rights Bureau, had direct access to Vance and Carter. The Bureau's staff was growing 'even during a time of budget pinching'. (Derian's original staff of two had grown to twenty-nine by 1979.) Each State Department bureau now had a full-time, permanent human rights officer who worked in liaison with Derian's bureau. A special interagency group – the Christopher Group – existed 'to factor human rights concerns' into aid and lending decisions. The National Security Council (NSC) staff also contained an officer charged with human rights duties. Ambassadors in the field were now 'personally responsible for the implementation of human rights policy' and the gathering of information. Derian's bureau had the right to review arms transfers, with, according to Schneider, a 'negative presumption' against transfers to countries 'engaged in gross violations of human rights'. The human rights initiative was 'comparable to acupuncture in that each of these individual developments is a needle inserted into the decision making process . . .'.[2]

Schneider's account was somewhat disingenuous. Rather than acupuncture needles, penetrating the foreign policy bureaucracy at sensitive points, the human rights officers were more like people trying to referee a rugby match which is veering out of control. The State Department has traditionally tended, especially at regional desk level, to identify with client regimes. It is often remarked upon that State suffers from having no constituency except foreign governments. Traditional, clientistic State Department attitudes did not disappear with the appearance of new, human rights referees. Moreover, as Joyce Starr, a White House aide concerned with human rights co-ordination, complained in 1978: 'Patt Derian is not perceived within the Department as a spokesperson for the President. Her wins and losses are essentially dependent on the consensus and support of Secretary Vance and Warren Christopher.'[3] Derian and Schneider declared all-out bureaucratic war on State Department traditionalism. Derian frequently collided with the career bureaucracy, who tended to resent what they saw as her arrogance and amateurism. As R. J. Vincent put it, the 'State Department is charged with guarding the national interest, not the human interest'. It tended to see it 'as no part of its duty to place the safety or well-being of American citizens in the service of some supposed obligation to humanity'.[4] It was not so much that State Department officers objected to what Congressman David Bowen (Democrat; Mississippi) called the 'McGovernite' principles of Derian and her associates. (In March 1977, Bowen also complained to Warren Christopher about 'opportunists' in the State Department 'trying to 'out-Carter' President Carter in the human rights area').[5] Rather, many Department personnel felt that the policy was imprecise, and that it cried out for an injection of career professionalism. D. C. McGaffey, a Foreign Service Officer, subsequently recalled:

No-one in the Foreign Service assumed that President Carter was politically naive, or totally cynical. Unfortunately, the human rights policy as enunciated did not give sufficient guidance or definition to determine exactly where between these extremes the real, desired policy would fall.[6]

The career bureaucracy was able, to a significant degree, to undermine the Human Rights Bureau. During 1980 in particular, with the turn towards a Cold War agenda on the part of the Administration, the Bureau became seriously weakened. (The situation was further complicated by Derian's illness in that year and the appointment, under some protest, of a senior Foreign Service Officer, Stephen Palmer, to take her place.) Even before 1980, however, the career bureaucracy won some important victories. For example, Warren Christopher effectively vetoed an early Human Rights Bureau proposal to have every relevant State Department agency produce a plan to promote human rights within each country.[7] According to Stephen Cohen, a deputy to Derian between 1978 and 1980, career bureaucracy resistance took further forms. At least until 1978 when Congress made section 502B of the Foreign Assistance Act unequivocally binding, the regional bureaux tended to question the direct applicability of relevant legislation. In addition, sections of the State Department used their control over information to influence the process. In Cohen's words: 'The extent of abusive practices was consistently underreported.' There appears, for example, to have been consistent underreporting of abuses in Argentina and East Timor. Moreover, Cohen alleges that the regional bureaux tended to overstate US security interests as a way of resisting calls to cut assistance. Most accounts suggest that the Bureau for East Asia was a particularly conspicuous exponent of such tactics. At one time, the East Asia Bureau suggested that the US might lose its bases in the Philippines unless aid to the Marcos regime was tripled. Derian and Assistant Secretary for East Asian Affairs Richard Holbrooke made little effort to conceal their mutual personal animosity.[8]

Beyond the boundaries of the State Department, the human rights bureaucracy encountered still more scepticism and resistance. The Pentagon underwent virtually no internal institutionalisation of human rights causes. The Treasury Department consistently opposed attempts to link US economic assistance, especially through the international financial institutions, to human rights. The Department of Commerce regularly conflicted with Derian's bureau over the sale of crime-control equipment to repressive regimes.[9] The National Security Council staff did have an institutionalised commitment in the form of a human rights officer working on its 'global issues cluster'. (Between 1977 and 1979, the officer was Jessica Tuchman Matthews.) In the early years, Tuchman was effective. Brzezinski's commitment to 'global issues' was clear from his academic writings. The compactness of the NSC staff also made it relatively easy, compared with the situation at State, for Jessica Tuchman to resolve disputes and present a clear human rights case to interagency meetings. By the same token, however, Brzezinski was able, relatively easily, to control his staff's output. There was no possibility that human rights causes could be advanced by NSC staff if these clashed with specific security concerns prioritised by Brzezinski. By 1979, in many areas a strong tradition of conflict had been established between Brzezinski, representing the NSC staff, and Derian's State Department bureau. Tensions between Derian and the National Security Adviser are evident, for example, in a 1979 NSC staff memo referring to 'a considerable amount of history' between the two 'on the subject of Argentina'.[10] As was the case with the Bureau of Human Rights, the non-security 'global issues' cluster at the NSC – traditionally denigrated by the staff as 'globaloney'[11] – found itself further marginalised during the frenetic events of 1980.

The formal arena for adjudicating interagency disputes was the Christopher Group. Its mandate was to 'examine our bilateral and multilateral foreign assistance decisions as they relate to human rights' and generally 'to coordinate the Administration's position in this area'.[12] The group's membership comprised interested parties from across the executive branch.

Meetings were usually held monthly, with often over forty people taking part, including representatives from the NSC staff and the Defence Department. 'Security' considerations were presented alongside human rights.

Though its formal purview was wide, the group tended to focus on the multilateral development banks, especially those covered by the International Financial Institutions Act of 1977. (This Act mandated that human rights be considered with regard to policy in the International Bank for Reconstruction and Development, the International Development Association, the International Finance Corporation, the Inter-American Development Bank, the Asian and African Development Banks and the African Development Fund.) The Christopher Group tended not to consider aid and loans made available through the Agriculture Department, the Export–Import Bank, the Agency for International Development and the International Monetary Fund. Even more crucially, military assistance and security supporting assistance programmes were also often not considered by the group. Decisions in these areas were made, in formal bureaucratic terms, in the Security Assistance Program Review Working Group (chaired by Under Secretary Lucy Benson) and its parent body, the Arms Export Control Board. (However, Derian's bureau was represented on these two bodies and regularly appealed military and security aid decisions direct to Christopher, who then adjudicated upon them.) The Christopher Group itself developed a formidable and coherent body of 'case law' on human rights decisions and elaborated an important body of principle: namely that 'integrity of the person' violations should receive particularly high priority; that human rights practices can be expected to differ from country to country; that other fundamental US interests must be considered alongside human rights; that policy must be influenced by the leverage available to the US in particular cases; that policy must be responsive even to incremental changes in the level of human rights violations; and that 'quiet diplomacy' was often more effective than formal sanctions.[13] The group's procedure was described in 1978 in the following terms:

For each country a bureau member in the Department of State lays out the human rights-related problems. Violations are listed and positive developments in the human rights area are outlined. The particular loan under consideration is briefly described. It is then decided whether to instruct the U.S. director to the [international financial institution] to vote yes, no, or to abstain on the particular project. It seems that normally the (regional) bureau people are more in favor of granting the loans or at least abstaining while Warren Christopher and others at the secretary and assistant secretary level and those in the human rights bureau will be less lenient.[14]

The Christopher Group provided the human rights policy with only a limited degree of cohesion. Contrary to the wishes of many of its participants, the group did not develop coherent overall policies for individual countries. This failure, together with the group's restricted purview, frequently led the policy into incoherence. As Caleb Rossiter, Congressional staffer on arms control and foreign policy, remarked, it made America 'look silly when' the United States 'blocks a loan to South Korea but gives them a thousand military helmets'.[15] The Christopher Group itself, supposedly a bureaucratic referee, was often forced to operate as a bureaucratic player. For example, it battled in 1978 against the Department of Agriculture's unilateral decision to extend a major loan to Chile. The group supposedly operated through consensus, yet its proceedings were often so chaotic and conflictual that Christopher felt himself forced to resolve disputes and produce outcomes. (According to Derian, it was 'one man, one vote – Christopher was the man and his was the vote').[16]

Bureaucratic conflicts, slippage and 'turf wars' inevitably impact on policy – this was as true of the Carter Administration as of all Presidencies. In seeking to build a new interest, human rights, into the policy process, both Congress and the Carter Administration were bound to encounter significant levels of bureaucratic inertia. In some areas, the inertia and resistance were profoundly damaging. Christopher Shoemaker, who served on the NSC staff, has, for example, described Carter's arms sales policies in the following terms:

After Jimmy Carter's 1977 decision to restrict the sale of military hardware on a worldwide basis, virtually the entire security assistance community within the government set about undermining the policy until it was effectively rescinded three years later.[17]

Unquestionably, as Jessica Tuchman Matthews later testified, many of the inconsistencies of the human rights policy are traceable to bureaucratic pulling and hauling.[18] Nevertheless, human rights perspectives had, however imperfectly, been incorporated into the process. Both Derian's bureau and the Christopher Group were highly visible and did give human rights a hitherto unknown bureaucratic legitimacy.

Assessing the human rights policy
In attempting an assessment, it seems useful to identify six criteria for judging the policy. Firstly, given its origins and motivation, it is important to assess the degree to which Carter's human rights initiative restored domestic foreign policy consensus. Secondly, the policy should be judged according to its success in achieving fairness and consistency between countries big and small, strategically important and unimportant, rich and poor, those in receipt of American aid and those not. Thirdly, there needs to be considered the balancing, so crucial in the case of Nicaragua, of the claims of non-intervention and self-determination versus those of positive intervention to promote human rights. In other words, the policy should be judged in relation to the degree to which it managed to avoid incorporation into American imperialism under another guise. Fourthly, means should be considered. How appropriately did the Administration use the various means open to it – verbal condemnation and encouragement, sanctions, 'quiet diplomacy', bilateral and multilateral action? Fifth, the relationship between human rights and 'national security' must be discussed. And, sixthly, the ultimate

query: did the policy actually do anything to alleviate human misery?

As noted in Chapter 5, the human rights initiative did achieve a temporary restoration of consensus in the first two years of Carter's Presidency. In their study of Congressional foreign policy, published in 1979, Thomas Franck and Edward Weisband concluded that, having legislated the 'broad outlines' of human rights policy and 'established a new and effective oversight', Congress was now 'inclined to leave the Executive to implement on a day-to-day, country-by-country basis'.[19] Important disputes did emerge, especially over efforts to require US representatives on international financial institutions (such as the IMF) to vote against loans to countries with records of human rights violations. The Administration held that such requirements infringed acceptable margins of executive discretion, and also tended to hurt the poor in Third World countries rather than their governments.[20] Generally, however, as Carter was keen to point out in post-White House interviews,[21] the Administration's record on foreign policy votes in Congress was rather good. (Indeed, with SALT never having been voted on, Carter never lost a single important foreign policy vote.) The early consensus on human rights was constitutive of this success. The human rights consensus was, as indicated in Chapter 5, to some extent a union of opposites, and its left- and right-wing factions were continually threatening to spin away. In February 1978, for example, Mondale was forced to call Congressional liberals from Manila in an effort to persuade them against cutting aid to the Philippines when the US was negotiating an extension on its lease on the Subic Bay naval base. In August 1978, Republican Senator Barry Goldwater declared that he was going to vote to condemn Idi Amin in Uganda: 'But, while we are at it, let us vote to condemn the People's Republic of China. Let us vote to condemn Cuba.'[22]

The human rights consensus began to unravel from the later part of 1978 onwards, and to disintegrate during 1979. Iran, the debate on SALT, and the Administration's own turn towards more orthodox Cold War policies all contributed to this process. In June 1979, Senator Henry Jackson actually compared the Vienna Summit to Neville Chamberlain's 1938 Munich agreement – 'appeasement in its purest form'. (On Carter's return from Vienna, he stood in the rain, declaring: 'I'd rather drown than carry an umbrella.')[23] On the liberal side, it was inevitable that many would feel that the early agenda was in 1979 and 1980 being abandoned. During 1979, it also became evident that public support for human rights was rather shallow. Polls tended to show high levels of public approval for the policy, but little actual enthusiasm. A 1978 Chicago Council on Foreign Relations survey, for example, found 67 per cent of the public favouring human rights promotion abroad. Yet only 50 per cent saw Soviet treatment of its minorities as 'our business', and only 40 per cent agreed that the US should actively oppose apartheid in South Africa. Only 1 per cent identified human rights among the two or three most important international issues. John Holum of the State

Department Policy Planning Staff gave his opinion in 1981 that the whole 'global community' agenda, including human rights, 'didn't have a popular foundation yet' – it was so 'precariously based' that it 'could come unravelled over something like Iran'.[24]

Regarding the second of the criteria outlined above – that of consistency – there were clearly many areas where, for security or economic reasons, the Administration appeared to soft-pedal human rights. Iran was one. Other candidates included Romania, South Korea, the Philippines, Cambodia, mainland China, Zaire, Morocco, Pakistan and East Timor. To any admirer of the human rights initiative, it is distressing to see the television footage of Carter welcoming President Ceausescu of Romania to the White House in April, 1978. Patricia Derian has subsequently expressed her extreme misgivings about the patronage of Ceausescu, who was regarded in Washington as something of an admirable individualist, pluckily facing down the mighty Soviet bear. The Carter Administration repeatedly, and successfully, appealed to Congress for Romania to be granted 'most-favoured-nation' trading status.[25] In the case of South Korea, whose human rights violations were better known in Washington than was the case with Romania, the US did on occasion vote against loans in the international financial institutions. Such behaviour appeared ridiculous, however, in view of the fact that US military aid, ranging between $130 and $276 million annually, was being extended to the South Korean regime. The campaign promise to withdraw US troops from Korea was itself withdrawn formally in July 1979. In the Philippines, President Marcos was able to use the military base lease renewal process to extract US aid and arms. Congressional disquiet over the Marcos human rights record was successfully shunted aside.[26]

The 1977 Vietnamese invasion of Cambodia created a dilemma for the Administration. Cambodia's ruler, Pol Pot, had, in effect, declared war on his own population. As Gaddis Smith has written: 'If standards of human rights alone had prevailed, the United States should have supported Vietnam.' Carter had made moves towards normalising relations with Vietnam. In 1978, however, the US opposed its old enemy in Hanoi. Brzezinski perceived the Cambodian–Vietnamese conflict as the 'first case of a proxy war between China and the Soviet Union'. The Administration tilted towards Cambodia and China, allowing the direction of policy to follow the lead taken by the Association of South East Asian Nations. (The Carter Administration was committed to developing economic ties with the emergent industrial states represented in ASEAN.) Regarding mainland China itself, Brzezinski's plans for closer relations also proceeded with, in effect, no concern for Beijing's record on human rights.[27]

In black Africa, Joseph Mobutu, ruler of Zaire, received substantial aid – over $10 million annually – despite notorious human rights violations. Carter wrote long letters to Mobutu, urging liberalisation of the regime. He was offered some gestures in return, such as local competitive elections. US policy was shaped by Zaire's importance as a cobalt supplier to the American aircraft industry. The centre of Zaire's mineral wealth, Shaba (formerly Katanga) province, was twice invaded by secessionist forces from Angola in this period. The second invasion – Shaba II (May 1978) – occasioned a particularly strong condemnation by Carter of Soviet and Cuban meddling in Africa. In a still obscure policy excursion, secret American aid appears to have been extended to King Hassan of Morocco in his war against the Polisario guerrillas in the Western Sahara. Again, aid was extended – at least in part with the aim of securing US bases – without concern for Hassan's human rights record. In Pakistan, Administration attitudes to the military dictatorship of General Zia changed dramatically after the Soviet invasion of Afghanistan. Before 1980, Zia had been condemned, especially with regard to the trial (and eventual execution) of former Prime Minister Bhutto. Aid was also cut off to Pakistan in April 1979 in line with the 1978 Nuclear Nonproliferation Act. (The Act barred aid to countries which refused to submit to international control over the acquisition of nuclear weapons.) During 1980, however, Pakistan's strategic importance persuaded the Administration that a change in policy was required. Zia was offered $400 million in military aid. (He famously dismissed this offer as 'peanuts'.) Carter welcomed the General in Washington, declaring (surely with irony) that Zia's 'knowledge of the sensitivities and ideals of American life make him particularly dear to us'.[28]

As the largest country in ASEAN and a clear 'regional influential', Indonesia occupied a pivotal position in US perceptions of South-East Asia. It was seen as a bulwark against Soviet and Vietnamese influence. Military sales were reduced for a time. However, American arms transfers were crucial in facilitating the genocidal war being unleashed by Indonesian forces against the people of East Timor. The American A-4 bomber was, along with the British Hawk, central to the saturation bombing campaigns of 1978–9. Robert Oakley, Deputy Assistant Secretary for East Asian Affairs, regularly informed Congress that reports of genocide were exaggerated, and that Indonesia had not – in the period since its 1975 invasion – infringed East Timor's right to self-determination! In fiscal year 1980, Indonesia received substantial US aid. It was one of six countries admitted to be violating human rights but whose aid was justified under statutory language which allowed aid which would 'directly benefit the needy people . . .'. (The other five countries were Guinea, Haiti, Liberia, Somalia and Zaire).[29]

Arms sales to Somalia, votes in the international financial institutions for loans to Syria, Overseas Private Investment Corporation programmes in Saudi Arabia and Malawi: it is not difficult to enumerate examples of the Carter Administration either ignoring, or applying inconsistently, its human rights injunctions. The Administration was allowed, under statute, to support multilateral loans for repressive regimes if they none the less met 'basic human needs' just as it could provide direct aid to such regimes if 'needy people' benefited. As Joshua Muravchik has argued, it is hard to see much consistency in the way these loopholes were used and interpreted. In 1978 three countries were singled out to have their loans opposed *despite* the objects of these loans satisfying the 'basic human needs' criterion. The countries were the Central African Empire, South Yemen and Chile – all notorious violators, but scarcely more or less worthy to be trusted to use money to serve 'basic human needs' than many others.[30]

Yet another area of putative inconsistency concerns the interface between public policy and private investment. The Administration generally supported American business investment as a liberalising and progressive force. Andrew Young's positive attitude towards corporate investment in South Africa was noted in Chapter 4. The Administration supported the Sullivan Code of Conduct for US corporations investing in South Africa, but did not seek to make it mandatory. In a speech made in Brazil in March 1978 Carter declared his outright opposition to 'any act of Congress' that 'would try to restrict the lending of money by American private banks . . . under any circumstances'. He denied 'any incompatibility between a belief in the free enterprise system where a government does not dominate the banks' and 'a deep and consistent . . . belief in enhancing human rights'.[31] The Administration was reluctant to adopt trade embargoes, opposing even the proposed embargo on trade to Idi Amin's Uganda until it was passed by Congress in 1978. Yet trading sanctions and economic boycotts were not ruled out altogether. One of the Administration's first acts was to appeal to Congress to strengthen the embargo against the Ian Smith regime in Rhodesia. It was estimated that in 1978 American businesses engaged in trade with Argentina lost over $800 million as a result of the human rights policy, especially as it related to the issuance of export licences. Commerce Secretary Juanita Kreps frequently complained about such losses, which totalled possibly as much as $10 billion every year. Business lobbies were organised to oppose – sometimes successfully sometimes not – specific inhibitions on free trade deriving from the human rights policy. Brzezinski himself took time in 1980 to explain to the chairman of the Eaton Corporation in the following terms how the policy:

entails the sensitive balancing of its several components, which often conflict. The process can and does involve the occasional decision to forgo a U.S. grant, loan or sale . . . In that sense, I could agree there is what you call a 'downside' to the human rights policy. But in fact the great majority of proposals are approved, either because they do not violate clearly established criteria, or fit clearly into an exception.[32]

Mindful of the policy's economic impact, President Carter in early 1979 explicitly ordered that the overall needs of US trade be considered when making and implementing human rights decisions.[33]

Despite Carter's order, it is clear that the policy did have some negative impact and, to the extent that it did, characterisations of it as mere painless symbolism are inaccurate. Moreover, returning more directly to our discussion of policy inconsistency, it is important to note a number of factors which set this inconsistency in context, though they do not 'excuse' it. Firstly, it will be appreciated that policy was always the product of the bureaucratic conflict already described. In addition, it should be emphasised that the Administration's commitment was never, except in an entirely token sense, absolute. Carter did occasionally, as in the Inaugural Address, use the word 'absolute' in the context of human rights. But such language never found its way into the developed and stated practices of the Administration (as encapsulated, for example, in Presidential Directive 30, issued in February 1978). In interpreting the Foreign Assistance Act, for example, the Administration frequently cited that part of Section 502B which referred to 'extraordinary circumstances' and to 'the national interest of the United States'. The weighing of human rights against security and economic considerations was built into the Administration's own rules of procedure and indeed constituted the Christopher Group's *raison d'être*. Commenting on inconsistencies in the policy, Arthur Schlesinger Jr. argued that 'the double standard' was 'inherent in the situation'.[34] There was no question of sacrificing 'security' to 'human rights'. The only question was where and how to achieve an acceptable balance. Inconsistency was inevitable, if not to the degree that was actually achieved.

Also relevant to the charge of inconsistency is the question of information availability and dissemination. As was the case with East Timor, information did not always make its way up the bureaucratic ladder. Confusion and uncertainty was also occasioned by the perception, built into the Christopher Group's working practice, that even small improvements should be rewarded. The Administration saw the policy as infinitely flexible, capable of being adjusted to reflect expectations as well as improvements or deteriorations in human rights practices. The problem here was that repressive governments, like Somoza's in Nicaragua, were able cynically to orchestrate Washington's responses.

Defenders of Carter's policy might also point out that, even in unpromising areas, some successes were achieved. Even in Indonesia, political prisoners were released. Romania did liberalise its emigration policy in response to US pressure. It can also be argued that the policy was reasonably even-handed in its application to left- and right-leaning regimes. It was, of course, an important facet of the Reaganite assault on Carter's policy to assert, as Jeane Kirkpatrick did, that the Administration favoured leftist 'foes' over right-wing 'friends'. Others have condemned the policy as irresponsibly anti-Soviet.[35] Analysis of the policy does not yield clear evidence of bias. The foregoing discussions of countries which 'escaped' the policy – Iran, Romania, South Korea, the Philippines, Cambodia, China, Zaire, Morocco, Pakistan (after 1979) and Indonesia – indicated their ideological heterogeneity. In terms of votes cast in the international financial institutions, the

Carter Administration opposed 34 per cent (in value) of loans to 'leftist' and 31 per cent to 'rightist' regimes.[36] Particular regional bureaux and bureaucratic actors did have clearly articulated ideological preferences. For example, Elizabeth Drew interviewed a State Department Africanist who 'says that . . . our first priority in Africa is elimination of racism, and human-rights deprivations are second'. The different forms of leverage available to the US in different countries – especially the existence or otherwise of aid (especially military aid) programmes – also contributed to the impression that the policy was ideologically selective. However, attempts to demonstrate such selectivity in terms of the overall policy are not convincing.[37]

Our next two criteria – the balance between non-intervention and active promotion of human rights, and the question of appropriate means – may be dealt with more rapidly. As discussed in Chapter 5, the human rights policy sought to address a world where US hegemony was no longer a fact of life and where self-determination and cultural pluralism would be respected. Robert Pastor wrote in 1979 that Latin America should no longer be regarded as America's 'region of influence' or, indeed, as a homogeneous region at all.[38] Carter acknowledged in April, 1977 that the US 'can't change the structure of governments in foreign countries'. The United States 'can't demand complete compatibility in a system of government or even basic philosophies with our own'. Nevertheless, 'we reserve the right to speak out firmly and aggressively . . .'.[39]

The Administration's answer to charges of cultural imperialism consisted, as was noted in Chapter 5, in appeals to international law. Beyond this, however, – as was made abundantly plain in the course of developing relations with Nicaragua – the boundary between interventionism and self-determination proved problematic. In fact, the whole policy, at least to the degree that it was based on unilateral action, had hegemonic overtones. After all, the policy's prospects of success were apparently brightest precisely in those areas where the US had maximum leverage – in other words in those parts of the world (notably Latin America) where the US was still the undisputed hegemonic power. (Republican Congressman Edward Derwinski once facetiously suggested that military aid be extended to the People's Republic of China in order that the US could obtain some leverage over that country's human rights practices.)[40] Congressman Tom Harkin put the point well in 1978:

We always hear it said, 'Well, we don't want to interfere in those countries. We don't want to go in there and mess in their internal affairs'. I don't see why not. We have been doing it for a hundred years anyway . . . We are going to influence Latin America . . . The question is how.[41]

Leftist critics of Carter's policy have interpreted it as a species of post-Vietnam 'world order' imperialism. James Petras wrote in 1977 that morality was the 'recurring ideological expression of U.S. imperialism in a period of crisis'. It is also pointed out that, during the Carter years, the US was still supplying repressive regimes from Indonesia to Brazil. Jenny Pearce has noted that much of this aid was channelled in such a way (through, for example, the Export–Import Bank and via arms sales) so as to circumvent the most rigorous Congressional review. The Carter Administration *was* still supplying repressive regimes. By the same token, Trilateralism clearly was a means whereby American capitalism sought to adjust to post-Vietnam conditions and to the rise of Japan and West Germany. Such an analysis reminds us that Carter's Presidency was adaptive of past practices and strategies, rather than seeking to deracinate them.[42]

The question as to whether the Carter Administration pursued appropriate means in pursuing human rights ends is impossible to answer with any precision. What is clear, however, is that the policy was not centrally co-ordinated to any great degree, and the development of appropriate means was largely *ad hoc*. The Administration did use a variety of means, ranging from aid cuts to 'quiet diplomacy'. Security assistance was terminated at some stage, owing to human rights violations, to Argentina, Bolivia, El Salvador, Guatemala, Haiti, Nicaragua, Paraguay and Uruguay. The following countries suffered aid cuts in at least one fiscal year: Indonesia, Tunisia, South Korea, Ethiopia, the Central African Empire, Guinea, Chile, the Philippines and Thailand. Assistance levels were raised as a 'reward' for improvements in the human rights field in India, Sri Lanka, Botswana, the Gambia, Costa Rica, the Dominican Republic and Peru. As we have seen, multilateral fora (the international financial institutions) were used alongside bilateral. Trade sanctions were used, albeit sparingly. The Administration banned the export of all equipment to the South African police and military, and prevented computers being exported to keep records pertaining to apartheid. In the discussions in Chapters 5 and 6, we saw various tactics of persuasion and condemnation being used. 'Quiet diplomacy' was used to dissuade the military in the Dominican Republic from aborting the result of an election. Assistant Secretary of State Philip Habib used quiet pressure in 1977 to negotiate the release of fourteen political prisoners in South Korea.[43] Patricia Derian was always anxious to argue that the policy was flexible, subtle and not entirely reliant on the carrot and stick. As Warren Christopher put it in 1979:

the most effective strategy for obtaining human rights improvements is one that combines the full range of diplomatic approaches with a willingness to adjust our foreign assistance programs as required. No element in the overall strategy can be as effective alone as in combination with others.[44]

The Deputy Secretary was here exaggerating somewhat the policy's conscious coordination. However, he was correct in his description of its potential for flexibility, sophistication and variety of methods.

The question of the policy's relation to national security concerns has to some extent already been discussed. The commitment to human rights was not absolute, nor was it intended to be. Legislation explicitly provided for exceptional circumstances and for security considerations. The 1976 International Security Assistance and Arms Export Control Act, for example, required the Secretary of State to provide reports both on the human rights status of relevant countries and on 'national interest' considerations. Patricia Derian explained to human rights workers in 1978: 'human rights objectives do not determine each and every foreign policy decision. They are . . . considered along with other vital U.S. interests such as promotion of national security, trade and arms control.' She told the House Foreign Affairs Committee during the early years of the Reagan Administration that she appreciated the need to 'maintain our bases at Subic and Clark Airfield' (in the Philippines), to 'prevent the repressive regime in North Korea from conquering South Korea', to 'keep ASEAN alive' and to enable Pakistan 'to withstand and discourage a Soviet invasion'.[45]

The neo-conservative critique of Carter's policy concentrated on its supposed indifference to the 'national interest'. According to Jeane Kirkpatrick, the Carter Administration was driven by 'a quasi-Marxist theory of historical development' which encompassed 'a conception of national interest in which U.S. power was, at best irrelevant', along with 'a tendency to suppose that history was on the side of our opponents'.[46] Speaking in Buenos Aires in 1978, Henry Kissinger condemned Carter's policy as 'romantic'.[47] In a 1984 speech, Reagan's Secretary of State George Shultz called it a 'cop-out': a way of 'making us feel better', but ultimately 'a form of isolationism'.[48]

Views such as these essentially encompassed two perspectives: the *realpolitik*, realist or 'national interest' orientation, and the more moralistic Cold War outlook. According to classical realist theory, the international order is inherently conflictual and potentially anarchic. The 'national interest' consists in the maximisation of national economic and security advantage, characteristically through the achievement of advantageous balances of power. Alongside the realist view, writers like Kirkpatrick pursue a more moralistic line of argument. American democracy is seen as the best possible form of government, and the best way of furthering global human rights is seen to lie in the consistent promotion of American liberal democracy.

As seen in Chapter 5, the early Carter policies were developed from an incisive and persuasive critique of both security-oriented realist and moralistic, Cold War perspectives. The 'national interest', in the context of interdependency theory, is held to be disaggregated and, indeed, at least as understood in traditional realist thought, largely illusory. Carter apologists, however, did not dispense with the idea of 'national interest'. Rather, they held that human rights policies *were* in the national interest. The US had suffered in the past by becoming identified with repression and reaction. As Vance wrote about the Third World: 'Change was and is sweeping through Africa, and those who identify with it will be able to influence its direction.'[49]

(Here Vance was making common cause with 'neo-realist' writers like Richard Feinberg and William LeoGrande.)[50] According to Andrew Young, one major goal of the human rights policy was international stability: 'Either we provide respect for human rights by democratic means, or we see the world disintegrate through violent means.'[51] Reasoning such as this, far from being 'romantic', sometimes assumed a very hard edge. For example, an Administration spokesman replied as follows to a complaint from Paraguay that the human rights policy was destabilising the regime there: 'we believe that a policy of promoting a wide range of human rights can help a government achieve a broader base of popular support and this can serve to enhance, rather than detract, from the stability of that government.'[52]

In assessing the human rights policy, it is important to appreciate that, to a considerable degree, the whole 'global community' agenda was dissipated in the policy turnaround of 1979–80. Human rights initiatives, however, were certainly not entirely abandoned. The Christopher Group continued its deliberations. Mark Schneider has admitted that 'heavier weight' was given to security considerations in the later years but also described this as being done 'without discarding the view that, in the long run, security interests benefited from a human rights emphasis'.[53] Nevertheless, the parlous condition of the Human Rights Bureau in 1980 has already been described. Derian turned her attention to disseminating information to non-governmental organisations concerned with human rights. Carter never, as Brzezinski testified, lost his personal commitment but did, following the Soviet invasion of Afghanistan, move back to a Cold War interpretation of international politics.[54]

Lastly, did it all make any difference? A Congressional Research Service study of 1981 concluded that the policy mitigated brutality only at the margins. It found only 'five or six instances' where 'actual or explicitly threatened reductions in aid' may plausibly be said to have effected human rights improvements.[55] Various attempts have been made to trace correlations between aid allocations and human rights conditions (as reported and measured by Amnesty International, Freedom House and the State Department itself) in recipient countries. The methodology associated with these exercises is highly complex and hotly contested. The situation is further complicated by the fact that some countries actually themselves spurned aid in protest at US interference in their affairs.[56] However, it is clear that there is no striking correlation between aid levels and human rights variables. Strategic importance and recipient need appear to have been more significant. More surprisingly, it cannot even be unambiguously demonstrated that aid allocation patterns shifted significantly during the Reagan years.[57] (The Reagan Administration, though it certainly downgraded human rights considerations in its public pronouncements, was still legally obliged to take them into account in recommending aid for Congressional approval.) Moreover, in the case of the multilateral banks, the Carter

Administration's opposition to money being lent to abusing countries was generally ineffective. Such loans were invariably approved, with US criticisms often being relegated to the status of gestures.

On the positive side, the policy did result in the release of small, yet significant, numbers of political prisoners. It has been suggested that the policy led directly to the moderation in behaviour of the Argentinian and Chilean military regimes, and that it contributed to the exit from power of the military in Ecuador.[58] The State Department's Country Reports on human rights rapidly became institutionalised and acquired a reputation for objectivity and accuracy. Under the Nixon and Ford regime, human rights legislation was, in Stephen Cohen's words, 'openly disregarded', largely owing to the opposition of Henry Kissinger. Though the Carter bureaucracy was capable of 'considerable flexibility' – even sharp practice – in applying the legislation, its good faith was far in excess of its predecessors.[59] Also, during the Carter years, the maxim no longer held that the US would automatically and unreflectingly support illiberal and corrupt anti-communist governments. In South Africa and Latin America, in particular, the US was now – not unequivocally, but on balance – on the side of change. In considering the positive side of the human rights policy, it is also worth recalling the encouragement given to victims of oppression. In words reminiscent of the letter sent to Carter by Anatoly Shcharansky's mother in 1978 (quoted in Chapter 5), Jacobo Timerman – the Buenos Aires editor imprisoned by the Argentinian military – declared in 1981: 'Those of us who were imprisoned, those of us who are in prison still, will never forget President Carter and his contribution to the battle for human rights.'[60]

Competence: the foreign policy process and the Vance–Brzezinski split

As in the domestic sphere, the Carter Administration's foreign policy system reflected the assumption that organisation matters, and that process structures policy. The system was the result of intense Presidential study and the object of continuous monitoring. Senior advisers consciously declined to sever considerations of process from those of policy substance.[61] The Carter Administration produced the most detailed internal studies – notably that by Philip Odeen – of Presidential foreign policy decision-making in decades.[62] The system was designed to enhance and reconcile Presidential control, openness, coherence, multiple advocacy and long-term planning. At its heart were two National Security Council committees: the Policy Review Committee (PRC), usually chaired by the Secretary of State, and the Special Coordination Committee (SCC), chaired by National Security Adviser Brzezinski. The PRC considered regional and international economic issues, as well as defence and functional policy (such as human rights). The SCC's purview included intelligence, arms control and crisis management. The main procedural device for formulating policy was the Presidential Review Memorandum, prepared by the NSC staff in the case of the SCC and by relevant (usually State) departmental staff for the PRC. (Within a month of Carter's inauguration, thirty Presidential Review Memoranda had been produced.) Many other Cabinet-level committees considered foreign policy issues under various chairmen. (Under Nixon and Ford, such committees would invariably be led by Kissinger.) Major issues were debated, and often decided, in weekly foreign policy breakfasts, involving Carter and the main foreign policy advisers – and increasingly personal domestic aides like Jody Powell and Hamilton Jordan.[63] The weekly 'VBB' luncheon also provided a forum for consultation between the Secretaries of State, Defence and the National Security Adviser.

In many respects this was a highly formalised and centralised system. Brzezinski later described it as 'perhaps formally the most centralised of all in the postwar era'.[64] For Carter, the guiding principle was centralised collegiality. Determined to play an active and decisive role, Carter saw himself (rather than the PRC, the SCC or indeed the National Security Council itself) as the deciding centre.[65] The system was also designed to guard against the premature shutting off of options. It was intended as a means of processing information without filtering out choice. The various Cabinet-level committees took it as their task, typically, to draw up options rather than make recommendations. Complaints about Presidential inaccessibility, familiar from previous Administrations, were relatively muted during the Carter years. Even those, like Alexander Moens, who question whether multiple advocacy did work under Carter, concede that opportunities for presenting and considering differing options did exist.[66]

The Carter system has, of course, been criticised far more for its putative incoherence and fragmentation than for any excessive centralisation. Such criticisms surfaced quite early in specialist journals.[67] Odeen felt that, though the 'open Administration' philosophy had brought a 'measure of freshness and vitality', it had also 'led to a perception of policy disarray'. Too often policy was made in an *ad hoc* manner by agency heads.[68] The roots of fragmentation were partially traceable to bureaucratic rivalries, of the type discussed above in the context of human rights policy. Such rivalries were always likely to upset pretensions to technocratic rationality. NSC staffer William Odom saw Odeen's report as 'a bureaucratic gambit to weaken Brzezinski'.[69] Carter's occasional fondness for using special envoys, like Robert Strauss (in the Middle East after Camp David) and Clark Clifford (dispatched to India in the wake of the Soviet invasion of Afghanistan) also tended to increase perceptions of fragmentation. Far more fundamental, however, and underpinning so many of the Administration's problems was the Vance-Brzezinski split. To some extent, this too had 'turf war' origins. As Stanley Hoffman wrote in 1980:

Even if the two dominant personalities . . . were saints and shared the same ideas, rivalry would loom up between them. One has at his disposal extensive resources including a large staff with information covering every corner of the globe; the other benefits from close, daily contact with the President and from a small team able to focus on timely and critical problems.[70]

Far more was at issue in the rivalry, however, than the 'natural' tendency for Secretaries of State and National Security Advisers to quarrel. Brzezinski did espouse 'global community' causes in the mid-1970s, and criticised Henry Kissinger's 'Lone Ranger' style of policy-making. However, by 1978 – the breaking point seems to have come over the Horn of Africa crisis – the President's two major foreign policy advisers were in open conflict.

On the question of foreign policy process, Vance stood for collegiality, a breaking away from the procedural legacy of Henry Kissinger and – in Hamilton Jordan's phrase – 'hard work and a steady course'.[71] Attempts to short-circuit the State Department generally, in Vance's view, led to problems. State's 'institutional memory' was an essential safeguard. The National Security Adviser's job was to 'act as a coordinator of the various views'. He 'should not be the one who makes foreign policy or who expresses foreign policy to the public'.[72] Despite some early promises to the contrary, Brzezinski had no intention of performing a mere 'coordination' role. He was, in his own words, 'advocate' as much as 'coordinator'.[73] Brzezinski felt the State Department to be incapable of the kind of policy innovation that both international economic developments and the changing Soviet threat demanded. According to later remarks by Brzezinski, 'large bureaucracies do not produce strategies – they produce shopping lists'. The State Department was simply unable to rise above its narrow, bureaucratic concerns. In remarks broadcast in 1990, the former National Security Adviser conceded that such views were in the Kissinger tradition: 'operationally, I have no objections to Kissinger's role.' He differed from Kissinger only to the extent that the Carter Administration 'placed more emphasis on openness, on human rights, on American commitment to principle'.[74]

Yet the Carter–Brzezinski relationship was not a replay of Nixon–Kissinger. Carter never backed his National Security Adviser to the extent that Nixon backed Kissinger. The Carter years actually saw a resurgence in the power of the State Department bureaucracy. The President leaned towards Vance on some issues (notably arms control and nuclear proliferation) and towards Brzezinski on others. Nevertheless, the influence of the National Security Adviser was clearly very strong after 1979. Brzezinski himself traced the growth in his influence to his success over the China normalisation policy.[75] The general crisis atmosphere of 1980 in particular also led to a magnification in the authority of the SCC. (Brzezinski and William Odom in fact took the opportunity to extend the SCC's remit well beyond its initially demarcated areas.)[76] The special difficulties faced by Muskie, Vance's successor, also contributed to Brzezinski's ascendancy. According to Carter, Muskie 'had an easier relationship than Vance with

Zbig'. The President appears, however, to have quickly developed doubts about the wisdom of the Muskie appointment. In the words of NSC staffer Madeleine Albright: 'He'd recreated a political figure.'[77] The former Senator from Maine did manage to win some bureaucratic victories over Brzezinski. The true power relationship was made clear, however, in August 1980, when it was disclosed that Presidential Directive 59 – embodying a major shift in nuclear strategy – had been developed and promulgated without Muskie's knowledge. Despite Brzezinski's unquestioned importance, it still should be emphasised that he never achieved the status of a Kissinger. The very fact that the critical Odeen report was promulgated in May 1980 – ostensibly at the height of Zbig's authority – testifies to this.

Returning to the Vance-Brzezinski split, it is clear that differences in belief regarding process and policy were compounded by a personality clash. Vance, according to Hamilton Jordan, 'didn't have an ounce of the self-promotor in him'; Brzezinski was the first National Security Adviser to employ his own public relations officer.[78] In Zbig's view, Vance was 'a quintessential product of the Eastern establishment', operating according to elite values and rules that 'were of declining relevance not only in terms of domestic American politics but particularly in terms of global conditions'. For the National Security Adviser, the Secretary of State exemplified the post-Vietnam loss of nerve which afflicted America's decadent ruling class.[79]

The 'basic fundamental split' on policy was, in Vance's view, 'on how to handle Soviet policy'. He and Brzezinski 'were deeply split on the question of linkage', with Zbig taking a more Kissingerian line.[80] For Vance, arms control was a goal in itself. To Brzezinski, the main goal was the containment of Soviet power. US policy on arms, on China, on regional disputes – all these could and should be used to promote containment.

Carter had severe difficulties in adjudicating and reconciling the split. In appointing Vance and Brzezinski, Carter seems to have had in mind not so much 'creative conflict' as a division of labour. 'Zbig would be the thinker', wrote Hamilton Jordan, 'Cy would be the doer, and Jimmy Carter would be the decider.'[81] In 1976–7, Vance and Brzezinski could be seen as representing different points on the post-Vietnam foreign policy spectrum, rather than as occupying contrary positions. Their appointments, although unpopular with the 1976 'peanut brigaders', also served the goal of consensus-building. Carter felt that a successful foreign policy would have to reconcile competing perspectives, which were in fact built in at all levels of the Administration. In the arms control arena, for example, Arms Control and Development agency head Paul Warnke, a conspicuous supporter of arms build-down, found himself opposed by the more hard-line Edward Rowny.[82] (Rowny eventually resigned in June 1979 from the SALT delegation, where he represented the Joint Chiefs of Staff.) To some extent, the slightly random appearance of the Administration's lower-level appointments reflected Carter's lack of insider contacts. However, it also represented a conscious desire to incorporate different views. Carter felt that his strong personal direction would hold competition in check.

At the highest level, effective Presidential adjudication of the Vance-Brzezinski conflict was lacking. From Vance's viewpoint, Brzezinski's unwillingness to observe proper limits was compounded by Carter's failure to enforce collegiality:

I do not feel the President adequately enforced what I think is essential in dealing with foreign affairs and national security issues – namely, to tell the principal players in the White House and in the departments that he expected them to work together in a collegial fashion . . .[83]

Vance has also accused Brzezinski of deliberately distorting the SCC and PRC summaries which the National Security Adviser prepared for the President.[84]

In Brzezinski's defence, it is clear that Carter did not seriously attempt to confine his adviser to a 'coordinator' or even a 'thinker' role. The President did not see Vance as a particularly adept public salesman for Administration policy. As Lloyd Cutler later recalled, Carter: 'felt unhappy that Vance was not being outgoing and quick on public retorts to what some Republican Senator said as he wanted. So more and more he urged Brzezinski to do that. Zbig loved it.'[85] Presidential acquiescence in Brzezinski's spring 1978 trip to China also effectively ended Carter's early determination that the Secretary of State should do, and the National Security Adviser should think. (Vance, incidentally, showed no more sign than Zbig of accepting this demarcation.) Carter also, in effect, acquiesced in Brzezinski's opening up, in the Kissinger tradition, of diplomatic 'back' channels outside the State Department's jurisdiction. The problem was not simply Brzezinski's personality or what Agriculture Secretary Robert Bergland later called his 'nutty ideas'.[86] Carter's attitudes were crucial. For the President, the approaches and personalities of his two top foreign policy advisers were compatible. (Carter continued to maintain this in post-White House interviews. In 1982, he declared that, though he should have fired Ambassador Sullivan and also Alexander Haig – from his post as NATO chief – there was no question of being dissatisfied with either Vance or Brzezinski.)[87] Even the move to Cold War orthodoxy in 1979–80 was regarded by Carter not so much as a victory for Brzezinski, but rather as a necessary, but temporary, postponement of the 'global community' agenda.

In retrospect, it seems that Carter underestimated the damage which the Vance–Brzezinski split was doing to his Administration. Carter's foreign policy process was bound to be more fractionated than that of his predecessors. Congressional reassertion, the collapse of the Cold War consensus after the defeat in Vietnam and the rise of the international interdependency agenda were all bound to leave their mark. Open feuding at the top could only make a difficult situation worse.

Vance's 1976 memo had urged Carter to make the Congress and the American people joint partners in foreign policy. Important gestures were made to achieve this end – notably the disclosure of Vance's disarmament proposals prior to his unsuccessful March 1977 visit to Moscow. The Carter Administration did far more than any of its immediate predecessors to involve Congress (especially in the SALT process) and to stimulate public debate. Again, however, the record was patchy and bore the imprint of the Vance–Brzezinski split. Carter himself became increasingly preoccupied with leaks of sensitive policy discussions, to an extent which Vance found excessive. Cyrus Vance also later criticised Carter for not involving Congress more than he did.[88] The Panama Canal treaties and Camp David accords were negotiated without any real Congressional input. As noted in Chapter 6, Presidential management of the Iranian crisis also involved a major accretion of authority to the executive.

At least one further area commands attention in distinguishing Carter's conduct of foreign policy: control of the CIA. The 1977 firing of George Bush as Director of Central Intelligence signalled the new regime's determination to break with the old ways. It was the first time an incoming President had dismissed an incumbent DCI. Bush's eventual successor, Admiral Stansfield Turner, displayed a clear determination to control and civilise the agency. He became immensely unpopular with CIA personnel. He oversaw personnel reductions and forced special project units to compete with other CIA components. He prioritised technical intelligence-gathering and deprioritised covert operations. Turner's policies, of course, reflected the post-Vietnam public suspicion of the CIA, and the determination of Congress to oversee the agency effectively. The CIA's wings had already been significantly clipped before Turner took over. During the early Carter years, the CIA's budget allocation for covert action fell to less than 5 per cent (compared to over 60 per cent in the late 1960s). Relations with Congress improved. Turner consciously used his channels to the new Congressional intelligence committees to recruit support for the agency. As a senior aide later put it, Turner 'felt it was important to share information and responsibility with the Congress'. Once on board, Congressional overseers would have to stifle their criticism: 'If other committees raise questions, you tell the intelligence committee to get the other guys in order. It's a very effective tactic.'[89]

Administration attitudes towards the CIA, however, did not escape the spin-off from the Vance–Brzezinski rivalry, and also changed significantly after 1979. In considering covert operations, Stansfield Turner found himself 'buffeted between Vance's scepticism and Brzezinski's enthusiasm'.[90] The Secretary of State favoured a maximum sharing of information with Congress. Brzezinski, through whom intelligence reports reached the President, condemned Congressional oversight as interference – 'like the liberum veto in the Polish Parliament'.[91] Carter himself was aware of past CIA horrors, but was also increasingly anxious about impeding effective intelligence. He never condemned covert action *per se* and supported the view that such operations should not be reported in detail to the Congressional committees. After 1979,

Congress itself became less concerned with intrusive oversight. The 1980 Intelligence Oversight Act, supported by the Administration, weakened earlier reporting requirements. By the latter part of 1980, as Stansfield Turner recalled in his memoirs, 'a wide variety of covert operations' – in Central America, Africa, Iran and Afghanistan – were in process.[92]

The myth that Carter and Turner had dangerously emasculated the CIA became an important part of Reagan's critique of his predecessor. The Reagan transition team accused the CIA under Turner of having lost the capacity to conduct effective covert operations, of consistent under-estimation of the Soviet threat and of failure to detect the Soviet brigade in Cuba. The last accusation was absurd.[93] Uncertainty about CIA estimates of Soviet strength did reinforce doubts about the SALT treaty. However, in 1984 the CIA itself admitted that it had greatly *over*estimated Soviet defence spending after 1976.[94] Covert operation capabilities were reduced, as was clear from the experience in Iran. However, in retrospect, the Carter–Turner era represented – in stark contrast to previous and succeeding periods – a responsible, competent effort to balance the claims of democratic control with those of effective intelligence.

The Carter Doctrine

Let our position be absolutely clear; An attempt by any outside force to gain control of the Persian Gulf region will be regarded as an assault on the vital interests of the United States of America, and such an assault will be repelled by any means necessary, including military force.[95]

The Carter Doctrine, promulgated in the State of the Union Address on 23 January 1980, amounted to a reaffirmation of containment and the formal ending of detente. During the first half of 1980, Carter repeatedly called up the memory of containment. In April he invoked America's firm stance in 1946 'against Soviet occupation of northern Iran'. The US needed to stand firm against current Soviet efforts 'to exploit unrest to expand its own dominion and to satisfy its imperial ambitions'. The impending Moscow Olympics even induced the President to disinter arguments deriving from 1930s appeasement. It was now Carter, not Senator Henry Jackson, who deployed the Munich analogy: 'It is extremely important that we not in any way condone Soviet aggression. We must recall the experience of 1936, the year of the Berlin Olympic games. They were used to inflate the prestige of . . . Hitler.'[96]

At the heart of the policy turnaround were new priorities for defence spending, new military postures and a new nuclear doctrine. These develop-ments were not born at the moment of the Soviet invasion of Afghanistan but derived from positions being adopted during 1978. Defence spending increases were recommended in January 1978, when Carter urged all NATO countries to implement 3 per cent increases in upcoming years. He committed the US to a 6 per cent real increase in fiscal year 1979 and to further rises in the future. In March 1978, Carter warned against Soviet interference 'in local conflicts' and vowed to 'match' Soviet power: 'We will not allow any other nation to gain military superiority.' In May 1978, the US led the remilitarisation of NATO, with the decision to endorse the Pershing II and cruise missiles as a theatre nuclear force.[97] The Yemeni crisis of early 1979 was something of a dry run for later events. The new post-1979 policy emphasis built upon these foundations. Negotiations to demilitarise the Indian Ocean were abandoned. Draft registration was introduced. The idea of a Rapid Deployment Force, to enable US military power to be injected quickly into crisis areas, was revived. 'Linkage' was no longer a concept restricted to one wing of the Administration. Vance attempted vainly to keep detente alive. He and Muskie (who yielded to no one in condemning the Soviet invasion of Afganistan) even made occasional references to the under-lying convergence of US and Soviet interests. Muskie did meet the Soviet Foreign Minister in Vienna on 8 May. However, in Vance's words, the scales were now 'tipped toward those favoring confrontation . . .'.[98]

Presidential Directive 59, signed in July 1980, indicated how remote notions of converging superpower interests were from the Administration's central concerns. The ideas behind PD-59 were not new. They went back at least as far as the early 1960s and had been advanced by the Ford Administra-tion, and supported within the Carter Administration by Brzezinski and his close associates. PD-59 did, however, appear to set the seal upon official acceptance of 'limited' nuclear war options and the abandonment of tradi-tional deterrence theory. The possibility of the US choosing the nuclear path with the intention of winning a war seemed closer. As Defence Secretary Harold Brown explained:

Besides our power to devastate the full target system of the USSR, the United States would have the option for more selective, lesser retaliatory attacks that would exact a prohibitively high price from the things the Soviet leadership prizes most – political and military control, nuclear and conventional military force, and the economic base needed to sustain a war . . .[99]

Brzezinski applauded this recognition of the prospects made possible by the new generation of accurate nuclear weapons: 'flexible use of our forces . . . on behalf of war aims that we would select as we engaged in conflict'.[100]

With PD-59, the Carter Administration seemed even to be teetering into 'war fighting' attitudes that challenged containment itself. In general, how-ever, the 1979–80 turnaround embraced a return to containment. Behind the new policy lay forces already explored in previous chapters: anxiety about energy sources, the reaction to the Nicaraguan and Iranian shocks, the overreaction to the Afghanistan invasion, the Carter Administration's internal rivalries. As noted in Chapter 5, President Carter interpreted the invasion as a direct grab for control of 90 per cent of the world's exportable

oil supplies. America's European allies disagreed. The West German leadership, in particular, blamed Carter for derailing detente. (The hysterical
reaction to Afghanistan also, in Bonn's view, threatened to divert resources
away from the 'real' threat – a Soviet attack across the European Iron
Curtain.) In the US, George Kennan himself, the architect of containment,
warned the Administration that it was overreacting.[101] The shifting power
balance within the Administration – Brzezinski supporters made significant
gains in securing lower level appointments during 1978 and 1979 – made
favourable reception of such views unlikely.

Above and beyond all this, the new direction in policy was shaped by the
anti-SALT elite mobilisation of 1978–80, by perceived changes in public and
Congressional attitudes, and by the imminence of the 1980 elections.

The anti-SALT elite mobilisation, led by the Committee on the Present
Danger, fed on the growing discomforted and beleaguered state of the Carter
Administration. Some criticisms of the SALT treaty were fair. It clearly lagged
behind developments in nuclear technology, failing even to mention the US
Pershing II missiles or the Soviet Backfire Bomber. However, depictions of the
Carter Administration as having neglected defence and opened a 'window of
vulnerability' were very wide of the mark.[102] Politically, however, the con-
vergence of New Right, Reaganite, neo-conservative and anti-SALT forces
pushed the Administration on to the defensive. In February 1979, Ronald
Reagan pronounced echoes in Carter's policy of 'the sorry tapping of Neville
Chamberlain's umbrella on the cobblestones of Munich'.[103] Some 'Henry
Jackson Democrats' were prepared to support the apparent post-Afghanistan
change of Presidential heart. In February 1980, for example, Senator
Moynihan welcomed the 'new American foreign policy'. According to the
New York Senator, the Soviets were engaged in 'five distinct colonial wars' –
in Angola, Ethiopia, the Western Sahara, Cambodia 'and now in
Afghanistan'. Carter's new policies were welcome, but he must bring 'into his
administration people who share the views he now propounds'.[104] The
neo-conservative writer Carl Gershman was less impressed. In July 1980, he
berated Carter's 'new foreign-policy establishment' of post-Vietnam
disaffected intellectuals, who had saturated US foreign policy with 'defeatism
masquerading as optimism . . .'.[105]

For the first half of 1980, of course, Carter's main political challenge came
from Kennedy and the left. In the fall election campaign, Reagan's bellicose
attacks on Carter's record appeared at times in danger of going too far.
Republican sabre-rattling frightened many voters and polls consistently
showed Carter ahead on the war and peace issue.[106] Reversing the parties'
traditional strengths, it was the economy that was assisting Reagan. Carter's
advisers urged the President not only to 'call into question whether Reagan
has the intelligence, grasp of complex issues, and temperament' needed for
the White House;[107] but also actually to focus on foreign policy. Hedley
Donovan outlined a position for Carter to adopt in June 1980:

The arms control process must continue. You hope it will be possible in your second term to carry forward the efforts made in your first term, and indeed in every Presidency from Eisenhower on. But there is no realistic possibility of continuing the process until the Soviets take some positive steps toward improving the international climate.

I think this position would make Reagan look recklessly hard-line, since he has been all-out against SALT all along, without reference to Afghanistan. Linkage is a deep-seated reality in American public opinion. Why not ally yourself with this fact of life, and let Reagan be against it?[108]

In the event, Carter's swing to the right on foreign policy in 1980 arguably had the effect of blurring the Reagan-Carter distinction in this area, and hence focusing the election – to the Democrats' disadvantage – on domestic economic issues.

Though many voters were worried by Reagan's bellicosity, there is no question that the 1979–80 Carter policy turnaround was rooted in perceived shifts in public opinion. The early Carter policies grew from the post-Vietnam dissensus. In 1978, the President had effectively used public opinion as a lever against conservative Congressional opposition to the normalisation of rela-tions with mainland China.[109] By 1979–80, however, poll evidence sug-gested that the anxieties and shocks of these years had led to a shift in public opinion. As Daniel Yankelovich and Larry Kaagan put it, the American public felt 'bullied by OPEC, humiliated by the Ayatollah Khomeini, tricked by Castro, out-traded by Japan and out-gunned by the Russians'.[110] Significant numbers felt that Fidel Castro had used US human rights policies to 'trick' Carter into admitting large numbers of Cuban refugees. Between mid-1979 and mid-1980, the percentage of poll respondents agreeing with the proposition that 'we are behind the Soviet Union in terms of military strength' climbed from 38 to 53 per cent.[111] Despite the Carter Doctrine, such sentiments did not accrue to the Administration's benefit, at least in so far as voters concluded that the situation had deteriorated under Carter's watch. Public support for defence spending increases was reflected in the new mood in Congress. The Carter Doctrine both fed from and stimulated increased public assertiveness in foreign policy attitudes, an assertiveness which redounded ultimately to Reagan's benefit. Voters in 1980 may have feared Reagan, but 77 per cent in a post-election poll in the *New York Times* expected the new President to 'see to it that the US is respected by other nations'.[112]

Notes

1   Subcommittee on International Organisations, House Committee on Interna-tional Relations, Committee print: *Human Rights Conditions in Selected Countries and the US Response*, July 1978, pp. 346–51. For further discussion along these lines, see A. Glenn Mower, *Human Rights and American Foreign Policy* (New York: Greenwood, 1987), ch. 2; Howard J. Wiarda, *The Democratic Revolution in Latin*

America (New York: Holmes and Meier, 1990), pp. 128–40; Lincoln F. Bloomfield, 'From Ideology to Program to Policy: Tracking the Carter Human Rights Policy', *Journal of Policy Analysis and Management*, 2, 1982, pp. 1–12; Jack Donnelly, 'Human Rights and Human Dignity: An Analytic Critique of non-Western Conceptions of Human Rights', *American Political Science Review*, 76, 1982, pp. 303–16.

2　Mark L. Schneider, 'Human Rights Policy under the Carter Administration', *Law and Contemporary Problems*, 43, 1979, pp. 261–7, at 262.

3　Memo to R. Lipshutz from J. Starr, 19 June 1978, box 46, S0: Lipshutz (folder, 'Soviet Jewry').

4　R. J. Vincent, *Human Rights and International Relations* (Cambridge: Cambridge University Press, 1986), p. 135.

5　Letter, D. R. Owen to W. Christopher, 18 March 1977, box FO-2, WHCF: SF: Foreign Affairs.

6　D.C. McGaffey, 'Policy and Practice: Human Rights in the Shah's Iran', in D.D. Newsom, ed., *The Diplomacy of Human Rights* (Lanham: University Press of America, 1986), pp. 69–79, at 69.

7　See Edwin S. Maynard, 'The Bureaucracy and Implementation of US Human Rights Policy', *Human Rights Quarterly*, 11, 1989, pp. 175–248, at 197.

8　Stephen B. Cohen, 'Conditioning U.S. Security Assistance on Human Rights Practices', *The American Journal of International Law*, 76, 1982, pp. 246–79, at 259.

9　Maynard, 'The Bureaucracy . . .', pp. 240–2; D. P. Forsythe, *Human Rights and U.S. Foreign Policy: Congress Reconsidered* (Gainesville: University of Florida Press, 1988), p. 53.

10　Memo to Z. Brzezinski from T. Thornton, 15 June 1979, box CO-10, WHCF: SF: Human Rights.

11　See Christopher C. Shoemaker, *The NSC Staff: Counseling the Council* (Boulder: Westview, 1991), p. 87.

12　T. M. Franck and E. Weisband, *Foreign Policy by Congress* (New York: Oxford University Press, 1979), pp. 93–4.

13　Mower, *Human Rights and American Foreign Policy*, p. 75.

14　Memo to P. Bourne from B. Angaena, 4 May 1978, box 33, SO: Bourne (folder, 'Human Rights').

15　Maynard, 'The Bureaucracy . . .', p. 217.

16　*Ibid.*, p. 210.

17　Shoemaker, *The NSC Staff*, p. 30.

18　J. Muravchik, *The Uncertain Crusade* (Lanham: Hamilton Press, 1986), p. 115.

19　*Foreign Policy by Congress*, p. 91.

20　*Ibid.*, p. 92; Forsythe, *Human Rights and U.S. Foreign Policy*, pp. 60–2.

21　Carter, MC transcript, p. 57.

22　*CQWR*, 5 Aug. 1978, p. 2050. See also G. D. Loescher, 'Carter's Human Rights Policy and the 95th Congress', *The World Today*, 35, 1979, pp. 149–59.

23　Cited in Robert D. Schulzinger, *American Diplomacy in the Twentieth Century* (New York: Oxford University Press, 1990), p. 328.

24　See Richard A. Melanson, *Reconstructing Consensus* (New York: St. Martin's, 1991), pp. 104, 117. See also Daniel Yankelovich and Larry Kaagan, 'Assertive America', *Foreign Affairs*, 59, 1981, pp. 696–713; Linda B. Miller, 'Morality in Foreign Policy: A Failed Consensus?', *Daedalus*, 109, 1980, pp. 143–58.

25 See Joseph Harrington, 'American–Rumanian Relations, 1977–1981', paper presented at the Eighth Presidential Conference, Hofstra University, Nov. 1990; J. Harrington and B. J. Courtney, *Tweaking the Nose of the Russians: Fifty Years of American–Romanian Relations* (New York: Columbia University Press, 1990); David B. Funderburk, *Pinstripes and Reds* (Washington DC: Selous Foundation, 1989), p. 33; J. Carter, *Keeping Faith* (London: Collins, 1982), pp. 298, 472.

26 Mower, *Human Rights and American Foreign Policy*, p. 40; C. Vance, *Hard Choices* (New York: Simon and Schuster, 1983), pp. 32, 127; Stanley Karnow, *In Our Image: America's Empire in the Philippines* (New York: Ballantine, 1989), pp. 398–401.

27 Gaddis Smith, *Morality, Reason and Power* (New York: Hill and Wang, 1986), pp. 97, 100; Michael Shaller, *The United States and China in the Twentieth Century* (New York: Oxford University Press, 1990), pp. 203–13.

28 Smith, *Morality, Reason and Power*, pp. 232, 148; M. G. Schatzberg, 'Zaire under Mobutu', in Daniel Pipes and Adam Garfinkle, eds, *Friendly Tyrants: An American Dilemma* (London: Macmillan, 1991), pp. 420–47; Schulzinger, *American Diplomacy in the Twentieth Century*, p. 319; Craig Baxter, 'The United States and Pakistan', in Pipes and Garfinkle, eds, *Friendly Tyrants*, pp. 479–506.

29 Muravchik, *The Uncertain Crusade*, p. 122. See also Jose Ramos-Horta, *Funu: The Unfinished Saga of East Timor* (Trenton: Red Sea Press, 1987), p. 91; John G. Taylor, *Indonesia's Forgotten War* (London: Zed Books, 1991), p. 175.

30 Muravchik, *The Uncertain Crusade*, pp. 125–30.

31 Cited in J. Pearce, *Under the Eagle* (London: Latin American Bureau, 1982), p. 119.

32 Letter, Z. Brzezinski to E. M. deWindt, 6 June 1980, box HU-3, WHCF: SF: Human Rights. See also Sandy Vogelgesang, *American Dream: Global Nightmare* (New York: Norton, 1980), p. 220; Lars Schoultz, *Human Rights and United States Policy Toward Latin America* (Princeton: Princeton University Press, 1981), p. 65; Richard H. Ullman, 'Human Rights and Economic Power: The United States versus Idi Amin', *Foreign Affairs*, 56, 1977–8, pp. 529–43.

33 See Loescher, 'Carter's Human Rights Policy . . .', p. 157.

34 A. M. Schlesinger Jr., 'Human Rights and the American Tradition', *Foreign Affairs*, 57, 1978–9, pp. 502–21 at 519.

35 Mower, *Human Rights and American Foreign Policy*, p. 55. The neo-conservative critique is presented in Jeane Kirkpatrick, *Legitimacy and Force*, vol. I (New Brunswick: Transaction, 1988), pp. 141–4; E. W. Lefever, 'The Trivialization of Human Rights', *Policy Review*, 19, 1978, pp. 11–34; R. W. Tucker, 'The Purposes of American Power', *Foreign Affairs*, 59, 1980–1, pp. 241–74; Michael Novak, 'Human Rights and Whited Sepulchres', in H. J. Wiarda, ed., *Human Rights and U.S. Human Rights Policy* (Washington DC: American Enterprise Institute, 1981), pp. 83–102; Muravchik, *The Uncertain Crusade*. See also S. P. Huntington, 'Human Rights and American Power', *Commentary*, 72, 1981, pp. 37–43.

36 Mower, *Human Rights and American Foreign Policy*, p. 106.

37 For differing views, see *ibid.*, p. 56; also, Stephen Cohen, 'Wrong on Human Rights', *New Republic*, 28 Mar. 1981, pp. 11–14. Elizabeth Drew, 'A Reporter at Large: Human Rights', *The New Yorker*, 18 July 1977, pp. 36–61.

38 Memo to Z. Brzezinski from R. Pastor (through J. Schechter), 4 May 1979, box CO-9, WHCF: SF: Countries.

39 *Public Papers of the Presidents of the United States: Jimmy Carter, 1977, 1* (Washington DC: US Government Printing Office, 1977), p. 782.

40 Muravchik, *The Uncertain Crusade*, p. 188.

41 Cited in Lars Schoultz, *National Security and United States Policy Toward Latin America* (Princeton: Princeton University Press, 1987), p. 290.

42 J. Petras, 'President Carter and the "New Morality" ', *Monthly Review*, 1977, p. 38; Pearce, *Under The Eagle*, p. 118; Noam Chomsky and E. S. Herman, *The Political Economy of Human Rights* (Boston: South End Press, 1979); Michael T. Klare and Cynthia Arnson, *Supplying Repression* (Washington DC: Institute for Policy Studies, 1981); M. T. Klare, *American Arms Supermarket* (Austin: University of Texas Press, 1984).

43 See Mower, *Human Rights and American Foreign Policy*, p. 103; Muravchik, *The Uncertain Crusade*, p. 44. For a critique of Carter's policy, see H. J. Wiarda and M. J. Kryzanek, *The Dominican Republic: Caribbean Crucible* (Boulder: Westview, 1982). See also L. M. Clarizio, B. Clements and E. Geetter, 'United States Policy Toward South Africa', *Human Rights Quarterly*, 11, 1989, pp. 249–94, at 251.

44 Mower, *Human Rights and American Foreign Policy*, pp. 90, 102.

45 Muravchik, *The Uncertain Crusade*, p. 140 (Derian, 1982); *American Foreign Policy: Basic Documents, 1977–1980* (Washington DC: US Government Printing Office, 1983), p. 415 (Derian, 1978).

46 J. J. Kirkpatrick, 'Dictatorship and Double Standards', in Wiarda, ed., *Human Rights and U.S. Human Rights Policy*, pp. 5–29, at 7.

47 *The Times*, 26 June 1978.

48 G. P. Shultz, 'Human Rights and the Moral Dimension of U.S. Foreign Policy', in Newsom, ed., *The Diplomacy of Human Rights*, pp. 213–222, at 216.

49 C. Vance, *Hard Choices* (New York: Simon and Schuster, 1983), p. 313.

50 See R. E. Feinberg, *The Intemperate Zone: the Third World Challenge to U.S. Foreign Policy* (New York: Norton, 1983); W. M. LeoGrande, 'The United States and Nicaragua', in T. W. Walker, ed., *Nicaragua: The First Five Years* (New York: Praeger, 1985), pp. 425–46; Tom J. Farer, 'On a Collision Course: The American Campaign for Human Rights and the Anti-radical bias in the Third World', in D. Kommers and G. Loescher, eds, *Human Rights and American Foreign Policy* (Notre Dame: University of Notre Dame Press, 1979), pp. 263–70; T. J. Farer, 'Manage the Revolution', *Foreign Policy*, 52, 1983, pp. 96–117; W. LaFeber, *Inevitable Revolutions* (New York: Norton, 1984). Also, Paula J. Dobriansky, 'Human Rights and US Foreign Policy', *Washington Quarterly*, 12, 1989, pp. 153–69.

51 Cited in L. M. Fasulo, *Representing America* (New York: Facts on File, 1984), p. 235.

52 Letter, V. L. Giannini to P. Meyer (Paraguay resident), 31 May 1977, box HU-4, WHCF: SF: Human Rights.

53 Mower, *Human Rights and American Foreign Policy*, p. 31.

54 Z. Brzezinski, *Power and Principle* (London: Weidenfeld and Nicolson, 1983), p. 49; Maynard, 'The Bureaucracy . . .', p. 181 (on Derian).

55 Muravchik, *The Uncertain Crusade*, p. 170.

56 US military assistance was rebuffed temporarily by Brazil, El Salvador, Guatemala, Argentina and Uruguay. See John Salzberg, 'The Carter Administration: An Appraisal', in V. P. Nanda, J. Scarritt and G. W. Shepherd, eds, *Global Human Rights* (Boulder: Westview, 1982), pp. 11–22, at 13.

57   See Steven C. Poe, 'Human Rights and Economic Aid Allocation under Ronald Reagan and Jimmy Carter', *American Journal of Political Science*, 36, 1992, pp. 147–67; S. C. Poe, 'Human Rights and US Foreign Aid', *Human Rights Quarterly*, 12, 1990, pp. 499–512; J. M. McCormick and Neil Mitchell, 'Is U.S. Aid Really Linked to Human Rights in Latin America?', *American Journal of Political Science*, 32, 1988, pp. 231–9; David Carleton and Michael Stohl, 'The Role of Human Rights in U.S. Foreign Assistance Policy: A Critique and Reappraisal', *American Journal of Political Science*, 31, 1987, pp. 1002–1118; D. L. Cingranelli and T. E. Pasquarello, 'Human Rights Practices and the Distribution of U.S. Foreign Aid to Latin American Countries', *American Journal of Political Science*, 29, 1985, pp. 539–63; M. Stohl and D. Carleton, 'The Foreign Policy of Human Rights: Rhetoric and Reality from Jimmy Carter to Ronald Reagan', *Human Rights Quarterly*, 7, 1985, pp. 205–29; M. Stohl, D. Carleton and S. E. Johnson, 'Human Rights and U.S. Foreign Assistance from Nixon to Carter', *Journal of Peace Research*, 21, 1984, pp. 215–26. See also David P. Forsythe, 'Congress and Human Rights in U.S. Foreign Policy: The Fate of General Legislation', *Human Rights Quarterly*, 9, 1984, pp. 383–404.

58   See Robert Wesson, *The United States and Brazil: Limits of Influence* (New York: Praeger, 1981), p. 151; G. W. Grayson, 'The United States and Latin America: The Challenge of Human Rights', *Current History*, 76, 1979, pp. 38–55; Mark Falcoff, 'Argentina under the Junta', in Pipes and Garfinkle, eds, *Friendly Tyrants*, pp. 153–76; Sol M. Linowitz, *The Making of a Public Man* (Boston: Little, Brown, 1985), p. 238.

59   Cohen, 'Conditioning U.S. Security Assistance . . .', p. 276. See also Forsythe, *Human Rights and U.S. Foreign Policy*, p. 53.

60   Cited in Carleton and Stohl, 'The Foreign Policy of Human Rights', p. 226.

61   See, e.g., Memo to the President from H. Donovan, 20 Feb. 1980, box 2, SO: Donovan (folder, 'Foreign Policy Study').

62   See Leslie H. Gelb, 'Why not the State Department?', in C. W. Kegley and E. R. Wittkopf, eds, *Perspectives on American Foreign Policy* (New York: St Martin's, 1983), pp. 282–98, at 292; P. Odeen, 'The Role of the National Security Council', in K. F. Inderfurth and L. K. Johnson, eds, *Decisions of the Highest Order* (Pacific Grove: Brooks-Cole, 1988), pp. 338–57; Dick Kirschten, 'Beyond the Vance-Brzezinski Clash Lurks an NSC under Fire', *National Journal*, 17 May 1980, at p. 814.

63   See Joseph G. Bock, *White House Staff and National Security Assistant* (New York: Greenwood, 1987), pp. 147–8.

64   *Power and Principle*, p. 74.

65   See E. C. Hargrove, *Jimmy Carter as President* (Baton Rouge: Louisiana State University Press, 1988), pp. 111–20; Robert E. Hunter, *Presidential Control of Foreign Policy: Management or Mishap?* (Washington DC: Washington Papers 91, (vol. 10), 1981), p. 26.

66   Alexander Moens, *Foreign Policy under Carter: Testing Multiple Advocacy Decision-Making* (Boulder: Westview, 1990), pp. 21–3; A. Moens, 'The Carter Administration and Multiple Advocacy', *International Journal*, 45, 1990, pp. 913–48.

67   See Stanley Hoffman, 'The Hell of Good Intentions', *Foreign Policy*, 29, 1977–8, pp. 3–26; T. L. Hughes, 'Carter: The Management of Contradictions', *Foreign Policy*, 31, 1978, pp. 34–55.

68   *National Journal*, 17 May 1980, p. 816.

69   Brzezinski, MC transcript, p. 49 (remark of William Odom).

70   S. Hoffman, 'Old Wine, New Bottles: American Foreign Policy and the Politics of Nostalgia', *Millenium*, 9, 1980, pp. 91–108, at 93.

71   H. Jordan, *Crisis* (New York: Putnam's Sons, 1982), p. 48.

72   'Sailing Without an Anchor', BBC (radio 3) broadcast, 14 Mar. 1990. (See also *National Interest*, 21, 1990, pp. 100–7.)

73   See Brzezinski, MC transcript, p. 85.

74   'Sailing Without an Anchor.' See also G. A. Andrianopoulos, *Kissinger and Brzezinski: The NSC and the Struggle for Control of US National Security Policy* (London: Macmillan, 1991).

75   Brzezinski, MC transcript, p. 73.

76   See Shoemaker, *The NSC Staff*, p. 68.

77   Brzezinski, MC transcript, p. 75 (remark of Albright); *Keeping Faith*, p. 521.

78   Jordan, *Crisis*, p. 49; C. W. Kegley and E. R. Wittkopf, *American Foreign Policy* (London: Macmillan, 1987), p. 354.

79   Brzezinski, *Power and Principle*, pp. 42–3, 480–1; Smith, *Morality, Reason and Power*, p. 42.

80   'Sailing Without an Anchor.'

81   Jordan, *Crisis*, p. 47.

82   See Dan Caldwell, *The Dynamics of Domestic Politics and Arms Control* (Columbia: University of South Carolina Press, 1991), p. 185.

83   K. Thompson, ed., *The Carter Presidency* (Lanham: University Press of America, 1990), p. 141.

84   Vance, *Hard Choices*, p. 37.

85   Cutler, MC transcript, p. 35. See also Carter, *Keeping Faith*, p. 54.

86   Bergland, MC transcript, p. 20. See also John Prados, *Keepers of the Keys: A History of the National Security Council from Truman to Bush* (New York: Morrow, 1991), pp. 389–445.

87   Carter, MC transcript, p. 15.

88   Thompson, *The Carter Presidency*, p. 141; Vance, *Hard Choices*, p. 37.

89   Cited in Frank J. Smist, *Congress Oversees the Intelligence Community* (Knoxville: University of Tennessee Press, 1990), p. 111. See also Rhodri Jeffreys-Jones, *The CIA and American Democracy* (New Haven: Yale University Press, 1989), ch. 12.

90   S. Turner, *Secrecy and Democracy* (Boston: Houghton Mifflin, 1985), p. 88.

91   Smist, *Congress Oversees . . .*, p. 110.

92   Turner, *Secrecy and Democracy*, p. 88; John Prados, *President's Secret Wars* (New York: Morrow, 1986), pp. 349–50.

93   See John Ranelagh, *The Agency* (London: Weidenfeld and Nicolson, 1986), p. 664.

94   See Walter LaFeber, *The American Age* (New York: Norton, 1989), p. 671.

95   *CQWR*, 26 Jan. 1980, p. 201.

96   *Public Papers of the Presidents of the United States, Jimmy Carter, 1980–81, 1* (Washington DC: US Government Printing Office, 1981), pp. 633–5 (10 Apr. 1980). See also D.L. Hulme, *The Political Olympics: Moscow, Afghanistan and the 1980 US Boycott* (New York: Praeger, 1990); Clark Clifford, *Counsel to the President: A Memoir* (New York: Random House, 1991), pp. 640–1.

97 See Thomas J. McCormick, *America's Half-Century* (Baltimore: Johns Hopkins University Press, 1989), p. 206.

98 Vance, *Hard Choices*, p. 394. See also Erik Beukel, *American Perceptions of the Soviet Union as a Nuclear Adversary* (London: Pinter, 1989), p. 87; Fred Halliday, *The Making of the Second Cold War* (London: Verso, 1983), pp. 224–6; A. Acharya, *U.S. Military Strategy in the Gulf* (London: Routledge, 1989), pp. 55–7.

99 Cited in Kegley and Wittkopf, *American Foreign Policy*, p. 90.

100 Brzezinski, *Power and Principle*, pp. 459–60.

101 See Cecil V. Crabb, *The Doctrines of American Foreign Policy* (Baton Rouge: Louisiana State University Press, 1982), pp. 351–2, 355; Helmut Schmidt, *Men and Powers* (London: Cape, 1990).

102 See Halliday, *The Making of the Second Cold War*, pp. 70–5; J. W. Sanders, *Peddlers of Crisis* (London: Pluto Press, 1983); Simon Dalby, *Creating the Second Cold War: The Discourse of Politics* (London: Pinter, 1990).

103 *New York Times*, 21 Feb. 1979.

104 D. P. Moynihan, 'A New American Foreign Policy', *New Republic*, 9 Feb. 1980, pp. 17–21.

105 Carl Gershman, 'The Rise and Fall of the New Foreign-Policy Establishment', *Commentary*, 76, July 1980, pp. 13–24.

106 See Albert R. Hunt, 'The Campaign and the Issues', in Austin Ranney, ed., *The American Elections of 1980* (Washington DC: American Enterprise Institute, 1981), pp. 142–76, at 157.

107 Memo to the President from Martin Franks, 26 June 1980, box 79, SO: Jordan (folder, 'Reagan').

108 Memo to the President from H. Donovan, 11 June 1980, box 2, SO: Donovan (folder, 'Memos'). See also Pat Cadell, 'The Democratic Strategy and its Electoral Consequences', in S. M. Lipset, ed., *Party Coalitions in the 1980s* (San Francisco: Institute for Contemporary Studies, 1981), pp. 269–85.

109 See R. Y. Shapiro and B. I. Page, 'Foreign Policy and the Rational Public', *Journal of Conflict Resolution*, 32, 1988, pp. 211–47, at 237; L. A. Kusnitz, *Public Opinion and Foreign Policy: America's China Policy* (Westport: Greenwood, 1984). See also M. Mandelbaum and W. R. Schneider, 'The New Internationalisms', in Kenneth Oye *et al.*, eds, *Eagle Entangled* (New York: Longman, 1979), pp. 34–88; O. R. Holsti and J. N. Rosenau, *American Leadership in World Affairs: Vietnam and the Breakdown of Consensus* (London: Allen and Unwin, 1984), ch. 4.

110 Yankelovich and Kaagan, 'Assertive America', at p. 696. See also L. Kriesberg and R. Klein, 'Changes in Public Support for U.S. Military Spending', *Journal of Political and Military Sociology*, 10, 1980, pp. 275–97.

111 Yankelovich and Kaagan, 'Assertive America', p. 701.

112 *New York Times*, 16 Nov. 1980.

8

Conclusion

Domestic and foreign policies

On leaving his job in the White House, Stuart Eizenstat was asked to evaluate the Carter Administration's domestic achievements. He drew attention to Carter's restoration of integrity to the social security system. Eizenstat expressed pride in the development of 'the nation's first comprehensive urban policy', attracting private investment to the cities. Carter had also, asserted Eizenstat, caused education and youth training funding to be increased. His energy policies would lead to increased incentives for the production of fossil fuels and would help conservation. Carter also, according to the DPS chief, achieved important legislation in the area of child welfare, especially concerning child abuse. Deregulation of transport and communications represented 'the most substantial change in the relationship between business and government since . . . the New Deal'. Civil service and farm price reforms were also mentioned by Eizenstat as constituting significant achievements.[1]

Some of Eizenstat's judgements were excessively optimistic. The plight of America's cities was not significantly alleviated during Carter's Presidency, though their condition was to deteriorate sharply during the Republican years to come. The deregulatory thrust begun by Carter was to give rise to calamities later, most obviously in the Savings and Loans sector but also elsewhere.[2] However, Eizenstat's judgement was essentially correct. Carter did point the country in new directions. His was not a stand pat regime, devoid of ideas. Though detailed development and implementation were often lacking, conservation, the environment and the rights of the consumer were now being taken seriously.[3] Carter was especially proud of having signed the 1980 Alaska Land Act, which set aside 104 million acres in national parks, wildlife refuges and wilderness areas. Similarly, despite the high political costs, energy issues were put firmly at the forefront of national thinking.

What the Carter Administration could not do was solve America's post-liberal dilemma. As Pat Cadell discerned in 1977, President Carter 'understood and shared the frustrations of most Americans' with the liberal versus conservative debate inherited from the 1960s. Though articulate, the debate 'offered little guidance . . . toward fundamental solutions of problems like energy, the economy, cities, welfare reform, government efficiency'.[4] It did not help in reconciling stark, cross-cutting interests, such as those of oil-producing and consumer states in the field of energy policy.

Carter's answer to political fragmentation and to the 'economic box'[5] of the 1970s lay in populism and transcendence of 'special interests', in fiscal conservatism and (preferably inexpensive) domestic human rights policies – competence and compassion. His populism was refreshing and drew from an authentic democratic well,[6] yet it failed to establish a new consensus. (Commenting on this failure in 1980, Amitai Etzioni noted that one should not 'disregard the fact that one cannot build much of a coalition when the building stones have been weakened'.)[7] The legacy of, in particular, American race relations points to the fact that social justice cannot be achieved without radical redistribution. From Carter's viewpoint, however, extensive redistribution of resources was made politically and administratively impossible by the exigencies of the 'age of limits'. His economic management, within these limits, was scarcely sure-footed. He faced the familiar trade-off between inflation and recession: between Democratic constituency demands and the imperatives of fiscal conservatism. Carter supported standby controls in the 1976 campaign, but subsequently rejected them. The year 1977 saw a stimulative approach, and 1978 a tax reduction. In 1979, Federal Reserve chief Paul Volcker announced newly restrictive monetary policies; 1980 saw two separate budgets in six weeks. The 'misery index' and the Iranian oil shock sealed Carter's 1980 electoral fate. Again, however, it is by no means clear that Carter's economic performance was inferior to Reagan's. Vast increases in the labour force hid the achievements of the 1970s in creating new jobs. Significantly more jobs were created in the Carter years than in Reagan's first term. Carter's record on the federal deficit was also manifestly superior.[8]

Jimmy Carter's post-liberal foreign policy floundered amid the shocks of 1979. Nevertheless, the attempt to transcend anti-communist containment and to achieve a foreign policy of leadership without hegemony was an insightful response to international change and to the defeat in Vietnam. The new agenda, it must be said, had not borne many fruits by the time it was substantially jettisoned in 1979–80. Individual initiatives, such as Carter's effort to reach international agreement on the use of the world's oceans, frequently stalled. The Trilateral agenda of inter-capitalist partnership yielded little. Japan welcomed American policies on mainland China, but the $12 billion trade surplus with the US remained. Relations with the West German leadership were poor, and a concerted Japanese–West German attempt to aid the US economy in 1977 fizzled out. At the 1979 Tokyo summit, Japanese and West German leaders urged Carter to reverse the fall of the dollar and halve US oil imports. Carter's nuclear non-proliferation policies led to further conflicts with Japan and West Germany. (The 1979–80 policy turnaround also impacted on the nuclear non-proliferation stance, particularly regarding the supplying to India by the US of enriched uranium in 1980.)

Despite these problems, the Carter Administration's 'global community' phase remains a vital point of reference for post-Cold War policy-makers. Like their counterparts a decade later, Carter's foreign policy team saw themselves (at least before 1979) as operating in a world in which old ideological labels were losing their meaning, and in which liberal democracy was gaining ground over both bureaucratic communism and rightist dictatorship.[9] The 'global community'/human rights approach – despite all its contradictions and problems – looked forward to a world no longer dominated by superpower conflict. It recognised the dangers of such a world succumbing to atavistic fragmentation. The concerns of the early Carter years – from nuclear proliferation to international environmental and economic co-operation – appeared also as the world's central concerns in the wake of the collapse of Soviet communism. Far from constituting defeatism, the interdependence agenda underpinned a responsible attempt – entirely at odds with Reagan's approach in the early 1980s – to manage America's relative international decline, and to foster (to some extent) non-colonial relationships with developing countries. Ratification of the Panama Canal treaties was an important step in this direction, and signalled Carter's willingness to take on issues that Eisenhower, Johnson, Nixon and Ford had considered too tricky. Camp David also, despite its limitations, was a major original success. (Of course, there was also continuity with previous Administrations – in policy towards China, for example, in the eventual resumption of containment and in the playing out of Henry Kissinger's policy starts in southern Africa.) On the debit side, it can be argued that the Carter Administration's penchant for comprehensive solutions did not always serve it well. Carter should, for example, have pressed immediately ahead with ratification of Nixon's 1974 and Ford's 1976 partial nuclear arms control treaties. Early analyses of long-term Soviet economic weakness were accurate, but perceptions of the Soviet regime were not always realistic. The reaction to the Afghanistan invasion was hysterical. Relations with Iran were badly mismanaged, though it is difficult to envisage exactly how a different outcome could have been achieved. The new policy of 1979–80 involved an unnecessarily drastic break with the 'global community' approach. (The journalist Dick Kirschten entitled a June 1980 report of the President ignoring recommendations from his own Commission on World Hunger, 'Let Them Eat Missiles'.)[10]

By the same token, the Reaganite charge that Carter left America defenceless and vulnerable was nonsensical. Some Presidential decisions, notably the B-1 cancellation, did upset the military, a group among whom Carter's stock was extremely low by 1980.[11] However, it was during Carter's

Presidency that defence spending began to rise once more after the post-Vietnam falling back. Augmentation and modernisation of America's strategic nuclear arsenal began in earnest. Also it should be remembered that Reagan's Administration not only retained the Carter Doctrine, but also adhered voluntarily to the SALT II limits until the late 1980s.

Competence and compassion

One term as governor of Georgia is far from being the best preparation for the White House. Carter's 'outsider' status was in many ways his strength, but it brought with it inevitable problems. Carter lacked familiarity with important Congressional, Democratic party and bureaucratic networks. When he entered the White House, he had never even met a Democratic President. (Carter's Trilateral Commission connections ameliorated his difficulties to some degree. It is ironic that the former Georgia governor was in some ways better prepared for the foreign policy side of his Presidential job than for the domestic.)

Yet contemporary journalistic accounts of the Georgians' cock-sure amateurism and inability to comprehend the ways of political Washington were exaggerated. Carter's political judgements were not always of the highest order,[12] and no doubt this was linked to inexperience. Yet the President and his staff learned quickly. They were not above oiling and stroking Members of Congress. The image of Carter as a leader paralysingly immersed in detail also needs revising. Indecision was sometimes a problem, notably in the Presidential reluctance to recognise and adjudicate the Vance–Brzezinski split. But Carter's own staff saw their boss as decisive and firm, in a range of decisions from the B-1 cancellation to the reaction to the Soviet incursion into Afghanistan. He was extraordinarily hard-working. He did occasionally become mired in detail, and failed to develop management structures entirely suited to his style. His White House office tried to absorb too much work, and on several occasions, as we have seen, the Administration's decisional circuits became badly overloaded. However, in contrast to Ronald Reagan, Carter interpreted the Presidential portfolio as requiring far more than a talent for public communication and reassurance.

When it came to public communication and reassurance, of course, Carter lacked Reagan's touch. The Georgian saw the Presidency as a focus for public education, primarily in the perceived realities of the 'age of limits'. His team, however, failed to develop sustained and successful means to achieve such ends. The public did not respond well to Carter's requests for peacetime sacrifices. The Administration's achievements were often undersold. Gerald Rafshoon warned the President in June 1977: 'You are running the risk of *boring* the people and you have 3½ years to go.'[13]

The technocratic focus on managerial efficiency was a way of attempting to compensate for Carter's particular 'outsider' difficulties, and to respond to the dilemmas of the post-imperial Presidency. It also offered a path through the otherwise apparently impenetrable post-liberal policy maze. President Carter was right to take problems of management and organisation very seriously. Yet managerial efficiency cannot, of itself, solve underlying problems of social justice and group conflict. As Bertram Carp of the DPS later noted, there was a danger of assuming that 'if we just do this under better procedures these conflicts . . . really don't exist.'[14]

The striking of technocratic attitudes also increased the Administration's vulnerability to what Rafshoon called 'the competence issue'. The Carter Presidency was not incompetent. Yet it was not so smoothly consistent in operation that it could afford to boast of its technocratic efficiency. In foreign affairs, in particular, the Vance–Brzezinski split destroyed the coherence of the decision-making machinery.

At home, the commitment to compassion and human rights was played out within the confines of the perceived post-liberal order and fiscal caution. Within these limits, as we have seen, the Administration strove in good faith to rise above a merely symbolic attachment to women's and black civil rights. In terms of international policy, the ending of the Cold War has shed new light on the human rights policy. The collapse of Soviet-style communism led former critics to look again at Carter's defence of liberal democratic and humanitarian values. Even Joshua Muravchik, neo-conservative critic of Carter's policy, acknowledged in 1991 that the 'uncharismatic Jimmy Carter did much to launch the global wave of democratization through his advocacy of human rights . . .'.[15] The human rights policy was a refinement of, rather than a radical departure from, past practices. It was rightly treated with a measure of cynicism by those who had felt the sharp edge of American foreign policy in the past. (Rafshoon advised the President before his 1979 trip to Latin America: 'The Mexicans respect our competence but doubt our compassion.')[16] Carter was neither able nor willing entirely to expunge support for repression from the repertoire of US foreign policy. US bilateral and multilateral assistance to the developing world increased significantly during Carter's term.[17] However, the Administration did not support any massive, unconditional redistribution of resources from the rich countries of the North to the poor countries of the South. Yet the human rights policy did at least begin to move the US away from the cripplingly hypocritical and counter productive legacies of the Cold War. Within the ambit of the 'age of limits' as he understood and interpreted that concept, it can be concluded that Carter kept faith.

Notes

1   S. Eizenstat, Exit Interview, 10 Jan. 1981 (Carter Library).
2   See D. L. Barlett and J. B. Steele, *America: What Went Wrong?* (Kansas City: Andrews and McMeel, 1992), ch. 6.

3 See M. K. Landy, M. J. Roberts and S. R. Thomas, *The Environmental Protection Agency: Asking the Wrong Questions* (New York: Oxford University Press, 1990), pp. 39–41, 279–88. Also, Dick Kirschten, 'Here's the Windup', *National Journal*, 8 Apr. 1978, p. 565; Garry Wills, 'Carter and the End of Liberalism', *New York Review of Books*, 12 May 1977, pp. 16–20; Mark E. Rushefsky, *Public Policy in the United States: Toward the Twenty-First Century* (Pacific Grove (California): Brooks/Cole, 1990), ch. 6.

4 Memo to the President from P. Cadell, undated (1977), box 3, SO: Speechwriters: SF (folder, 'Carter Administration – Political Themes').

5 W. B. Cutter (executive assistant director, OMB), cited in J. Fallows, 'Is It All Carter's Fault?', *Atlantic Monthly*, Oct. 1980, pp. 45–8, at 47.

6 See Christopher Lasch, *The True and Only Heaven* (New York: Norton, 1991).

7 A. Etzioni, 'The Lack of Leadership', *National Journal*, 23 Feb. 1980, pp. 334–7, at 336.

8 See S. Woodcock, 'The Economic Policies of the Carter Administration', in M. G. Abernathy *et al.*, eds., *The Carter Years* (London: Pinter, 1984), pp. 35–53; Ann Mari May, 'Economic Myth and Economic Reality: A Reexamination of the Carter Years', paper presented at the Eighth Presidential Conference, Hofstra University, Nov. 1990; John E. Schwarz, *America's Hidden Success* (New York: Norton, 1988); E. C. Hargrove and S. A. Moreley, eds, *The President and the Council of Economic Advisers: Interviews with CEA Chairmen* (Boulder: Westview, 1984), pp. 463–95 (Charles Schultze). See also Leo P. Ribuffo, 'Jimmy Carter and the Ironies of American Liberalism', *Gettysburg Review*, 1988, pp. 738–49.

9 See Address by W. Christopher to American Bar Association, 9 Aug. 1977, *American Foreign Policy: Basic Documents 1977–1980* (Washington DC: Department of State, 1983), pp. 412–17, at 416.

10 *National Journal*, 14 June 1980, p. 985.

11 Richard A. Stubbing, *The Defense Game* (New York: Harper and Row, 1986), p. 357; John G. Tower, *Consequences: A Personal and Political Memoir* (Boston: Little, Brown, 1991), p. 239.

12 E. C. Hargrove comments: 'The most telling criticism against Carter as president is that he did not calculate the political consequences of action beforehand and thus often squandered limited political resources.' (Hargrove, 'Jimmy Carter: The Politics of Public Goods', in Fred I. Greenstein, ed., *Leadership in the Modern Presidency* (Cambridge (Massachusetts): Harvard University Press, 1988), pp. 228–59, at 258).

13 Letter, G. Rafshoon to the President, 14 June 1977, box 34, SO: Jordan (folder, 'Images'). Rafshoon did not actually join the staff until 1978, but prior to this he was an active member of Carter's 'political family'.

14 B. Carp and D. Rubinstein, MC transcript, p. 84 (Carp).

15 Joshua Muravchik, *Exporting Democracy: Fulfilling America's Destiny* (Washington DC: American Enterprise Institute, 1991), p. 226; see also Cyrus Vance, 'The Human Rights Imperative', *Foreign Policy*, 63, 1986, pp. 3–19.

16 Memo to the President from G. Rafshoon, 5 Feb. 1979, box 28, SO: Rafshoon (folder, 'Memoranda').

17 See William Ascher, 'The World Bank and U.S. Control', in M. P. Karns and K. A. Mingst, eds, *The United States and Multilateral Institutions* (London: Routledge, 1992), pp. 115–40, at p. 119.

Index

DATE DUE

12-01-05			